WORKING
WITH
DREAMS

WORKING WITH DREAMS

Montague Ullman, M.D.
and
Nan Zimmerman

DELACORTE PRESS/ELEANOR FRIEDE

Published by
Delacorte Press/Eleanor Friede
1 Dag Hammarskjold Plaza
New York, N.Y. 10017

Designed by Giorgetta Bell McRee

LIBRARY OF CONGRESS CATALOGING IN PUBLICATION DATA

Ullman, Montague.
Working with dreams.

Includes bibliographical references
and index.
1. Dreams. I. Zimmerman, Nan, joint author.
II. Title.
BF1078.U44   154.6'3   79–12866

ISBN 0–440–09282–5

To all who by sharing their dreams
deepened our appreciation of dreams

Acknowledgments

We are deeply grateful to many people, more than we can mention by name, who helped in various ways in the preparation of this book. Our heartfelt thanks go

to the dreamers whose dreams appear in this book;

to our respective spouses, Janet and Howard, who, each in their own way and with much selfless energy, helped us see the book through completion;

to Richard Jones, Allan Rechtschaffen, Doris Bartlett, and John Sunderland, who were kind enough to read the manuscript, or portions of it, and make helpful suggestions;

to Laura A. Dale for her careful check of the proofs;

to Hadley Smith for her help with the typing, her concern, and her encouragement;

to Eleanor Friede for rescuing this book from oblivion and for arranging for us to work with Jeanne Bernkopf, whose editorial judgment and general good sense account for a good many of whatever virtues this book may have.

The authors also wish to acknowledge the kind permission of the publishers of the Swedish magazine *Ord & Bild* to quote from *Tre kvinnors drömmar,* as translated for us by Ulla Löfgren; of Harcourt Brace Jovanovich, Inc., for permission to quote from *Modern Man in Search of a Soul* by Carl G. Jung; and of Alfred A. Knopf, Inc., for permission to quote from Wallace Stevens, "Thirteen Ways of Looking at a Blackbird," copyright 1923 by Wallace Stevens, renewed 1951 by Wallace Stevens, from *The Collected Poems of Wallace Stevens.*

The Dream is a law to itself; and as well quarrel with a rainbow for showing, or for not showing, a secondary arch.
The Dream knows best, and the Dream, I say again, is the responsible party.

De Quincey

Contents

WORKING
WITH
DREAMS

Foreword

There are probably about a dozen people in the world who know everything that is known about the psychology of dreams and dreaming. Montague Ullman is surely one (he may be the first) of these. His many books and professional articles contain some of the most original contributions to our knowledge of these subjects as have been made in the last quarter century. Nor have these contributions been limited to a particular esoteric niche in theory, or in laboratory research or in clinical practice. He has been equally prolific as a theorist *and* as an investigator *and* as a clinician *and* as a teacher of theorists, investigators, and clinicians.

It may therefore come as a shock to some of his colleagues that Monte Ullman had the senior hand in the writing of this down-to-earth book, whose primary objective is to restore to the everyday authors of dreams a sense of their native authority over them. It is a demystifying book; healthily and happily so. It will persuade you that if you want to learn how to appreciate and learn from your dreams there are some straightforward ways of doing so. These ways require some effort and some courage, and, sometimes, some friends; but they do not require any expert knowledge of dream theory, of dream research, or of clinical technique—nor do they require the help of anyone who possesses expertise in any of these specialties.

It once occurred to me, when writing one of my own articles on dreams, to say: "Analyzing a dream is like investigating air; very important for meteorological research, but not much of a way to enjoy a spring morning." I said this partly out of exasperation, because, at the time, the knowledgeable literature on dreams was exhausted on theories and methods of analysis and clinical interpretation. Nothing existed then on how to appreciate, enjoy, and learn from dreams—as we appreciate, enjoy, and learn from related functions of human imagination in responding to literature and poetry. The book before you corrects this deficiency in spades, and I am grateful to the authors for having so thoroughly removed this erstwhile source of personal irritation.

Ullman and Zimmerman's work will stand alone for a long time: It speaks with an authority which needs not, and does not, proclaim itself; for all the simplicity of its prose, there is not an antiintellectual line in it; it is devoid of zealotry. In practicing the arts of dream appreciation, as Ullman and Zimmerman describe and illustrate them, the dreamer either learns something that he didn't know he knew, or he doesn't. That's all. But what a world of new visions on the meaningfulness of dreams is opened by this economy of purpose!

Don't be misled by the simplicity of the chapter headings. "A Backward Glance" is as comprehensive a history of how humans have responded to dreams as exists. Whole books on the subject cover no more material. "What's in a Dream?"

answers almost all of the questions that almost any contemporary person could think to ask about dreams. "Psyche Asleep" does the same with respect to dreaming. "The Way a Dream Is" presents a phenomenological view of the dreamed dream which reawakens the truth of the old saw that a dream unappreciated is like a letter unopened.

"Guidelines to Dream Work," "Picturing Our Predicaments," and "Dispelling Self-Deception" constitute the pragmatic how-to-do-it core of the book, wherein we are instructed in the fundamentals of the art: how to recall dreams, how to record dreams, and how to enlist them in the refreshment, enrichment, and expansion of our waking lives. Nothing is left to the reader's naked imagination in any of this. Not a principle is enunciated, not a method is suggested, not a concept is introduced, not a category advanced that is not lavishly illustrated from the common world of appreciated dreams.

Not only do persons become stunted by dysfunctional myths; so do societies. And in "The Dream and Society," "Dream Appreciation in Public," and "Dreams People Share," notwithstanding their ascientific posture, the authors make an exceedingly valuable contribution to a social science of dreams. For too long, since Freud succeeded in earning scientific legitimacy for the study of dreams, has this legitimacy been tacitly assumed to be restricted to the private enterprises of the consulting room. Perhaps, because dreams have proven to be so rich in potential personal value within these confines, it has not occurred to us to ask if dreams may also have potential public values. Thus we have failed to explore the educational and recreative benefits that may accrue to reflection on dreams in ordinary communal settings. For example, a woman who dreams of herself as a cow will, in her efforts to appreciate the dream, likely gain some fresh perspectives on her personal development; she will also likely be hard pressed to ignore the social stereotype which provided the dream its analogy. But so are the friends with whose respectful efforts she might have been helped to arrive at these fresh perspectives, likely to share in them by way of raised consciousness (personal and social) on the realities of sexism. In pointing to this "bidirectionality" of some dream images ("inwardly, to some unfinished bit of emotional business that is unique to ourselves; and outwardly, to some unsolved problems in the society of which we are a part"), and further, in describing a simple process by which small groups of students, friends, or family members may mutually perceive these bidirectionalities, Ullman and Zimmerman have gone a very long way toward meeting a memorable injunction stated in 1966 by Roger Bastide: "Freud repersonalized the dream; now we must resocialize it."

Some words on the special contributions to the book of its coauthor: while Ullman is a seasoned psychoanalyst and a world-renowned expert on dreams, Zimmerman is a writer and a teacher. In the realm of dream work, she is a nonprofessional—a gifted and experienced one, to be sure, but still not a professional. Not only does she not claim more, she revels in her nonprofessional status and shows how much she knows about dream work in her own very persuasive chapters. Nothing could have more effectively carried the book's main message, that professional authority is not an essential ingredient to the art of dream appreciation, than this unusual duality of authorship.

RICHARD M. JONES, Ph.D.
author of
The New Psychology of Dreaming

Montague Ullman's Introduction

A number of years ago I set out to write a book about dreams meant for anyone interested in the subject. I had always had a strong theoretical interest in dreams, felt challenged and excited when working with them in my clinical practice, and as time went on I became more and more convinced that the skills involved in understanding them could be shared with people who had no professional background. My head was filled with thoughts and ideas about dreams and dreaming that I had accumulated for almost three decades and so the words, pages, and chapters came easily even though, up to now, my writing had been confined to short communications to scientific and clinical journals.

I was convinced I was writing a book about dreams for the layman. A chance encounter with Nan Zimmerman showed me otherwise.

I met Nan in Virginia where she and her husband, Howard, were attending the same convention I was, a meeting of the Parapsychological Association. At one of those small, informal gatherings that provide relief from the concentrated scientific input, the subject of dreams came up and it soon became apparent that Nan had as lively an interest in dreams as I did. She had had a dream the night before and was anxious to share it to learn how I worked with dreams. She seemed so serious about this that, despite the informality of the atmosphere and the presence of others, I began working with her to help her find the answer, not from me, but from somewhere within herself. Nan was a very willing subject. Then and there we pursued her dream imagery back to the immediate life situation that led to it. I was pleased and so was she. I thought that was the end of the matter.

But dream work has a slightly addictive quality to it and Nan was hooked. The following morning, as we were on our way to another session of the convention, she had a new dream to tell me about. By the time we reached the meeting we had established some of the important connections between the imagery and her life.

The convention came to an end. Nan and Howard went home to Virginia and I to New York. We parted with my encouraging her to work on her dreams and to feel free to write if she needed help. Nan responded by writing frequently and frankly about her dreams. I found this an opportunity to test my ideas of how to get across to someone else my thoughts about dreams and how to work with them. But Nan was more than a dreamer catching on to her own dreams. She began to read extensively and familiarized herself with dream literature. And she soon was clarifying, simplifying, criticizing, and adding to what I was tossing at her. She gradually moved from the role of disciple (and at times, I am afraid, guinea pig) to that of a valued colleague.

Our working together gave me a fresh new perspective on the few chapters I had already written and led ultimately to our collaboration on this book. The goal I had in mind remained but now I was working with someone who could help me achieve it. Though we use the pronoun "I" throughout the book to relate my experiences and views, Nan made many contributions to the shaping of both.

Our hope is to share with you our experiences with dreams, convince you of the accessibility of your own dreams, and stimulate your interest in working with them.- But first let me explain what has led me to want to help dreamers deal with their own dream imagery. There have been four discrete, though at times overlapping, kinds of experiences. They include my experience as a practicing psychiatrist and psychoanalyst, my experience as a community psychiatrist, my experiences as a dream researcher, and finally, beginning with Nan, my experiences in working with nonprofessionals.

Every psychiatrist, particularly one interested in dreams, owes a debt to Freud. Mine is an ambivalent debt. Certainly Freud's remarkable book on dreams established once and for all the therapeutic usefulness of dreams, and all psychotherapists since Freud have been the legatees of this heritage. There are, however, strings attached, and that is what bothers me. Freud's way of looking at dreams derived in large measure from his way of looking at neurotic symptoms. As a result people tend to link dreams and psychoanalytic theory and thereby to believe—wrongly, I feel—that only an expert can work effectively with dreams.

Of course dreams are useful in therapy, because they tell the truth about the dreamer. Confronting the truth about oneself and accepting it without being defensive about it or frightened by it is the essence of psychological healing. Dream images derive from the feelings we have about issues that are of some importance to us. And feelings don't lie. They simply are. The images of the dream convey the source and context of these feelings in relation to our present as well as our past. When read correctly these images tell us who we are instead of who we think we are. They speak to us about our actual impact on others, not about what we would like that impact to be. In short they are honest, no-nonsense assessments of the immediate predicament in which we are at the time we are dreaming. There seems to be an insistent honest aspect to our being that uses the dream to register our emotional temperature as well as to point to causes and contexts. And this accounts for the healing potential our dreams hold for us.

But why do dreams assume these bizarre shapes and forms? At the risk of oversimplification I would suggest that we have two ways of apprehending reality. When we are able to organize our experiences in time and space, as we do when we are awake, we relate to the world around us through the use of language. When we are dreaming, it is the world of our inner being that concerns us. It is expressed in a sensory mode, and in sighted people this is most often a visual one. (In those who have been blind from birth the dream is developed through the use of senses other than vision, e.g., touch, smell, hearing, the sense of movement.) I should emphasize that the linguistic and the sensory modes are not mutually exclusive. Both are always present. It is a question of relative dominance at any given moment.

In what way does imagery honestly mirror the self? Again, to short-circuit, I would suggest that human beings have learned how to shape images into visual metaphors, how to express their feelings and thoughts by using an image metaphorically rather than literally. A metaphor, as anyone interested in poetry learns, can be a powerful form of expression. In our dreams we have this power. The pictorial metaphors are created with seemingly effortless ease and, once created, they stand in a confronting relationship to us. We are the witnesses to, as well as the participants in, our dreams.

When, in a dream, we select an image out of the virtually limitless repertoire of social images available to us and use it to convey a sense of what we are feeling and going through, then, it seems to me, we engage in a highly creative act. We do what any artist does with the raw material of his medium. We rework the social images available to us, combine them with each other in unique arrangements, and mold them to the point where they fit with what we are feeling.

The difference between the dreamer and the artist lies not in the element of creativity but in the nature of the audience for whom the creative product is destined. The artist links himself to an outside audience, other people, the world at large. The dreamer is engaged in fashioning a communication to himself. That the message appears puzzling and strange doesn't negate the fact that it is intended for the dreamer alone. The artist is self-consciously the artist. The dreamer is an unconscious artist, an artist in spite of himself. The artist is aware of his relationship to the work he has created. It takes some effort before the dreamer can bring that relationship into focus. But it is there regardless of whether or not the dreamer accepts his own authorship. There is excitement, challenge, joy, at play in creativity and this is no less true in dreams than in any other form of artistic expression.

These were some of the ideas that I gravitated to in the course of my years of private practice.

The second lap of my journey as a psychiatrist brought me into what has come to be known as community psychiatry. In 1967, as director of a community mental health center, I participated in a national program initiated to bring a full range of psychiatric services to communities where such services were not available. Such facilities were not only mandated to provide direct patient care but also to initiate preventive services in an effort to lessen the alarming extent of psychiatric disability. Because there were not enough trained personnel to implement such an ambitious program, we professionals shared our skills with each other and set out to train a competent corps of paraprofessionals. Part of my skill-sharing program was to help fellow professionals in psychology, social work, and psychiatric nursing realize the importance of working with dreams in therapy and to teach them the skills necessary to do so. It was this teaching experience that convinced me that such skills could be shared and that effective dream work was within the grasp of anyone who wished to reach out for it.

My work at the Maimonides Medical Center provided me with the opportunity to do something I had long wished to do: to establish a dream laboratory in which I could study and experimentally assess the reality of ESP in dreams and in other altered states of consciousness. My experiences with dream telepathy both in my clinical practice and during these laboratory investigations profoundly influenced my notions about the dreaming state, the role it plays in our lives, and the connections we can sometimes make with others when we are in this state. (The timing and circumstances of such connections remain unclear; the fact of dream telepathy is not.)

In 1974 I resigned from my position as director of psychiatry at Maimonides. The years I had spent there had been rewarding in terms of personal growth. I learned a great deal by moving out of the sheltered cloisters of the consulting room and into a community beset with racial tensions, economic deprivations, and inadequate social support systems. But ultimately I experienced a sense of diminishing returns and the knowledge that administrative responsibilities were weighing too heavily. I am by nature more of a conceptualizer than a doer. It was easier for me to innovate than to implement. When an establishment reaches its full growth it is the implementation that becomes important.

I longed to get back to teaching and took advantage of an opportunity that presented itself immediately after my resignation to teach in Sweden for the next year and a half. I spent most of the time in the lovely city of Gothenburg helping a new psychoanalytic program get under way. I also worked closely with the Holistic Psychoanalytic Society in Stockholm. My determination to teach dreams through an experiential approach was as new for me as it was for the people I worked with in both institutes. It involved a radical shift in focus from their patients' dreams to their own. But my enthusiasm must have been contagious, for they began to respond to the power of the process we were engaged in. We continued in this manner all during the time I was there. The structure I developed is the same one I use now when working with lay people and in teaching psychiatric residents and psychoanalytic candidates.

The final phase of my dream journey began with a weekend of experiential work at Esalen followed by a few experiences at other growth centers. It picked up steam in my work with Nan and has resulted in my present full-time commitment to dream work. I had started with exploratory intuitive forays based more on conviction than on structure and skill. It was Nan who made me acutely aware of what had to be explained to someone new to the field, and how to get the material across.

Ever since my return to the States I have felt as if I am engaged in an ever-deepening learning experience. I have reassessed the relative merits of dream work in the one-to-one relationship of therapy compared to that of small groups—and I have learned what there is in the group approach that can be carried over with advantage to individual work. Most important, I reassessed the role of theory and the role of the expert in connection with dreams.

Many years ago at a workshop on dreams a psychoanalytic colleague, Marianne Eckhardt, stated her preference for the term *dream appreciation* rather than the more common term *dream interpretation.* This immediately struck me as felicitous and I have used it ever since. We appreciate art and we can learn to appreciate our dreams. Interpretation strikes me as a technical term with a more limited application. A psychoanalyst can bring his technical and theoretical knowledge to bear on an interpretation of a dream. He can *help* us appreciate it but he cannot, regardless of the accuracy of the interpretation, appreciate it for us.

When we are awake it isn't easy for us to see ourselves with the same honest vision that our dream projects. We are too easily seduced into one or another self-protective mechanism. We like to think of ourselves as "nice guys." We are not like that jealous, greedy, or aggressive character who happened to turn up in our dream. We have to live up to the image we think others have of us or that we want others to have of us. These personal and social expectations and pressures wreak havoc with our capacity to deal with the truth about ourselves. And so when we undergo the transformation from dreaming to waking we move from the realm of honesty to a realm where expediency comes into play.

I do not mean to imply that it is only the bad things about ourselves that are difficult for us to accept. Our dreams are also adept at pointing out resources and assets that we have been unaware of or have neglected. But we are more apt to pull away from the negative than from the positive. What we do not realize is that in the dream we are presenting ourselves with these truths so that we can become more whole. **Healing begins with an acceptance of what it is that has to be healed.**

Ignoring it will not make it go away and it can only be ignored up to a point.

The fact that dreams are often so difficult to repossess has been a major factor in the perpetuation of the cult of the expert, the person who knows what dream symbols mean and who, by virtue of that knowledge, can offer an interpretation to the dreamer. Psychoanalysts are the last in a long line of such experts.

I take strong exception to the notion that anyone can be an expert about anyone else's dream. We can become experts only about our own dreams. But we can *help* others to become experts about their dreams. That, in fact, is the purpose of this book.

The role of helper derives from two basic facts about dreaming. First, it is useful to have support as we struggle to bring an honest perspective to our dreams. Second, others who are not personally involved in the dream can often "read" our metaphors better than we can, simply because they do not have to deal with the consequences of their reading. These two facts are the basic underpinning of my approach to dreams. But whatever help comes from others does not in any way compromise the dreamer's authority over his own dream. His role remains that of the expert. The paradox of dream work is that the dream, the product of our most private and intimate being, can best be brought to fullest realization through being shared with another or others. The helpful outside emotional support and the stimulation of imaginative input brings the dreamer closer to his own production.

Does this imply that dream work can only be done in the presence of others? No, it doesn't—only that it is easier. The purpose of this book is to help the individual dreamer connect to his dream images whether he chooses to go into a group or not. The group work is presented in detail because it illustrates the process one has to go through to make these connections. But the steps involved can be applied by the individual working alone. It is simply axiomatic that with help one may go a little further. I enjoy working on my own dreams and profit a great deal by so doing. When I have the opportunity to share a dream in a group, I often go beyond the point I can get to on my own.

Part of our lack of preparedness for and our neglect of dream work, it seems to me, results from a syndrome I have labeled "dreamism," an irrational prejudice against dreams and dream work. Our energies are directed at mastering the world outside ourselves and we are left to manage as best as we can the aftereffects of this cultural heritage on our inner state of being—our subjectivity, our feelings—that occupies us in our dreams. And so we lose a valuable mechanism for healing our fractured subjectivity.

Why should there be an aura of mystery about our dream life? Dreams are natural events. They are a normal universal dimension of human existence. Were more attention paid to them, more social support offered to encourage dream work from an early age, we would all have had a much closer sense of connection with our dreams and a much higher level of sophistication in dealing with them. We need our dreams to help us cope with the complexities of living that characterize our existence as human beings, that make us the unique individuals we have it in us to be.

Nan Zimmerman's Introduction

My interest in dreams became focused in 1960 when I began keeping a journal. Recording my dreams became a natural part of writing down my experiences and thoughts and reflecting on my inner life. I read a little Jung, and others on Jung, and was awed, if not a bit intimidated, by the grand scope and universal implications of dream images. Then I came upon Frederick Perls's *Gestalt Therapy Verbatim.* My husband and I even managed to see a film of one of his workshops. I was intrigued by his method and combined it with the hodgepodge of other techniques that I accumulated. With these rather disorganized skills I pecked away at the meanings of my dreams, but they remained distant.

Then came that chance encounter described by Monte. I was in the habit of asking experts in the field of psychology how they worked with their own dreams, almost always with interesting results. And so I asked Monte Ullman. He explained that it was more clarifying to talk about a dream than to talk abstractly about methods of working on one. I offered mine of the previous night—and we were off.

In my dream I was furious with a friend who continued to expect me to do something I couldn't do, despite my protests. Later I saw his wife (in waking life a slim and graceful lady), who had grown very fat. I was horrified by her clumsy, disproportionate appearance.

Monte questioned me about the day before the dream. I had felt bombarded by all the stimuli of the conference. I knew little about parapsychology and less about the technical language of scientific investigation used in the research briefs and papers that were being presented. And who, Monte asked, is responsible for putting you in the position of feeling this bombardment? Well, it was Howard's conference. Was I angry with Howard for asking that I come with him to a conference where I would feel stretched out of shape? Frankly, yes! But I hadn't admitted it. I was ashamed of myself. I hadn't set realistic limits on the number of meetings I attended and the data I absorbed. After all, if I overeat to the point of obesity, it is my responsibility to change my eating habits. So the friend in my dream was Howard, and I was the fat wife!

It had never occurred to me that my dream could be a reflection of what was happening to me at the conference we were attending. I had thought of dream meanings in more general terms. Monte made me see that my dream was reflecting the experiences which brought me to that day: what I feared at the conference, exactly how put upon I felt. Every part of the dream conspired to make the message explicit. No image or transition was too minute to be considered. I was exhilarated and exceedingly hopeful, for there was something about the way that Monte talked with me about my dream that made me believe that I could learn his process.

It was natural and whole, an organic rather than a complicated or superimposed theory.

The correspondence that followed and the collaboration that grew out of it provided me with an education far more beneficial (and strenuous) than I would have expected from graduate school. Monte was a relentless taskmaster in requiring that I do the work on my dreams while he guided me and enlarged the possibilities and constantly clarified the process.

For "midterm" exam he sent me one of his own dreams. This was the beginning of our collaboration. We were in the same boat, struggling to understand ourselves more fully through the help of our dreams. And we were soon committed to the joint endeavor to share this process with others.

Before meeting Monte I had been involved in a great deal of work with small groups—church, school, music, and literature—both as participant and leader. I knew something about the need for structure when no professional leader was present. I also believed, from my experiences within these groups and as a music teacher, that genuine learning takes place when we understand the process from which conclusions and techniques are drawn and thus can own, change, or discard the conclusions for ourselves. As Monte began sending me chapters of the book he planned to write for lay people, I knew they would have to be translated into a language which those of us with limited scientific background could comprehend. And I knew that I must learn the precision that the language of science demands. I made diagrams illustrating the main theoretical points. I read the books assigned to Monte's psychoanalytic students and listened to the tapes of his lectures and workshops. And along the way I dreamed dreams of self-doubt and of coming upon a house with doors and rooms I had never seen before.

My excitement about dreams was spreading. Friends were calling up telling me, "I had the craziest dream last night."

And I found that I could share what Monte was teaching me: you *can* learn to appreciate your own dreams. Your dream images are a part of an intrinsic self-healing that is available to you. Their meanings become clear not through gimmickry but through steady honest work. And the reward of finding the meaning embedded in the images is often joy and hope.

My first dream group was the Tower House. My husband and I, using Monte's techniques, worked together with eight other people without professional leadership. The impact of that experience was so great that we continue to meet (four years later) on an irregular basis.

While the Tower House group was shaping up, I began working with the Anderson family and thereby extended my interest in dream work to include children. Through my piano teaching I had learned already how often children express unguarded excitement at discovering some new ability within themselves. How would they respond to the discovery of their dream creativity? Several of my older students confided their dreams to me, and through them I saw a natural way to bridge the distance between teenagers and adults. The possibilities for deepening self-understanding and relationships seemed endless.

Besides, Howard and I had just gone through the tortuous process of an international adoption, and were adjusting to suddenly becoming parents of a toddler who understood only Korean. We had less time alone and together, but we found that sharing our dreams helped us to keep the distances from building up and allowed us to describe our real problems. We found ourselves looking forward to the time when our little daughter could tell us what pictures she saw in her sleep. Working on dreams as a family seemed to us a natural outgrowth of caring for one another.

The Andersons were our friends. We went out as couples, knew their daughters, and were, for a period, in a growth group together. I helped both parents with dreams and then they began sharing their children's dreams. They worked as a unit, with me as their helper until they were comfortable with the skills needed to work alone. Part of their story is told in "The Family That Dreamed Together." We remain friends. Occasionally one of them will tell me a dream, but most of their dream appreciation is now contained within their private family life.

I continue to lead workshops, continue to find that no two nights are alike, except for the consistent excitement that comes whenever a dreamer finds a message within a dream.

What was begun years ago in Virginia continues to grow. It has given birth to this book, to many workshops, and to groupings of people earnestly looking more deeply into themselves. Monte has said many times that we are all experts in regard to our dreams. But as I look back on what he has generated by his experimentation, perception, and compassion, I believe that in the realm of dreams Montague Ullman is the "first among equals."

1

What's in a Dream?

Every time I, Monte, begin a new group in dream work, I ask what questions are uppermost in the members' minds. So let's start with those: the most common and the most general questions concerning the nature of dreaming. I will deal later with more specific questions.

90 min/ ½

Does everyone dream every night?

Yes. Every adult, unless interrupted, maintains a fairly regular sleep cycle every night. The first period of dreaming occurs approximately ninety minutes after we fall asleep and lasts five to ten minutes. The sleep cycle continues in ninety-minute segments, the dream periods getting longer with each cycle. The final one before awakening may last up to forty minutes.

Scientis

Do children have the same sleep and dream cycle as adults?

No. Babies spend most of their time in that part of the sleep cycle that is associated with dreaming. The ratio shifts as the child grows.

Do animals dream?

All mammals studied thus far in the laboratory are known to have the cyclical physiological changes in sleep that are associated in humans with dreaming. Because we cannot communicate directly with animals we don't know what their subjective experiences are during these periods. There is indirect evidence, however, that animals do experience imagery. Sleeping animals have been observed to move their paws, as in running, and even to growl as if they were participating in some sort of activity that seemed real to them.

Does color in a dream have special significance?

Most dreams have some color in them, but the color usually fades quickly when you awake unless you make a special effort to recall it. Everything in a dream, including color, is important from the point of view of meaning. A particularly vivid color or a color repeated in several images may provide an important clue to the meaning of the dream.

What kind of dreams do blind people have?

This depends on how long they have been blind, and whether or not they have been blind from birth. Where there has never been any visual input, there is no visual imagery. The blind person uses all of his other sensory modalities (touch, smell, hearing, sense of movement) to construct his dreaming experience. Perception of the dream environment as experienced through hearing, touch, or movement seems real to the blind dreamer. Helen Keller writes of "seeing" in her dreams much as she does when awake but, of course, with a much richer array of fantasy and imagination. In those not blind from birth, visual imagery tends to diminish over time.

What are the effects of drugs on dreams?

Both stimulants and sedatives, if taken over a long period of time, tend to diminish the amount of time spent in dreaming sleep. Alcohol, for example, depresses dream time.

What is the effect of hypnosis?

Hypnotic suggestion can extend or diminish the time spent dreaming, but only within narrow limits. The basic cycle is biologically controlled and is not easily manipulated psychologically. Hypnotic suggestion can influence dream content to a certain extent. It is as if a posthypnotic suggestion becomes operative at the dream onset.

Do dreams solve problems? Can we get answers from our dreams?

If the issue is one which genuinely concerns us and if, somewhere in our past experience, we had the resources needed to deal with it, we can, in our dreams, discover those resources and restructure them to highlight their bearing on a current problem. But the content of our dream is drawn from our real-life experience and so, if there is nothing in our past experience that can help us cope with the present issue, dreams may be able to do no more than call attention to that fact.

Can we use dreams to enhance our creativity and inventiveness?

I generally respond to this question by pointing out what a remarkably creative and inventive occurrence the dream itself is. Every dream is unique. The dreamer is expressing what has never been expressed before. He is effortlessly, but nevertheless creatively, transforming something vaguely felt into a visual display which both captures and radiates the feelings involved. Everyone has a touch of the poet in him, even if it only comes out in a dream.

Then too, there have been many reports about inventions, discoveries, poems, stories, and pictures that began with dream imagery. Some people with special artistic talent seem to be able to use the creative energies of their dreams. Our dreaming self responds to the concerns of our waking self—not as slave to master, but as a resourceful ally with a will and intention of its own. We cannot, then, ask command performances of our dreams, but we can count on them to help us, to link their natural creativity with our specialized creative pursuits.

Can we program or control our dreams?

No, not *consciously*. If we look upon a dream as a kind of natural resource flowing within us, if we liken it to a river, a river shaped by our life experience, then its flow will not be changed simply by having someone on the shore urge a new direction on it. But if the person on the shore does the work necessary to make a change in direction possible, the flow will alter as desired. The point of the analogy is that there has to be more than conscious intent to influence the flow. There has to be a genuine emotional investment. Our dreams are there to further our emotional investment in living, regardless of how we choose to make that investment.

How much can we find out about ourselves through our dreams?

The answer to this depends largely on how systematically and how effectively we work on them. There is something to learn about ourselves in each of our dreams although the importance and significance to our lives will vary from dream to dream. Our dreams tap into our experiential and emotional reservoirs and bring something new to our current perspective. Working with them increases our store of knowledge about ourselves.

What effect do remembered dreams have?

In other words, does just the fact that a dream is remembered influence our lives?

When a dream spills over into the waking state as a remembrance, the feelings that accompany it will certainly influence our mood and may do so very profoundly if they are intense or unusual in any way. They may leave us with positive feelings of wonder, excitement, and elation, or negative feelings of foreboding, dread, and fear. We can sense the significance of these feelings and their connection with things going on inside of us even when we don't understand the content of the dream and sometimes even when we don't remember that content clearly.

What is the effect of an unremembered dream?

Before the days of laboratory monitoring of dreams the answer would have been that we have no way of knowing. But in the laboratory we awaken a sleeper five or six times during a night and thereby listen to dreams that would ordinarily be forgotten by the morning. What we consider the effect of such dreams really depends upon what we think is the function of dreams. If we take the Freudian position, then, regardless of whether a dream is remembered or not, it serves as a kind of safety valve, releasing instinctual energies that have been stirred up. If, however, we think of dreaming as a time when we assess the impact and importance of recent events in our lives to determine whether or not we have the resources to deal with them without having to awaken, then the fact that the dream did not interrupt the cycle means that we have found some way of coping with the situation, and so that dream is less likely to be remembered than one in which more intense or unresolved feelings are mobilized.

Any dream, even an emotionally neutral one, assumes importance simply by virtue of being recalled, and thereby made available for the rewarding work that can be done with it. There are, of course, people who manage to recall a good many dreams every night, but even of their dream life, much is simply not remembered.

What are nightmares?

What are ordinarily called nightmares are severe anxiety dreams leading to one's awakening in fright. The issues in the dream are too overwhelming to be contained while asleep and so awakening occurs. True nightmares, in which one

nondreaming Phase of sleep

feels caught up in an uncontrollably terrifying experience, occur in the nondreaming phase of sleep and often have very little remembered content. They are seen most characteristically in the night terrors of children where even after they are seemingly awake it remains difficult for them to shake off the terror.

Are there dreams that come true? *telepathic Precognitive*

A dream dealing with an unresolved problem does not "come true," but it *is* true as a symbolic depiction of a real-life situation. Its truth may subsequently be experienced by the dreamer and in that sense may be said to come true. But there are, in my opinion, two very special kinds of dreams which may be said to come true: the telepathic dream, which incorporates into the dreamer's account a truth about another person that he would have no ordinary way of knowing; and the precognitive dream that depicts unexpected events that do later occur. I will deal with both of these further on.

Why do we sometimes repeat the same dream?

All of us have emotional residues from our past that we haven't quite disposed of: particular areas of vulnerability that get bruised from time to time in the course of our lives. When this happens, we often have a dream which depicts the problem and shows where we are in relation to it. If we fail to make progress in the particular area that is giving us trouble, we are apt to encounter the same problem again in our lives and to dream about it in the same way. The imagery with which the issue was first depicted in the dream served us well in stating the problem and so, what we do on subsequent encounter is, in effect, to plagiarize the very images we previously used and reuse them to express the same situation.

What does it mean when, in a dream, you realize you're dreaming?

That is referred to as "lucid" dreaming. Almost all of us have had a lucid dream at some time or another and some of us have them quite often. In any dream the setting is always involuntary; we do not will the opening scene. We experience it initially as an audience of one, witnessing the images that are thrust upon us. As a dream progresses, however, more and more voluntary or volitional elements enter the picture. We are in the dream actively or as a spectator; we are acting as well as reacting to what is taking place. As we become more and more aware of our own role in the dream we may suddenly experience the awareness that it is all a dream. Some lucid dreamers are able to take the next step and begin to shape the subsequent course of the dream, making it a playful exercise of fantasy and omnipotence, and some can even take an additional step and use the lucid dream experience as a stepping-off point for an "out-of-body" experience: can feel themselves separating from their physical body and can view themselves sleeping peacefully. Those adept at this feel they can travel considerable distances from the body they have left behind. But the reality of the out-of-body experience has still to be convincingly demonstrated in the laboratory.

Although the dreamer can influence the subsequent course of a dream once it becomes a lucid dream, the element of control occurs only within certain limits. An analogy might be Living Theater where, after the actors have created a certain framework, the audience is invited to influence the subsequent course of the play.

Are there universal symbols?

People often ask me: Are there universal symbols in dreams? Although both Freud and Jung respected the individuality of dream symbols, each in his own way gravitated toward a concept of universal meanings which they associated with particular symbols. Since repressed sexual wishes played so important a role in Freudian theory, he tended to regard all oblong objects as phalluses and all hollow structures as vaginas. Though Jung felt we use our own specific images to represent the contents of our personal unconscious, he attributed universality to the archetypal images welling up from the collective unconscious.

I myself always begin with the assumption that the meaning of a dream image is the meaning attributed to it by the dreamer. Dreamers can use the same image in many different ways, even though many people will give similar meanings to the same or similar images. We borrow the images in our dreams from society at large, and since we all swim in the same social sea, it should come as no surprise that we may use the same imagery to express the same meanings. Nevertheless even seemingly obvious meanings should never be assumed. A snake may mean a phallus in a dream interpreted along Freudian lines, and an archetypal reference to the fall of man when interpreted along Jungian lines. But neither may be the place the dreamer is at in his selection of a particular image.

It is important, therefore, not to lock any image into a general meaning without first exploring the specific ways the dreamer may have experienced that symbol. Take, as another example, a cross appearing in a dream. For an atheist it may signify emotionalism; for a Jew, discrimination; for a Christian, judgment or love or bearing troubles. But even these connections may overlook the dreamer's meaning. He may be at crossroads in his life or attempting to cancel, that is, cross off, some problem. If the dreamer is traveling, there may be a connection with crossing the line: the equator. The Red Cross is important to a great number of people. Then there is the emotional condition of being bad tempered and cross. The possibilities must be considered in the light of the dreamer's reaction to the image within the context of the dream, and then related to what he has been experiencing in his waking life.

With so many possible meanings, which one is correct? The only reliable guideline is the feeling response of the dreamer. Does the dreamer get a gut reaction to the meaning given an image? Does the particular meaning carry with it a sense of recognition and discovery? One sure guideline to the closeness and rightness of the fit between meaning and image is whether it has a liberating impact on the dreamer, leading to further insights about the dream.

Why do we dream in images?

Imagery is a primitive way of apprehending reality, one that, possibly, we share with other mammals. As humans we have learned to refine it, use it not to reflect reality directly, but rather the world and our relationship to it *metaphorically*. We have learned, then, to use images the same way a poet has learned to use language: to play with them and recombine them in new ways to express feelings, moods, and stirrings within us that cannot be adequately expressed in any other way. A metaphor is an attention-getting, powerful device and we wield it skillfully in our dreams.

Is our dream life a reality in itself?

Our dream life does seem to have a reality of its own. Whatever the nature of this reality is, its relationship to what we call "waking reality" remains to be defined. We do, though, sense that there is some kind of unity between these two realities. We are the same person awake or asleep despite the fact that we experience ourselves and the world about us differently in each state. In our existence as dreamers we seem to be experiencing ourselves and the world outside of the time and space reference that characterizes our self-awareness while awake.

Our brains are divided into hemispheres. The dominant hemisphere—usually the left—organizes our experience logically, linearly, makes it ordered in space and time and expressible in language. This is the hemisphere that controls our waking life. It has been hypothesized that in dreaming, the nondominant hemisphere, usually the right, comes to life, becomes dominant, and we unleash our intuitive, empathic, and creative faculties. We grasp things in their interconnectedness at a feeling level, their unity, holistically. And we order our experience at a feeling level rather than in terms of cause and effect, time and space. The result is that we see more of our world—the same world we move about in while awake—but we see it in a different way. The true expression of our humanity depends upon the skill with which we learn to orchestrate these two ways of being in the world.

What is real and what is symbolic in a dream?

Real events can seemingly be replayed in a dream, but their importance for us goes beyond the limits of what they literally seem to be. Our dream is saying to us that there is more to these events than immediately meets the eye. It is in this sense that everything in a dream is symbolic; it is just that some elements are more obviously so than others.

How much in a dream is trivial?

Nothing in a dream is trivial. Every detail, no matter how potentially insignificant it may seem, has to be taken into account, even though dreams vary greatly in the importance of the issues involved and their significance for the life of the dreamer. There is no dream trash. We should never junk a symbol just because we don't understand its value.

What about walking or talking in our sleep?

Actually neither of these seems directly linked to dreaming. They occur in the nondreaming phase of sleep and represent transitory releases of speech and motor mechanisms for reasons which are not yet understood. By the way, a sleepwalker, contrary to popular belief, can injure himself.

Are dreams wish fulfilling?

Wish fulfillment is certainly an aspect of dreams but, in my opinion, is by no means their sole instigator. I don't think there is any one need that shapes a dream. I think that dreaming is a naturally recurring period of partial arousal during sleep, which occurs when our brain is awake enough to give us the opportunity to react to any tension arising out of our recent life experience.

What is the source of our dreams?

The real answer is that we do not know. We most commonly refer to it as our "unconscious," basing this on

Freud's conception of the dynamic role unconscious strivings play in our lives. Jung spoke about the collective unconscious and the contributions it might make to the dream in
the form of archetypal images. Parapsychological investigations support the notion that altered states, like dreaming, do
on occasion enable us to tap into information sources that
extend beyond the normal spatial and temporal boundaries
of our existence.

Is dream work dangerous?

No. Not as long as we remember that dreams are the
property and responsibility of the dreamer and that anyone,
professional or otherwise, who intervenes, has to respect this.
The caution of professionals has led to a concern with the
possible danger of dream work. Whatever danger there may
be is not around dream work per se, regardless of the depth
or seriousness of its pursuit, but rather in the manner in
which it is carried out. If theoretical formulations take prece-
dence over a dreamer's felt response and if they are offered
in an authoritarian manner, then a dreamer can be hurt. Our
dreams are available to clarify what we are already experiencing. By becoming more known to ourselves we become stronger, not weaker. It is not dangerous to work with
dreams. It may be dangerous not to.

In a midwestern museum hangs a painting entitled "Waiting for the Chinook." A blizzard has trapped a cow in a deep
drift and she is immobilized, either by the snow or by her
instinct warning of deeper drifts all around her. Her only
hope is the Chinook, a warm wind which blows across the
plains, sweeping away the drifts and freeing the animals as
if by magic. However, huddling in the back of the scene is
a pack of starving wolves. The danger is that the wind that

frees the cow will also release her enemy, exchanging one form of destruction for another.

There are many people who feel that part of their creativity and spontaneity, their zest for life, is immobilized, trapped in unmanageable confusion or destructive patterns, and that they are bound by their own psychological landscape. They wait for some magical future to melt away the bonds and, at the same time, dread the possibility that any movement will bring about more danger.

If dream work remains exclusively in the hands of the expert, the message to the public is that it is better to remain immobilized than to use dreams without professional counsel. But I think it is time to rejoice over the Chinook. Let the warm winds blow. Let us find ways of using the resources of dreams. Let the expertise of the analyst join forces with the creativity of others who want to view life with increasing openness and expectancy.

2
A Backward Glance

The question of where dreams come from and why is hardly new. For thousands of years there have been theories. The questioning has continued for one simple reason: People are impressed by the mystery and power of their dream images. So let's take time out for a short history of how others have dealt with dreams.

In ancient times dreams were seen as supernatural: messages from the gods to warn, advise, prophesy, and encourage. The "good" dreams were welcomed and heeded, and the "bad" ones—the work of demons—were ignored or avoided at all costs.

One of the first organized glimpses into dream concepts came from Egypt in 2000 B.C. in what is called the Chester Beatty papyrus. This "dream book" deals with "good" and "bad" dreams, the idea of contraries (if you dream of death you will have long life), associations, and play on words. For example, the Egyptian word for *buttocks* resembled the word for *orphan* and so to dream of exposing your buttocks meant that your mother or father would die.[1]

Dreams were seen as devices of the gods to communicate helpful and heuristic information to man. Obviously this sort of aid was greatly to be desired, but for a man to have a dream worth remembering required special incubation practices and the help of priests devoted to invoking and interpreting these dreams. In Egypt these men were called "Masters of the Secret Things," or "Scribes of the Double House."[2] The procedure for dream procuring was relatively simple. A sick or disturbed person would sleep in the temple, after swallowing a potion to foster dreaming. Afterwards the priest would interpret the dream and administer any cure prescribed by the dream.

The Babylonians saw nature replete with gods to be placated and demons to be warded off. Dreams were essential to their prosperity and protection. Since the Babylonians were constantly seeking clues to the future, their dreams were connected to waking experiences and became omens. If a dream of dead cattle was followed by an actual season of draught, the next dream of dead cattle might be considered a foretelling of another dry period. It is easy to see why the role of the interpreter or priest was held in such high esteem: Someone had to keep the omens straight.

As Freud points out in his introduction to *Interpretation of Dreams,*[3] there were basically two prescientific methods of interpreting whether a dream was divine, good or bad, and of determining what it meant. The first method was to envisage the content of the dream as a whole and then try to find some other context for the meaning of what was being said. Freud cited the Old Testament as illustration of this approach. For example, in Genesis Joseph dreamed he and his brothers were in the "field binding sheaves, and my sheaf rose on end and stood upright, and your sheaves gathered

round and bowed low before my sheaf."[4] His brothers took
that as a prediction from Joseph that one day he would be
king over them.

The second method was by use of a "cipher," that is, by
treating the dream as if every image was a separate sign. For
this a dream book was consulted. The Nineveh tablets, found
in the library of an Assyrian king of the seventh century B.C.,
contained dream formulas based on assumptions about the
meanings of symbols dating from the beginnings of history.

The dream theories of the early Jews were similar to those
of the Egyptians, which is not surprising because the He-
brews were captives of both Egypt and Babylonia. The Jews,
however, had developed a monotheistic faith. It was through
their one holy Yahweh that all divine and good dreams were
initiated. Yahweh used dreams to make direct contact with
his chosen people and to give them guidance. Dreams as the
voice of God attempted to reveal truth to man so that he
might have a fuller and freer life.

Throughout the Bible there are cautions about selecting
and believing an interpretor. False prophets often made up
dreams for their own gain or were paid to by others for
manipulative purposes.

Dream interpretation was used by the rabbis and sages of
the Talmudic period for the purpose of molding religious,
social, and political behavior and thoughts. Dreams were
considered to have an external source—from God and his
associates, or from demons—and an internal source which
shows the dreamer what he thinks in his heart.[5]

The Talmud advised the dream interpreter "to consider
the dreamer's personality, his various life circumstances, his
age, his occupation, economic circumstances, state of happiness or unhappiness, how troubled or relaxed he was at the
time of dreaming, etc. The dream can then be interpreted
from many angles and in different ways."[6] But the assump-

tion remained firm that only the interpreter provided the interpretation of a dream, never the dreamer.

The most complete dream of the Old Testament is in the Book of Daniel, written in the second century B.C. Daniel interprets this dream of King Nebuchadnezzar:

> I saw a tree of great height at the center of the earth; the tree grew and became strong, reaching with its top to the sky and visible to earth's farthest bounds. Its foliage was lovely, and its fruit abundant; and it yielded food to all. . . .
>
> A Watcher, a Holy One coming down from heaven . . . cried . . . "Hew down the tree, lop off the branches, strip away the foliage, scatter the fruit . . . but leave the stump with its roots in the ground . . . let him cease to be a man's mind, and let him be given the mind of a beast. Let seven times pass over him"[7]

Daniel interprets it this way: Nebuchadnezzar has great authority and influence. His possessions and those dependent on him spread far across the earth. But Nebuchadnezzar sees himself as the author of his own success. In his heart the earthly king has set himself up as God. Yahweh will have none of that and will chop him down. Daniel attempts to use the dream therapeutically, urging the king to change his ways "so may you long enjoy peace of mind." Nebuchadnezzar refuses to let the dream be the instrument for healing his megalomania, and thus fulfills its prophesy.[8] For seven years he is lost in insanity and "ate grass like oxen . . . and his nails [grew long] like eagles' talons." At the end of seven years the king returns to his right mind and "blessed the Most High . . . praising and glorifying the Ever-living One."[9]

Mohammed had a great respect for dreams; in fact much

of the Koran, the holy book of Islam, was dictated to him
in a dream. As in Judaic dream theory there is in Islam a
distinction between divine and false dreams. Interpreters are
necessary and false prophets warned against. Each morning
after prayer Mohammed asked his disciples what they had
dreamed, then interpreted those dreams which appeared to
strengthen the faith. He felt that some dreams had a physiological cause which eliminated their value. Such dreams were
those of wine drinkers, people with evil personalities, eaters
of certain foods (lentils and saltmeats), and the dreams of
small children.[10]

The ancient Greeks took what they considered the best of
the Egyptian and Babylonian heritages, and adopted whatever was found to be of value from their associations through
trade and conquest. During Homeric times, following the
traditions of the past, they saw dreams as god-sent. It was
from a dream that Zeus received instructions to find Agamemnon. Nestor was sent to provide Agamemnon with the
wisdom which led to Greek military action against Troy.

Later the Greeks began limiting their focus on dreams
more and more to the problem of healing. Cults specializing
in sickness and cure were established. The *chthonic* deities—
gods of the body—were confined to specific locations. This
meant a pilgrimage to a shrine if you wanted help. The most
famous of these oracles was Aesculapius of Epidaurus, whose
cult spread to more than three hundred centers of incubation. The dream-procuring process inherited from the Egyptians was used by the Greeks for diagnosis and cure of
chronic physical complaints often associated with sterility.
The symbol of Aesculapius was the snake, closely associated
with ancestor worship in many primitive societies. Centuries
later Freudian theory would associate the snake with the
male sex organ.

To incubate a dream, a Greek citizen, unless dying or near

term in pregnancy, would go to the temples and after certain sacrifices and rites of purification would go to sleep. If he dreamed the "right" dream he awoke cured. Sometimes the god Aesculapius, in the guise of a bearded man or as a boy, came to the dreamer. Or the god might appear as a dog or snake touching the dreamer in the region of the body where healing was needed. If the dreamer was not healed, the blame was placed on the preliminary sacrifices. It became the custom to stay at the temple until the sacrifice was favorable and healing occurred. The cured became firm believers in the power and kindness of the god. This was probably a determining factor in making the cure permanent.[11]

The Greeks were the fathers of new approaches into the inquiry of the nature of dreams. In the fifth century B.C. Heraclitus stated that when man sleeps he retreats into his own world—a remarkable opinion given the weight of divine influence previously accorded dream content. Democritus, father of the atomistic view of the universe, held that some persons and objects might have the ability to emanate in a way that penetrated the sleeper's consciousness, thus hinting of ESP phenomena.[12]

Plato, in the fourth century B.C., was concerned with how dreams affected peoples' lives. He recalls Socrates' last days and describes how he spent many hours putting Aesop's fables into verse. When questioned why he would perform such a strange task in the precious time remaining to him Socrates related a dream instructing him to undertake such an endeavor.

The master innovator, however, was Aristotle, who struck down the theory that the gods were the source of dreams. He pointed out that, since the gods have complete command of the reasoning process, they would, if they sent dreams, send them only to those who could make use of them: the wise and rational people. But dreams are visited indiscriminately on all people. Therefore the gods had nothing to do with the occurrence of the dreams!

Aristotle reduced dreams to the activity of the senses. He studied and came to understand some of the characteristics of the dream life. For example, he saw that a dream incorporates the slight sensations experienced while one is asleep and changes them into intense sensations. Aristotle wrote, "One imagines that one is walking through fire and feels hot, if this or that part of the body becomes only slightly warm." His conclusion from this observation was that dreams might be used by physicians as an indicator of an ailment or malfunctioning of the body that has not yet manifested itself in outward signs.[13]

Hippocrates, founder of modern medicine, had previously come to the same conclusions through consideration of the dream symbols. These dreams came to be known as "prodromic" dreams from the Greek work *prodromos* which means "running before."[14]

Dreams have played a significant historical role in attempts to resolve the dilemma of what is reality. Primitive societies, both ancient and contemporary, hold the belief that the spirit of the person leaves the body and wanders about during sleep, visiting places and people and having adventures. A classic ancient reply to the question of what is real comes from Taoist Chuang-tzu around 350 B.C. For the Taoist all things are relative. "And one day there will come a great awakening, when we shall realize that life itself was a great dream."[15]

Chuang-tzu tells his dream:

> Once upon a time I, Chuang-tzu, dreamed I was a butterfly, fluttering hither and thither, to all intents and purposes a butterfly. I was conscious only of following my fancies as a butterfly and was uncon-

scious of my individuality. . . . Suddenly I was awakened, and there I lay, myself again. Now I do not know whether I was a man dreaming I was a butterfly, or whether I am a butterfly now dreaming I am a man."[16]

In the twentieth century Bertrand Russell, the English mathematician and philosopher, put the problem like this: "I do not believe that I am now dreaming but I cannot prove I am not."[17]

In the middle of the second century A.D. there appeared on the scene the Roman, Artemidorus of Ephesus. Drawing from experience and every book and tradition on dream interpretation available to him, he compiled five books which were to become the basis for most comprehensive interpretation systems until the time of Freud. Artemidorus focused on a practical approach to the understanding of dreams. He asserted that dreams were often a continuation of the activities of the day. He took into account the local customs, the dreamer's occupation, birth, economic status, and physical characteristics, including health. He tried to refine the interpretation of a dream according to the special conditions of the dreamer:

If a young woman dreams that she has milk in her breasts, it signifies that she will conceive, carry, and bring to birth a child. But for an old woman, if she is poor, it prophesies riches; if she is rich, it indicates expenses. For a maiden in the bloom of youth, it means marriage, since she could not have milk without sexual intercourse. But for a girl who is quite small and far from the time of marriage, it prophesies death. For all things, with few exceptions, that are out of season, are bad. But for a poor man without a livelihood, it foretells an abundance of money and possessions so that he will be able to feed even others. . . . But for an athlete, a gladiator, and for everyone in training, it means sickness, since it is the bodies of the weaker sex that have milk. Furthermore, I have known it to happen that a man with a wife and children, after this dream, lost his wife and brought up his children by himself, demonstrating toward them the combined duty of both a father and a mother.[18]

Artemidorus spent several paragraphs discussing the sun as symbol, primarily as the giver of life and enlightenment. But if the sun is presented in an unnatural way (if, for example, the sun itself comes directly into a house—an unbearable event), then misfortune will follow.

The coming of Christianity did little to alter ancient dream theories. It did, however, have to deal with the old enigma in light of Christian philosophy and morality.[19] Where do dreams come from? Why do they come? Let's look at some of the men who shaped the Christian view of dreams.

Clement was a Christian of the late second century educated in the Greek school. He believed that true dreams came from the soul's depth and revealed the relationship between man and God. He concluded that in sleep the soul, freed from sense impressions, has a heightened ability to reflect on itself and come to a truer hold on reality.

Until 313 A.D. the Christian community was under constant threat of annihilation by its rulers. Then came the conversion of Constantine and persecution all but stopped. According to some sources the reversal was due to a dream.[20]

In the late fourth century St. John Chrysostom preached to the Greek church in Constantinople that God revealed himself to his people through dreams and furthermore that we are not responsible for the content of our dreams, and so no images disgrace the dreamer.[21]

In the beginning of the fifth century Synesius, who became bishop of Ptolemais, wrote that the dream was the product of imagination, which lies halfway between reason and the world of sense experience. His description of the imagination bears resemblance to Jung's collective unconscious.

For Augustine (354–430) dreams were an important tool in grasping both the inner workings of the mind of man and his relationship with God. His own conversion was foretold in his mother's dream.

Jerome, a contemporary of Augustine, was a gifted but troubled church father. In his younger days he was entranced with the intellectual excellence of the classics, to the extent that he preferred them over the Bible. Then he became very ill and had a dream that reversed the direction of his attention. He dreamed that he was before the judgment seat and was condemned for being a "follower of Cicero and not of Christ." He suffered excruciating torture and mental torment, culminating in a vow never again to read "worldly books." The remainder of his life appears to be one of increasing fear of being attacked. His focus seemed to be particularly on warning against false dreams, and the possibility of demonic influence. With a subtle twist dreams now became reclassified almost exclusively with witchcraft and any attention paid to them was viewed as superstitious.[22]

A sort of stagnation characterized the following centuries. Care was taken to encourage the belief that dreams were not from God and must be ignored. The medieval church—the dominant influence on thought and behavior—was the authority. Any experiences that fell outside its doctrine were looked on with suspicion or condemnation. The word of God had been given to the church. No further word was needed.

The people did not need God to speak to them through dreams, if indeed He ever did. The church embodied all that was necessary.

The thirteenth century Italian theologian Thomas Aquinas resolved the conflict between his study of Aristotle, who did not believe in a divine source for dreams, and his allegiance to the teachings of the church and Bible, which said dreams came either from God or the devil, by deciding to ignore dreams as much as possible. He accepted Aristotle's view that we can know only through sense experience. His disavowal of the possible meaning of dreams sprang from his concern with free will. He could not reconcile God's speaking to man in a dream with man's freedom.

Near the end of the Middle Ages Martin Luther, the German Reformation leader, came upon the scene. He believed dreams could further self-knowledge by showing us our sins, "the friends and fathers of filthy dreams." But he himself was so upset by his dreams that he prayed that God no longer speak to him through them.[23]

With the advent in the mid-fifteenth century of Gutenberg's moveable type, printed material became cheaper. Books, previously the property of the elite or the church, came into the hands of ordinary people. A proliferation of dream booklets, primarily dream dictionaries based on the works of the second century Roman Artemidorus, were carried into villages by peddlers. The pamphlets provided meanings for dream images and instructions for private incubation rites. For example, sleeping with a sprig of mistletoe under the pillow, or eating a salted herring, were believed to procure dreams of the future, particularly of future husbands.[24]

As the dawn of the scientific approach to the acquisition of knowledge cast its shadow before it, intellectuals and rationalists became adamant in their attack against this sort of thinking. Nevertheless, consideration of dreams began to appear in the literature of the educated. Much of the history of dreaming had been traced for several centuries in religious literature; now it was found in the works of the great secular writers and poets.

John Bunyan's *Pilgrim's Progress* begins, ". . . as I slept, I dreamed a Dream. I dreamed, and behold I saw a Man clothed in Rags, standing in a certain place, with his face from his own house, a Book in his hand, and a great Burden upon his back."[25]

The nineteenth century American poet Edgar Allan Poe feared, as did Hamlet, that the "sleep of death" was not dreamless, and pushed the dilemma of reality one step further. "Is all that we see or seem but a dream within a dream?" ("Dream Within a Dream")[26]

Man was coming to grips with the possibility that dreams, like other products of the imagination, might be born out of necessity and experience.

For almost two thousand years man had done little but amplify and rearrange his notions about the nature and meaning of dreams. By the nineteenth century rationalism had become openly antireligious and, by implication, in many minds, antidreams. But the power and emotion attached to dreams could not so easily be put aside. The age of science began to batter down superstitions and old assumptions. Dream theories began reflecting the thesis that man was an intelligent, logical being, capable of controlling his own destiny. Dreams were innate to the psyche and could describe to man something about himself.

It was the German philosophers, Johann Fichte, Friedrich Schelling, and others, who developed the concept of the unconscious. By the time Freud began his studies, it was a well-established theory in Austria and Germany. German scholars grasped the logical relationship between the unconscious and the dream. From this grew the investigation of dreams as a clue to some buried portion of human personality. At the same time, English physiologists, such as David Hartley, were concerned with the *cause* rather than the nature of dreams. They concluded that dreams might reflect impressions made upon the waking consciousness, or indicate the state of the dreamer's health.

The ferment and intellectual investigation of the later nineteenth century set the stage for the conception and publication of Freud's masterpiece, *The Interpretation of Dreams.*

3

From Freud On

Until Freud's *Interpretation of Dreams* (1900), there had never been a truly scientific approach to the understanding of dreams. Freud's classic work provided an assessment of earlier contributions to dream theory and focused on wish fulfillment as the motivating force behind dreaming. In Freud's theory current wishes gain expression in our dreams because of their connection to unconscious conflicts caused by the repression of earlier infantile wishes. These wishes stem from the unfulfilled yearnings of the child at the very earliest stages of development: the oral, anal, phallic, and genital stages.

Freud explored the way the unconscious realm of our lives is reflected in our dreams. He used the technique of free association to get at the thoughts behind the dream images. He would ask a dreamer to say whatever came to mind in connection with each of the elements of the dream, thereby shifting the focus from the dream as remembered (the mani-

fest content) to the thoughts and feelings portrayed symbolically in the dream (the latent content). He then proceeded to
help the dreamer identify those underlying wishes.

In line with his emphasis on the importance of sexual
strivings in dreams, Freud tended to view certain symbols as
specific sexual referents: the penis symbolized by long,
pointed objects and the vagina by hollow objects or recepta-
cles.

According to Freud repressed impulses are aroused during
sleep by a recent experience (referred to as the day residue)
and seek release. Since the dreamer has no access to the
motor system, they are expressed not in outward action but
in imagery, the primitive language of the unconscious. To
gain access to consciousness in an acceptable form, these
images emerge as disguised representations of the forbidden
wish. In this way the dream protects the dreamer from being
disturbed by the unacceptable impulses, and thus fulfills its
role as the guardian of sleep. One has to get behind the
disguise to get at the meaning. It is as if the expression of and
the concealment of the wish went hand in hand.

Let me take a dream from one of my own dream groups
to illustrate Freud's theory.

Mary's Dream:

I was in an office in the old Teachers' Union building,
at a time prior to my marriage. I left the office together with a woman I knew only slightly. She was
questioning me as to why I had given an unsatisfac-
tory reference for "Millie" or "Nellie." I explained
my reasons. I then found myself alone on the street
and I suddenly realized I didn't have my handbag.
I thought I might have left it at the office. I felt
uncertain about how to get back there. I wandered

around endlessly, making many wrong turns. The harder I tried to find my way back, the more bewildered and lost I felt. I asked someone for directions. I tried to follow the directions but I found them confusing and frustrating. Finally I asked someone for bus fare, thinking I might as well go home. I was given a dime. I felt indignant and insulted. What could I do with only a dime? I then found myself talking with my uncle, Walter, perhaps on the phone. He told me he had found two things from my handbag. One was a picture of my husband, myself, and our sons (taken many years ago) and the other was some form of identification card. He thought maybe I had lost the bag in a taxi rather than in the office.

Mary, the dreamer, was a married woman in her fifties, with two grown sons living in distant cities. At the time of her dream there were several emotional crosscurrents in her life. She was in a still-unresolved marital situation. Two years before, her husband had moved into a separate apartment, having become involved with a much younger woman. Though that affair had now ended, Mary and her husband were still not living together though they saw each other frequently. Neither wanted a divorce.

This was a difficult and depressing time for Mary, but she was determined to carry on with her personal and professional life and work gradually toward a better definition of the marital relationship. She had even suggested that the two of them take a trip to Africa together. Her husband was interested and asked her to get more details. But after she had, he announced that he preferred to go on the trip alone. She felt hurt, disappointed, and angry, but unwilling to show her emotion for fear of jeopardizing the gains that had recently been made in their relationship.

Several days prior to the dream the two of them had been visiting friends in the country. Their host commented to Mary: "I hear you're going to Africa." Mary indicated briefly that only her husband was going. Then, overcome with feelings, she left the room and burst into tears.

An important fragment of Mary's past suddenly surfaced as she reexperienced the anger and helplessness she felt. As a young girl she had been disappointed, angry, and dismayed (all feelings she had suppressed) when it had been necessary for her father to leave for a prolonged stay in Africa as a member of a diplomatic mission. She had felt abandoned, since her father's absence meant she had to give up her plan to go away to college. Instead she had to take her father's place in caring for her mother, who was chronically and seriously ill. Mary's father was a dedicated and strongly supportive figure. She knew the necessity of his going could not be questioned since it was in such a worthy cause, and so she had been unable to recognize or express all her troubled feelings. The circumstances of her husband's trip, though quite different, evoked similar feelings and the same sense of impotence about expressing anger.

The "Millie" image also came out of the past, but from a more recent period. Millie was a housekeeper and mother substitute in a family Mary knew in which both parents worked. Though kindly and well meaning, Millie was bland and unimaginative and, in many ways, inadequate as a parent substitute.

A Freudian would take this dream and use it to explore what light the past could shed on the present. His theoretical position would orient him to the sexual development of the child and the role that development played in defining the nature of the past and the present wishes being frustrated. He would begin with the question of what current strivings are blocked in order to get to earlier, more deeply repressed wishes. He might, for example, liken her feeling of rejection by her husband about her going to Africa to her earlier frustration at the time of her father's departure for that continent. In each instance there were feelings of hurt, abandonment, and anger. That, in turn, might lead the Freudian to the still earlier Oedipal* strivings for possession of her father and her feelings of competition with her mother. Her failure in these struggles may have led to unresolved feelings of dependency (seeking help and bus fare) as well as to her experiencing herself as an inadequate woman (missing her purse) and as an inadequate mother (the Millie-Nellie image). She may have had problems earlier in her life working out her feelings of frustration and dependency caused by her mother's invalidism. Since Mary could not count on her mother for help, the Freudian might feel she tried to resolve the conflict between dependency and separation by introducing a substitute father figure in the person of an uncle. She succeeded only partially in overcoming the impasse. Her self-esteem as a professional and a mother was restored but the purse, symbol of her sexual adequacy (to a Freudian, a bag suggests a vagina-like receptacle), is still not in her possession. The symbolic characters portrayed in the dream were intended to conceal the wishes and feelings involved in this earlier struggle.

Freud elaborated on the manifold and ingeniously artful ways in which the dreamer expresses meaning in imagery. He turned dreams into powerful therapeutic instruments by his emphasis on their links to our past and their preoccupation with tensions and conflicts that linger on from childhood. He offered a systematic approach to uncovering their meaning

---

*In females this is often referred to as the Electra Complex.

by using free association. And he emphasized the perceptive and supportive role of another person in working with a dream.

I regard these as Freud's most enduring contributions to our knowledge of dreaming, but I find it difficult to accept a number of his more specific formulations. To me dreams reflect a broader array of tensions and concerns than can be lumped under the heading of wish fulfillment.

In contrast to Freud's emphasis on the more primitive and releasing aspects of the dream, I respond more to the dream as a healing experience because of its power to confront and by confronting, to reveal important aspects of ourselves that we are not attending to while we are awake.

I also feel that free association is a limited tool in working on dream imagery. Certainly the imagery can stir up significant memories that go back into our past, but it can also convey meanings that derive from the specific attributes or qualities of the images. I myself would place greater emphasis on the way these specific attributes lend themselves to metaphorical expression. A woman dreams of herself wearing a scarlet gown. The images show metaphorically the feelings she had about herself as a "scarlet woman."

Although Freud's writings on dreams are widely read by the laity, they do little to make dreams accessible outside a clinical setting. Indeed, they do much to discourage the spread of dream work. Specialized psychoanalytic knowledge was held to be needed to decode the symbols and to understand the dynamics of their appearance. Freud fitted dreams into a restrictive set of theoretically derived categories that posed too formidable a structure for anyone to tamper with without professional guidance.

Finally, to me the Freudian approach fails to do justice to the dream as a unique expression of the self that can elude any theoretically structured efforts to capture its meaning.

ny particular theory, including Freudian theory, is just one
ʹa number of possible systems of meanings that the dreamer
ιn explore. No theory should be allowed to assume priority
ʋer the dreamer's own felt responses to the imagery. The
ɾeamer, not the theory, is the authority over the dream. The
ɾeam is the dreamer's own theory of who he is and what he
going through at the time.

Carl Jung, contemporary with Freud, felt that Freud's
pproach oriented dream work too heavily in the direction
f hidden erotic difficulties. He considered the notion of wish
ιlfillment as altogether too small a container. He wrote:

> It is certainly true that there are dreams which em-
> body suppressed wishes and fears, but what is there
> which the dream cannot, on occasion, embody?
> Dreams may give expression to ineluctable truths, to
> philosophical pronouncement, illusions, wild fanta-
> sies, memories, plans, anticipations, irrational ex-
> periences, even telepathic visions, and heaven knows
> what besides.[1]

According to Jung, our dreams make us more whole by
ιsing images that tell us about parts of ourselves that we are
gnoring, suppressing, or simply not using, and so our uncon-
cious is a partner, not an opposing force. It is not a danger-
ιus monster, but a natural part of our being, a vast reservoir
ʹf the unknown. In a dream some part of that unknown seeks
ɾecognition and acceptance by our conscious self. The images
ʋe produce are not the products of camouflage or disguise
ιut are messages to be acknowledged. The intrinsic value of
he dream lies precisely in the honesty and accuracy of its
ɹortrayal of our subjective state at the time. Whereas in
ℸreud's view a dream is meant to conceal, in Jung's it is
ɴeant to reveal.

Jung stressed how important it is to abandon any preconceived opinions and theoretical predilections in working with dreams. He urged the therapist to ". . . stand ready in every single case to construct a totally new theory of dreams."[2]

To Jung dreams are concerned with more than origins and causes. He spoke of them as serving an anticipatory or prospective function: helping a dreamer to shape his future. Dreams are dreamed for a reason, so that it is proper to ask the question: "What impact will the dream have? Why did I have the dream?"

Jung saw our dreams extending beyond the realm of the personal unconscious to tap into what he referred to as the "collective unconscious." He felt that the deepest layers of our unconscious harbored certain tendencies that were common to the human race. These predispositions were genetically determined responses to the critical events we all face in the course of our lives (birth, individuation, struggle with evil, and so on). These responses make their appearance in consciousness in the form of what he referred to as archetypal imagery. The archetype itself is the inherited predisposition. The images derived from them have much in common with myths, folklore, and superstitions; e.g., images of creation, paradise, the earth mother, the powerful father, the monster. Jung denoted a special category of dream the archetypal or "big" dream which characteristically includes references to mythical figures, ineffable visions, and other elements that do not turn up in ordinary life. He regarded these as of special import and indicative of major shifts taking place in the dreamer's unconscious.

Jung pursued the meaning of the images through a process he referred to as "amplification." The color, shape, texture, and function of the object displayed are explored for their possible reference to the life of the dreamer.

Jung built an elaborate theory of the structure of the collective unconscious, peopled it with constructs of his own (the shadow, the anima, and the animus), and linked his explorations of its domain with alchemy and astrology. I have never been able to follow Jung into these domains.

In general, though, I feel more comfortable with Jung's approach than with Freud's. If a Jungian took the same dream I gave earlier, he would be oriented to the compensatory rather than to the sexual aspects of the dream. He would focus on the feelings and the images most prominent in the dream and through their "amplification" try to understand what the dream was saying to the dreamer. On the surface Mary was trying to contain her feelings about the way her husband handled the African trip. The dream reveals how she really felt.

Amplifying the images of the union building and being on the street would lead to the conclusion that she felt out in the cold and separated from the "union." In the dream she is confronted with the true intensity of her anger as she reacts with indignation and insult at being "short-changed" (given only a dime). The dream, to a Jungian, is prospective in that it points up the futility of pursuing paths going back to the past (the dream confronts her with the painful truth that there is no way of getting back to the "union" as it once was). Instead it orients her to her own identity as an individual and to her family relationships as these are validated by Walter. The dream in its honesty ends on a note of both hope and uncertainty with regard to her identity as a wife.

I do not think a Jungian would classify this as a "big" dream, or one containing archetypal imagery, except, perhaps, for the allusion to the rescuing father figure in the person of Uncle Walter.

I believe that Jung's fundamental emphasis on the directness and honesty of the dream as a message to be acknowl-

edged is correct. I agree with his view of the personal unconscious as the general realm of the unknown rather than as the
playground of instincts. I do not hold to his view of the
collective unconscious and its archetypal structuring. Yet I
resonate to whatever it is about dreams that suggested this
universal aspect to Jung. It does seem to be in the nature of
being human to feel our ties to the human race and to empa-
thize with the various crises that characterize life on this
planet. While awake we tend to take a limited view of these
ties and concern ourselves mainly with people of immediate
significance to us. Our dreaming self has never lost sight of
a basic truth, namely that, despite the manifold ways in
which the human race has fragmented itself in the course of
history, we are, nevertheless, all members of a single species.
There are times when this larger vision comes through and
takes the form that Jung refers to when he speaks of mythic
images appearing in a dream, images that capture an important aspect of the human predicament.

Jung swept away most of the categorical restrictions inherent in the Freudian view. In so doing he took a giant step
toward making dreams potentially accessible to the nonprofessional. He felt we should see dreams as natural events
bearing messages that are meant to be understood. His categories are looser and more ambiguous than Freud's and tend
not to detract from the simplicity of his approach. What
Jung did not do was develop a way of actually placing dream
work in the hands of the ordinary person. Dream work and
training in dream work still remained largely within a thera-
py-oriented setting.

This brief reference to Freud and Jung does not do justice
to the range and originality of their thinking about dreams,
but it is undertaken to assess each one's contribution to the
task of making dreams accessible.

My way of working with dreams derives from what I learned from them plus some original ideas of my own. Although these ideas will be developed elsewhere in the book it may be helpful now to make some of the differences more explicit by the following three-way comparison:

	Freudian View	*Jungian View*	*My View*
Function of Dreaming	a) To discharge repressed instinctual impulses. b) To modulate these instinctual tensions so as to preserve sleep (the dream as the guardian of sleep).	a) To orient the dreamer to unacknowledged aspects of the self. b) Compensatory —to help achieve psychic equilibrium. c) Prospective— to have a guiding influence.	a) To explore and assess the emotional impact of recent experiences and to bring about awakening if the feelings aroused go beyond a certain level of intensity. b) The dream is potentially available as a natural emotionally healing mechanism.
Motive for Dreaming	Wish fulfillment. An infantile wish connects with a current wish.	Goes beyond wish fulfillment to include all other concerns.	Agree with Jung that the single criterion of wish fulfillment is untenable. Dreaming is simply the form our consciousness takes at night to make us aware of our feelings.

	Freudian View	*Jungian View*	*My View*
Concept of the Unconscious	a) Unconscious as the container of the repressed. b) The dream as the royal road to the Unconscious.	a) The Personal Unconscious—Repository of higher aspirations as well as instinctual needs. b) The Collective Unconscious—that part of our unconscious that has been genetically determined, that is not directly knowable, and that manifests itself through archetypal images.	a) Unconscious as the realm of the unknown but not unknowable. b) The unknown consists of what we are ignorant of and what we defend ourselves against knowing.
Fixed or Universal Symbols	Gravitated to the idea of fixed sexual symbols.	No fixed symbols in personal unconscious. Archetypal images are universal.	No fixed or universal symbols.
Structure of the Dream	Latent and manifest content. Latter is a disguised rendering of the former.	The "manifest facade" is the dream. No disguise is intended.	Agree with Jung.

	Freudian View	Jungian View	My View
Language of the Dream	Imagery as the language of the unconscious—preverbal and prelogical.	Imagery as archaic figurative mode of thought.	The archaic capacity for imagery is transformed into a vehicle for expressing feeling as visual metaphors.
Role of Current Life Situation	Day residue touches off an earlier conflict.	Day residue opens up an area not attended to while awake. More stress on the present predicament of the dreamer.	No essential difference with Jung.
Technique of Working with Dreams	Free Association.	a) Amplification. b) Limited free association.	Assessment of the metaphorical potential of the imagery in relation to the life context that precipitated the dream.
Role of the Other	Authority working with specific structured point of view.	Authority functioning as a guide. No structured theory of Personal Unconscious, but structured view of the Collective Unconscious (Archetypes).	Helper who sees the dream as the dreamer's uniquely personal view of what is unconscious to him. No a priori structured container.

There have been many contributions to dream theory since the work of Freud and Jung, but for the most part they have been refinements and modifications of these two different ways of looking at the meaning of dreams: Are dreams meant to reveal or to conceal? Among the early analysts, Wilhelm Stekel[3] and Emil Gutheil[4] differed from Freud in matters of technique. Both worked more intuitively with dreams and both felt that the use of free association was a cumbersome and unreliable approach to the understanding of dreams. They emphasized the extent to which the patient's associations are not truly free, but are influenced by the theoretical predilections of the therapist. The images that appear in dreams are likewise influenced so that sexual symbols appear more often in the dreams of patients being analyzed by Freudians and archetypal images in the case of Jungians. Thomas French and Erika Fromm,[5] working within the Freudian framework, emphasized the problem-solving nature of dreams and the way in which the dreamer calls upon earlier solutions to help cope with what French referred to as the current "focal conflict."

Erich Fromm, in *The Forgotten Language,* took issue with Freud's emphasis on the irrational nature of the forces at work in our dreams and with Jung's preoccupation with the higher wisdom to be found in dreams. Taking a mid-position he felt that dreams revealed both our irrational and our rational nature: ". . . we are not only less reasonable and less decent in our dreams but . . . we are also more intelligent, wiser and capable of better judgment when we are asleep than when we are awake."[6]

Existentialists like Medard Boss in *The Analysis of Dreams* (1958) jettison all theory. As with Jung, the manifest content is the important aspect of the dream but, unlike Jung, Boss sees that content neither as reflecting a structured unconscious (individual and collective) nor as having a specific function (compensatory). It is regarded simply as another way of being-in-the-world. The dreamer is in a realm where his potential for being-in-the-world is experienced as perceptible images.[7]

Samuel Lowy in *Foundations of Dream Interpretation* introduced a number of new ideas about the role that dreams played in maintaining an emotional equilibrium.[8] He saw dreams as primarily serving the needs of the sleeping organism and doing it by generating feelings and regulating the emotional life of the dreamer. Past and present come together in the dream as part of the effort to maintain the unity of the psyche. Lowy also felt that free association had its limitations and that dreams required an intuitive response. I found Lowy's ideas most stimulating and helpful in the development of my own theoretical views. I, too, felt it important to emphasize that dreams are a form of consciousness oriented to our needs while we sleep.

For those who are interested in both a scholarly appraisal of the various contributions to dream theory and a careful and original integration of theory and laboratory data, there is the recent volume by Richard M. Jones, *The New Psychology of Dreaming.*[9]

The Gestalt approach, introduced by Frederick S. Perls, has moved in an innovative technical direction.[10] Here the work on a dream takes place in a group setting where the dreamer, by means of a role-playing arrangement, enters into a dialogue with every element of the dream, animate or inanimate. Perls considered each such element as signifying some unfinished emotional business left over from the past. He referred to them as "emotional holes." The Gestalt technique is an effective way of leading into the feelings behind the imagery and allows the group to play both a stimulating and supportive role. I have not pursued this approach because I felt it introduced too many extraneous elements into dream work and seemed to fragment and fracture the natural sequences of the dream. To me, elements of a dream often assume more specific meaning when looked at in relation to preceding and subsequent imagery.

If I were to sum up these various approaches by means of analogies, I might use the steam kettle for the Freudian-related approaches, a rotating mirror for the Jungian approach, and someone filling in holes in the ground for the Gestalt approach. In the case of the steam kettle, something under pressure succeeds in getting out, but in a different form. In the case of the mirror, the rotation of the mirror reflects an unknown side of the self. The Gestaltist is busy preparing solid ground by filling holes left over from the past.

The existence of diverse schools of thought suggests that no one theroretical structure encompasses all that we can discover in our dream life. A therapist's ability to work with a dream hinges, in my opinion, not on his particular theoretical knowledge of symbolism (either Freudian-Sexual or Jungian-Archetypal) but, rather, on his skill in detecting the various ways in which the dreamer awake evades the message from the dreamer asleep. Some people do require professional help to get at the truth of what their dreams are saying. For most people, however, the truth of their dreams is not beyond their reach. The help and support that may be needed do not have to be of the professional variety.

This book dispenses with all theoretical categories in working with dreams. Or rather, it is open to all categories, but only as possibilities that may help the dreamer learn more about his or her personal dream glossary.

But it is not enough to approach a dream without a theoretical bias. An educative and a retraining process is also needed. We have to learn about the metaphorical nature of the dream communication and the way it derives from a very real and immediate life situation. We must also learn something about the various ways we have of not allowing ourselves to know what the dream is trying to tell us. Armed with this knowledge we can take a more honest look at ourselves as we are now and as we have been in the past. These are the areas we shall be exploring together.

I should like to end with a few notes of caution. Most of us are tempted to look outside ourselves for the meaning of the images we create. We have been indoctrinated to seek outside, authoritative sources for the key to the images we come up with. So we seek out experts and dream dictionaries and fail to consider that no outside source can tell us why we have chosen a particular image. All that any outsider can do is to supply some ideas which may or may not have any relevance to the meaning our images hold for us.

Since interest in dreams is universal, the subject provides a fertile field for exploitation. Popular writers often take one or another of the remarkable qualities of dreams and package it for public consumption in a one-sided way. There is much that we can learn to do with our dreams, but there are also limits to what can be done. We can derive great benefits by working seriously with our dreams, but dreams alone cannot solve our problems in living. Our dreaming self does seek ways of coping with tensions, but the answers it supplies come somewhere out of our life history and they are limited by that life history. Dreams will often provide answers to problems we face, or point in a direction where an answer might be found, but they cannot promise solutions to life situations when no solution yet exists. The promise to use dreams to solve one's problems in any blanket way is an empty promise.

Another empty promise has to do with the possibility of controlling our dreams. Dreams liberate spontaneous, creative, life-enhancing energies in us. We can relate to those energies and benefit from them but we cannot control them. It is fortunate for us that our dreams cannot be manipulated or controlled by our conscious intent. They would be a lot less honest if they could.

4

Psyche Asleep

We do not know for certain why we sleep or why we dream, but we do know that our dreams are embedded in our sleep. So let's consider where we are and what we are like while asleep.

Since we feel refreshed after a good night's rest, it would seem that sleep is a period of bodily recuperation. But there is no physiological or chemical evidence that this is so. Sleep seems to be essential, but the amount people need varies tremendously from extremes of less than three hours to over ten hours. Yet when volunteers have been kept awake for long periods of time, irritability, confusion, and occasionally hallucinatory and even psychotic episodes have set in.

New laboratory approaches that involve electroencephalographic monitoring of the activity of the brain during sleep will, undoubtedly, shed more light on the nature of sleep. We have already begun to make considerable progress in understanding the various kinds of insomnia and other sleep disturbances.

There are profound physiological and psychological changes that accompany the shift from waking to sleeping. As we go off to sleep our body automatically disengages from the outside world by disconnecting our sensory apparatus and inhibiting voluntary control over our motor apparatus. Experiments have shown that when we block our sensory pathways mechanically so that no intimation about the outside world reaches us, there is a profound change in the way we experience ourselves. The effect of the absence of external stimuli on the brain is a consciousness in which imagery begins to prevail, imagery that may be experienced as real. When such imagery in the waking state is experienced as real, it is called an *hallucination.* When it occurs in the course of sleep it is called a *dream.*

When we sleep we separate ourselves from the world, but we assume that our relationship to it will not change very much during these brief nightly vacations from it. We assume, in other words, that it is safe to take a temporary leave. When we go to bed in strange surroundings, our sleep sometimes tends to be lighter, as if we had to be more vigilant. In our own beds our expectancy of unusual or intruding external events is minimal, so we turn our attention to ourselves totally and to the serious business of sleeping and dreaming. There are, of course, times when a special channel is left open to the outside as, for example, by the young mother who can sleep soundly but be selectively sensitive to even the faintest sound of her baby.

Going to sleep seems like a simple and innocuous event, but it is accompanied by major shifts and rearrangements. The onset of sleep is generally experienced as a lapse into unconsciousness. Occasionally we experience imagery during the transitional period between waking and sleeping. These are known as *hypnagogic images.* They reflect visually the last thoughts that occupy our mind before we drift off. For example:

Last remembered thought:

I had been asked to get a certain job done that was not my responsibility. I, in turn, assigned it to a coworker, Bob. Much to my chagrin, he made a mess of it.

Hypnagogic image:

We were playing football. I tossed the ball to Bob, feeling certain we would make a touchdown. Instead he fumbled the ball.

These images tend to be more simple and static, less vivid and less chaotic than true dreams. Most of us remain unaware of them unless we happen to be awakened as they occur.

In the laboratory, sleep is registered on the electroencephalogram as a change in the electrical activity of the brain in the direction of lower frequencies of brain waves and higher voltage patterns. There appear to be four distinct EEG stages during the descent into deep sleep. They are known as Descending Stage I and Stages II, III, and IV. By Stage IV the rhythm is predominantly slow with high voltage waves. Although dreams are occasionally reported from these stages, more often what comes out of them are the thoughts and preoccupations of waking life.

Once Stage IV is reached, the process returns back through Stages III and II to what is now called an *Emergent*

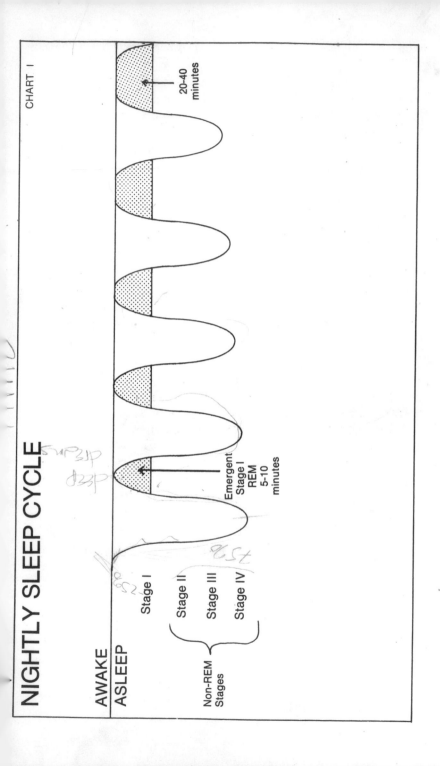

NIGHTLY SLEEP CYCLE

CHART I

AWAKE

ASLEEP

Stage I

Stage II

Stage III

Stage IV

Non-REM Stages

Emergent Stage I REM 5-10 minutes

20-40 minutes

Stage I. (See Chart 1.) Emergent Stage I is where most dreaming occurs. It comes approximately ninety minutes after falling asleep and recurs every ninety minutes thereafter. Depending on how long we sleep, there may be four to seven repetitions of this cycle, with each succeeding period of dreaming in the cycle lasting longer than the preceding one. The initial period is five to ten minutes while the last one may go on thirty or forty minutes.

During the period of dreaming there are sudden bouts of rapid movements of the eyes horizontally and vertically. These eye movements are so characteristic of the period that this phase of the sleep cycle is also referred to as the REM (rapid eye movement) state.

It is apparent that the REM state is a distinct and separate phase of the sleep cycle, differing physiologically from the other or non-REM phases. Even though we seem to be sleeping peacefully, our brain is aroused to the point where the EEG shows a resemblance to a normal waking record. And there are other characteristics of an aroused state: The pulse rate increases and breathing becomes more irregular. But there is at the same time a lessening of muscle tone, almost as if the body wants to insure that the motor apparatus will not be set in motion by whatever is being experienced in dreams during the REM state.

The onset, duration, and changes in duration of the REM-non-REM cycle are controlled by centers in the brainstem, but the amount of time spent in REM sleep varies with age. The average adult spends about one and a half hours in dreaming sleep every night—about twenty percent of total sleep time. This diminishes to about fifteen percent in old age, while sixty to seventy percent of a newborn's sleep is REM sleep and the percentage is even higher for prematures. Obviously we can't ask an infant about dreams and so we are judging only the physiological changes of REM sleep.

Not all of our dreaming experience is confined to the REM state—certainly dreams occur during brief daytime naps—and so when I speak of REM as the dreaming phase I simply mean that most dreaming takes place then, and if a dreamer is awakened during a REM period there is an eighty to ninety percent chance of dream recall. The memory of a dream fades rapidly, shortly after the termination of a REM period.

Though we can, and often do, interrupt our dreams, we cannot start a dream. The effect of a stimulus upon a sleeper depends upon its intensity and when it is introduced in the sleep cycle. A stimulus applied to a non-REM stage will either have no effect at all, or will awaken the sleeper, depending on its intensity. But when a stimulus introduced during a REM period is strong enough to register but not strong enough to awaken the individual, it may enter the dream in a symbolic form, often in an exaggerated way. A draft of air on the exposed skin of a dreamer may be depicted in the dream as a raging tornado. The reason for this effect may be that, since the stimulus is intruding on a relatively quiet sensory field and is not competing with other sensory stimuli, it looms larger than it would ordinarily.

We can use these findings to explain and dispute some popular beliefs about dreams. For example, eating something that doesn't agree with us doesn't *cause* our dreams, though it may *affect* them. One of the effects of a bout of indigestion is that we may sleep more restlessly, more lightly, and therefore be more prone to remember our dreams. Then, too, if we undergo discomfort during a dreaming period, it may influence the dream content and be reflected in the dream. But, remember, such discomfort cannot initiate a dream. Bodily positions by themselves have very little to do with dreaming.

Often a single theme runs through the dream sequences of one night, even though the imagery may depict it in ways that, at first glance, show no relation. First and shorter dreams of the night tend to be more present-oriented, less emotional, and less disordered in terms of time and space than our later dreams. Our recall is greatest from the REM period of early morning because this is the longest period of dreaming and our general arousal level is higher. We are, after all, at the end of a night's sleep.

If we are to deal with dreaming and dreams, we need some definitions. Dreaming is a unique display, usually visual, that occurs during the night in order, I feel, to assess the impact of recent events on our lives. A dream is a remembered residue—in the form of creatively assembled visual metaphors.

Dreaming

To me the fact that REM periods are biologically controlled and that we share them with other animals has interesting implications. It is conceivable from an evolutionary point of view that an animal when asleep was more vulnerable to danger than when awake, and so a biological arrangement insured fixed periods when the animal was closer to arousal, even though asleep: somewhat like having a built-in watchman check out the situation for possible dangers. I call this explanation of the function served by dreaming the "vigilance hypothesis."

Although we undergo the same vicissitudes of the sleep-waking cycle as do other animals, we do so under infinitely more complex circumstances. As humans we are oriented more to changes in our immediate social environment than to predators threatening our physical existence. The vigilance hypothesis suggests that we use the dreaming phase of the sleep cycle to explore the potential impact of such changes upon our lives.

Imagine, if you will, a soldier guarding an encampment at night, sitting before a radar screen ready to detect any approaching enemy planes. When a blip appears on the screen signaling an approaching plane he has to identify it for what it is and not for what he wishes or hopes it to be. He must keep it in focus until he has gathered enough information to be able to assess the situation. The dreamer is in a somewhat analogous situation. His attention is drawn to some residual feeling. He, too, is faced with a challenge that is too ambiguous to act on without further information. He, too, has much at stake in assessing the issue for what it is. The soldier decides about arousing the camp; the dreamer, about arousing himself. This is no small decision. It involves interfering with an important biological need and results in a radical transformation in state. It cannot be undertaken lightly. It must rest on solid facts. The solid facts in the case of the dreamer are the truthful reflections of the feelings of the dreamer. He appears in the dream as he is, not as he imagines himself to be. The dream reflects the way he is with others, not the way he likes to think he is. After all, vigilance operations would have no meaning unless they were able to get at the truth.

Say that a recent event results in a tension that continues to trouble us. The feelings connected with it surface during dreaming sleep and are represented as the initial images of a dream. (See Chart 2.) It is as if we are asking: Now that I have the opportunity to be conscious, what is it that I should be conscious of? What is happening to me right now? Faced with the decision of whether or not it is safe to remain asleep, we have to check out the intruding stimulus by exploring what light our past can shed on it. The next question, then, is: What information do I need to assess the tension I

DREAM STRUCTURE: Setting

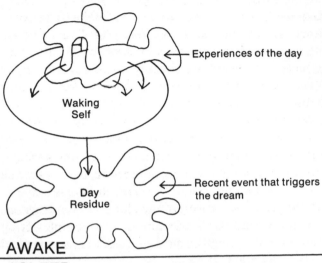

Experiences of the day

Waking Self

Day Residue

Recent event that triggers the dream

AWAKE

ASLEEP

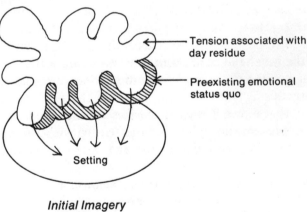

Tension associated with day residue

Preexisting emotional status quo

Setting

Initial Imagery of the Dream

Questions Confronted in Setting
What is happening to me?
What do I feel?
What might happen?

CHART 2

feel? The brain is a computer with a remarkable memory bank which we program with the initial images of the dream and the feelings associated with them. Out comes a flock of images from various epochs of our past. (See Charts 3 and 4.) These images sometimes go back to early childhood—but all are in some way related emotionally to the current issue. Once we have expressed in imagery the information we need to assess the current predicament we can turn to the last question: What can I do about it? At this point we move on to create relevant imagery to explore new solutions. (See Chart 5.) If we fail—that is, if the feelings connected with the imagery are too intense to be compatible with the continuation of sleep—we awaken. So, in a sense, all we are doing during a REM period is forming a basis for a yes-no decision about interrupting this state. Dreaming is a complex and remarkable way for getting the data we need to arrive at this decision. (See Chart 6.)

The Dream

Since I used the term *creative* for my definition of a dream, let me go into those qualities a dream has in common with art, expecially with the art form which relies heavily on metaphor: poetry. The poet rearranges language in order to convey metaphorically the feelings that he wishes to express. When poet Wallace Stevens writes

> *Among twenty snowy mountains,*
> *The only moving thing*
> *Was the eye of the blackbird*[1]

he is conveying more about the quality of aloneness than he could by any factual statement. The dreamer, too, is con-

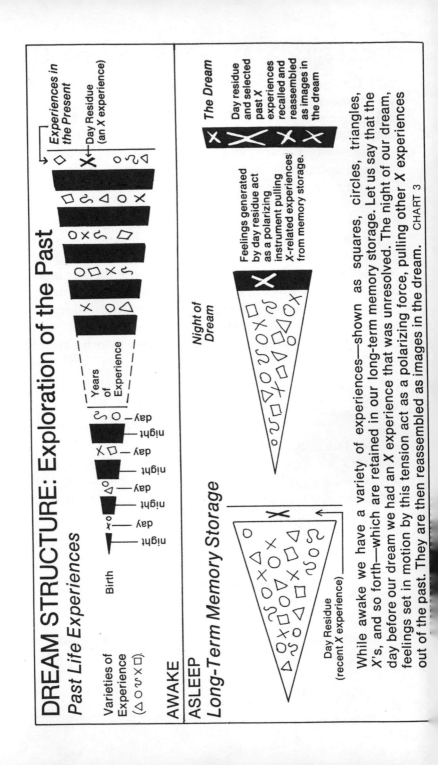

DREAM STRUCTURE: Exploration of the Past
Past Life Experiences

Varieties of Experience (△ ○ ▽ × □).

Experiences in the Present

Day Residue (an X experience)

Birth — Years of Experience

night — day — night — day — night — day — night — day

AWAKE

ASLEEP
Long-Term Memory Storage

Day Residue (recent X experience)

Night of Dream

Feelings generated by day residue act as a polarizing instrument pulling X-related experiences from memory storage.

The Dream

Day residue and selected past X experiences recalled and reassembled as images in the dream

While awake we have a variety of experiences—shown as squares, circles, triangles, X's, and so forth—which are retained in our long-term memory storage. Let us say that the day before our dream we had an X experience that was unresolved. The night of our dream, feelings set in motion by this tension act as a polarizing force, pulling other X experiences out of the past. They are then reassembled as images in the dream. CHART 3

DREAM STRUCTURE:Development

AWAKE
ASLEEP

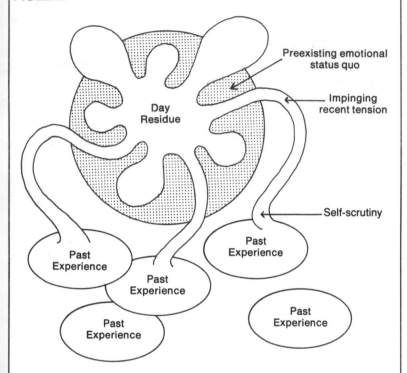

Preexisting emotional status quo

Impinging recent tension

Day Residue

Self-scrutiny

Past Experience

Past Experience

Past Experience

Past Experience

Past Experience

Rerepresentation of past:
1. Makes possible new arrangements
2. Exposes unrecognized aspects
   of past strengths and vulnerabilities

Questions Confronted:
What information and what benefit can my
past experience contribute toward solution
of the problem?
What resources, both healthy and defensive, can be
mobilized to cope with it?

CHART 4

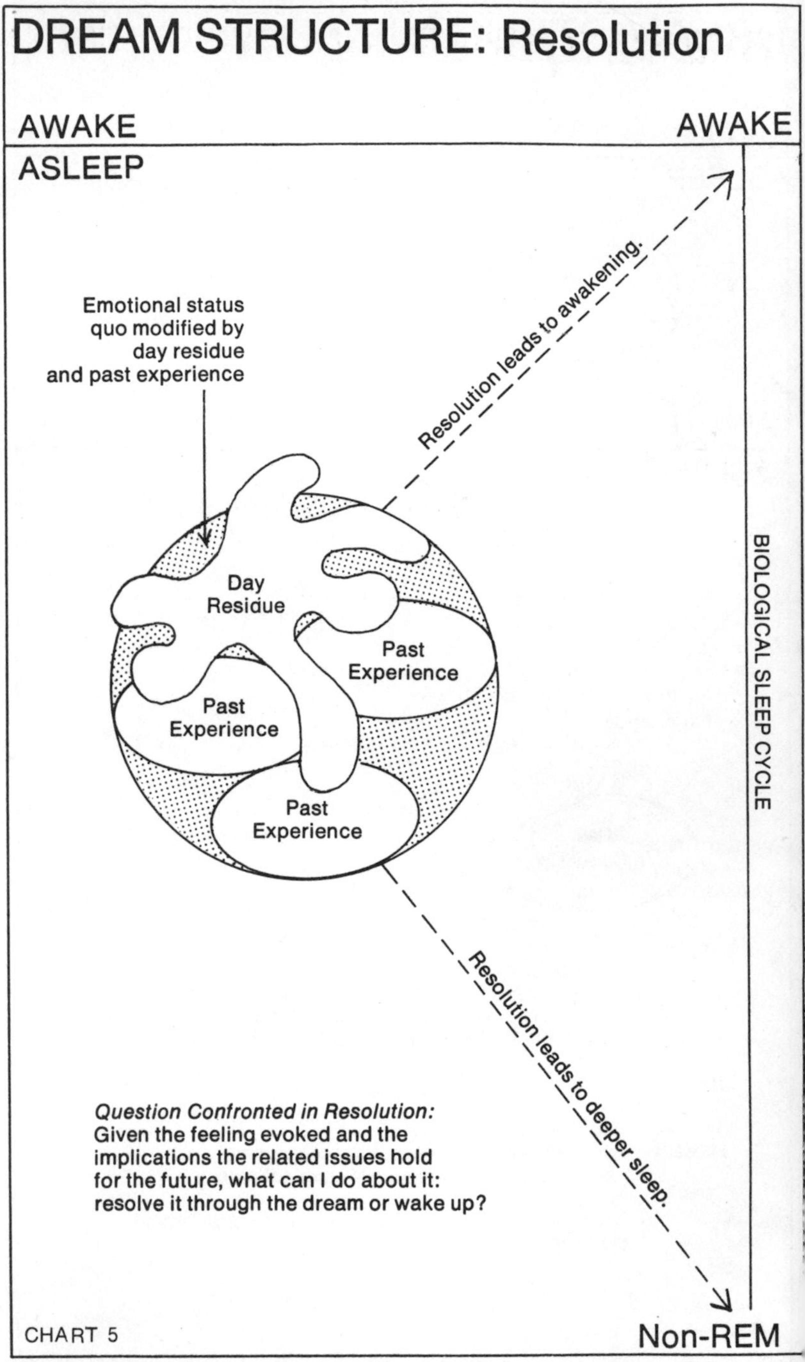

DREAM STRUCTURE: Resolution

AWAKE   AWAKE
ASLEEP

Emotional status
quo modified by
day residue
and past experience

Resolution leads to awakening.

Day
Residue

Past
Experience

Past
Experience

Past
Experience

BIOLOGICAL SLEEP CYCLE

Resolution leads to deeper sleep.

Question Confronted in Resolution:
Given the feeling evoked and the
implications the related issues hold
for the future, what can I do about it:
resolve it through the dream or wake up?

CHART 5   Non-REM

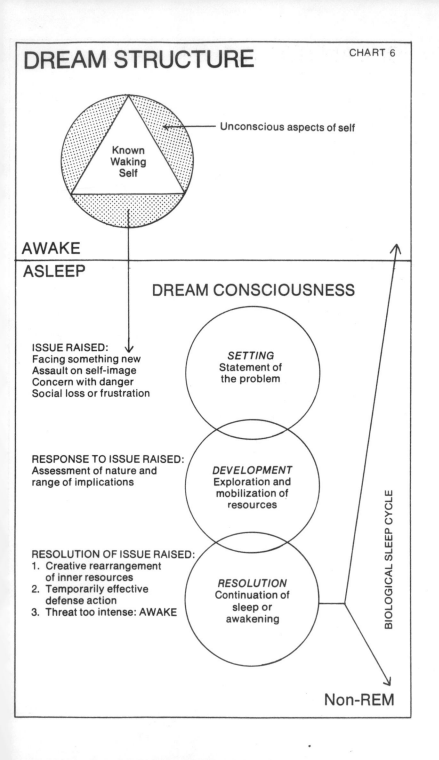

DREAM STRUCTURE

CHART 6

Known Waking Self

Unconscious aspects of self

AWAKE

ASLEEP

DREAM CONSCIOUSNESS

ISSUE RAISED:
Facing something new
Assault on self-image
Concern with danger
Social loss or frustration

SETTING
Statement of
the problem

RESPONSE TO ISSUE RAISED:
Assessment of nature and
range of implications

DEVELOPMENT
Exploration and
mobilization of
resources

RESOLUTION OF ISSUE RAISED:
1. Creative rearrangement
   of inner resources
2. Temporarily effective
   defense action
3. Threat too intense: AWAKE

RESOLUTION
Continuation of
sleep or
awakening

BIOLOGICAL SLEEP CYCLE

Non-REM

METAPHORS

CHART 7

WAKING METAPHORS	DREAM METAPHORS	MUTUAL CHARACTERISTICS
1. Verbal form	1. Visual form	1. Metaphors come into being with need to convey feelings
2. Known meaning immediately apparent	2. Unknown meaning— puzzling and unfamiliar	2. Reasons for need: a) Intensity and impact of feelings b) Subtlety, complexity, and unfamiliarity of feelings
3. Accepted mode of communication	3. Strange and private language	3. Object of metaphor: Recognition and identification of feelings
4. Consciously contrived	4. Unconsciously assembled	4. Source: Our creative imagination
5. Subject to conscious manipulation	5. Ruthlessly honest	
6. Owned	6. Frequently disowned	

CHART 8

METAPHORS

WAKING
Verbally Expressed

Rose

→ Connection directly made

Deliberate
Voluntary
Expressive of known feelings
Conveys more than ordinary speech

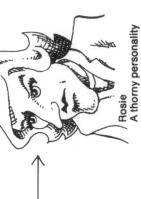

Rosy cheeks

DREAMING
Visually Expressed

Rose

→ Connection must be uncovered

Involuntary
Unwilled
Expressive of unknown feelings
Conveys more than simple
descriptive speech

Rosie
A thorny personality

cerned with expressing feelings, but he uses a different medium and addresses a different audience. (See Charts 7 and 8.) He digs into his personal repertoire of available images and rearranges them so that they become metaphorical expressions of the feelings and concerns he has at the moment. But whereas the poet is addressing himself to an audience outside of himself, the dream is a private communication intended to be personally, not universally, meaningful. We can pick up a poem written hundreds of years ago and find ourselves responding to the feelings being expressed. Isolated from its personal context, a dream will have more limited meaning. And there is one other interesting difference: What the dream does is done effortlessly, unconsciously, and seemingly spontaneously.

5

The Way a Dream Is

Sleep is the natural habitat of the dream, but what we call a dream is actually a pale facsimile of the original episode of dreaming. When we pull a fish out of the sea we can't expect to see it, feel it, and understand its way of life as if it were still swimming about freely, but we can learn something about it before it dies. And so it is with the dream. We have a brief time in which to learn something about it before it becomes frozen into a lifeless memory.

The remembered dream is like that flapping fish we were lucky enough to have caught. We have to do something with it or throw it back into the sea. And that brings up the first and perhaps most important difference between the way we relate to a dream while asleep and while awake. In our sleep we have no choice but to attend to the pictures that appear before us and involve us in the action. Once awake, we have the option of attending or not attending to the memory of these nocturnal images. Should we choose to attend to the dream, we become the accidental beneficiaries of a vast amount of research done during the night shift while our body was deciding how safe it was to remain asleep. As I see it, we do not dream a dream for the benefit of the waking state, but the waking state can nevertheless benefit from it. If, then, we are fortunate enough to recall the dream on awakening, we have the opportunity to look at the amount of information about ourselves that has been amassed and to dive back into the unfamiliar waters where the dream came from and learn more about the habitat that shaped the images.

 We know very little for certain about the source and function of our dreams. My view is a pragmatic one. It seems to me that the imagery generated and displayed during dreaming is meant to explore and assess the emotional impact of recent experience—and that that same imagery can be replayed during the waking state for our appreciation and understanding.

Once awake we have available to us the information that has gone into the shaping of our dream images. By exposing connections between the present and the past, our dreams shed light on both the strengths and weaknesses of our emotional heritage. In this sense they may be said to be a mechanism for emotional healing.

We seem to have no difficulty in understanding the concept of physical healing, but what does emotional healing mean? Simply, the repair of our relationships to people. While it is different from the physiological in that it takes place in interaction with others rather than within the confines of our own skin, it is just as real and equally important. Emotions register the state of our relations with others. It is this aspect of our lives that dreams monitor most sensitively.

The images we create at night intrude upon our sleep and

confront us with a dramatic display that evokes feelings. When this experience is carried over into the waking state we have the opportunity to explore the full range of meaning as well as the feelings contained in the imagery. In doing this we come upon less familiar and often disowned parts of ourselves. Dream work and the self-learning that goes with it are essentially the reestablishment of our connections to these aspects of our self.

The experience of dreaming is linked to healing by virtue of the honesty that shapes the images, the range and relevance of the information they contain, and the opportunity they afford for a growth-enhancing encounter with other aspects of ourselves. The healing power of the dream, then, is related to the information it contains and the manner in which it is expressed. Dreams often appear puzzling in the waking stage, not because they are intended to be, but because of our reluctance to come to terms with these other aspects of our nature.

To me, then, a remembered dream is an invitation to an emotionally healing experience. We become more "whole" as we learn how to read the messages to ourselves contained in our dreams—when we are able to cut through the personal myths, the self-deception, and just plain ignorance that have obscured the real nature of an issue of importance to us. We grow emotionally as we allow ourselves to face the truth of the matter.

Our emotions work to link us to other human beings and to safeguard those linkages. We cannot talk about emotional well-being except in terms of our connection to and relatedness with significant others in our lives. But often we don't understand those connections. Things sometimes go astray in childhood, so that we all carry unfinished emotional business from our past. Our dreams keep reflecting back to us the poorly understood, the dimly grasped, the disowned and avoided—all that is unknown and/or frightening, all that is alien to our waking self. To get at the truths involved may mean disrupting an emotional status quo, whether the truths are painful or not. All I can say is that it is worth it.

Let's look at the healing process in detail and see how the specific attributes of a dream lend themselves to it. To do so we'll use another dream from one of my groups:

Paula's Dream

There was to be a piano contest with various prizes, five hundred dollars being the biggest. I went to that place. My family was somehow there also. I felt too old to really compete and felt quite strange as I haven't played the piano that much in years. I felt awkward and went half-heartedly. I looked at a few pieces of music in a book and started to play one of the pieces. Down the street I saw a little black boy, very cute, about four or five years old. He was leaving his home, saying, in wide-eyed naiveté: "They really give people five hundred dollars?" His mother was explaining it to him. In the midst of this my family is expecting that I'll be in the contest. I know it's inappropriate. I seem too old for this sort of thing.

There are five aspects of dreams that have to do with healing: the relevance to a current predicament; the mobilization of pertinent information from the past; the honesty with which the information is presented; the bearing it has on our state of connectedness to significant others; and finally, the self-confronting and expressive way in which we present all of this to ourselves. Let's go through them with this dream.

Relevance

The content of a dream is triggered by one or more recent events. Referred to as the day residue, such events play a role because of the reverberations they set off into our past. The term is a rather loose one, since it may include events from the recent past, and not just from the day before the dream. Some aspect of a current happening strikes us as challenging, unfamiliar, or novel in some way. For such an event to gain admission to our dream life, it has to possess another quality —emotional intrusiveness. The event itself, or the feelings connected with it, persist and often surface to consciousness in the moments before we fall off to sleep.

The dreamer, Paula, is a young, unmarried professional woman in her mid-thirties, living in New York. On her mind at the time of the dream were major changes she was contemplating concerning where she would live and the kind of work she would be doing. The evening before the dream she received a telephone call from her parents. They live in Chicago and their calls were infrequent. Her father had seen an ad for a position in Indianapolis that he thought might interest her. Paula took this not as a disinterested suggestion but as a veiled hint that it was time she came back to some place closer to home. The more she protested that she was not interested because her own desire was to remain in the East, the more insistent her father became. She found herself reluctantly responding to this pressure by yielding to his insistence that she at least take down the information.

The telephone call and the feelings it evoked were immediately connected to the dream. Once again she was in a situation so familiar to her as a child, a situation in which her parents tried to influence her without really understanding her point of view. As she began to see this connection more clearly, some of her present concerns came into sharper focus.

Her anxieties centered about the move she was contemplating. It involved decisions as to which city to settle in and what direction to pursue in her career. One of her concerns was having enough money to make the move which would force her to buy a car. She had also gone through an illness recently which had left her in a physically debilitated state. The telephone call came, then, at a time when she felt drained physically and financially and when she was experiencing considerable anxiety about her future. Her parents had occasionally made offers to help in the past but she had refused for fear that there would be strings attached. She had been independent of her family financially since the day she had started college. As she spoke to her parents on the phone that night she again felt resistive to their overtures. This time, however, there was a certain poignancy about it because, after many years of separation, she did want to get back to her family. She just didn't feel ready right now.

Mobilizing Information

The new information in our dreams may be something from the past that we have forgotten or it may be something known and familiar but rearranged to appear in a new light.

The piano contest took Paula back to her childhood and to the authoritarian upbringing she had been subjected to. It reminded her of the many situations she had been in as a child when she had had to perform in areas which met some need of her parents, but which had no relationship to her needs or abilities. Piano playing was one of these. It was her father's thing, not hers.

The five-hundred-dollar figure in the dream had several

meanings for her. It was the amount of money she had once borrowed from her father and had never repaid. The memory of it brought back old uncomfortable feelings of obligation and indebtedness to her parents.

The figure five hundred also brought to mind the famous Indianapolis 500 auto race and conjured up images of dangerous competition and the excitement of winning. Competing and excelling were important values in her home. It also had reference to Indianapolis where her father wished her to be.

When a single element in a dream, such as the figure five hundred, conveys multiple meanings, it is said to be overdetermined. This is a common feature of our dream life.

The image of the incredulous black boy reminded her of her own naive acceptance of her parents' way of life. Being black and a boy emphasized for her the fact that, despite her acceptance of the situation, she experienced herself as different.

The situation depicted at the end of the dream was a familiar one to her. The expectations of her family made her acutely aware of how inappropriate those expectations were to her own needs and how little her family understood her.

Honesty

We have emphasized the honesty with which our emotional life is revealed in dreams. As we get into the metaphorical ramifications of Paula's dream imagery we see that all aspects of the conflict are brought into view exactly as the dreamer is experiencing them at that moment. Here is the message that is telegraphed to the dreamer: "Live up to my parents' expectations and I can go after the grand prize. The fact that what they expected and what I need are poles apart escaped them just as much now as it did when I was a child. Even though I know this and feel the old awkwardness and inappropriateness, part of me does get drawn into the situation." She finds herself toying with the idea of responding to her parents' overtures. At the same time her recollections of the way things have turned out in the past make her wary of compromising her present independence. She still feels vulnerable in relation to her parents.

When emotional sore spots persist, they do so because we continue to have misconceptions about ourselves. These misconceptions distort the way we see ourselves and others. I will use the term *personal myth* to refer to the basic misconception and the term *self-deceptive strategy* to refer to the misperceptions that help to keep the myth alive.

It is in the nature of dreams to expose and puncture personal myths so as to shed light on the self-deceptive strategies we use to hide truth from ourselves. Once the myth can no longer obscure them, the underlying realities come into view. Paula was struggling with a not uncommon myth in young people: that she needs to be Superwoman, to excel, to star in all undertakings. And to be able to do it on her own, with no help from anyone. The myth could be perpetuated only through misperceptions of her own resources as well as the resources and intentions of others. Her experience in her family led her to distrust the intentions of others and to hold the conviction that the price for help from others would always be too high. She had come to a turning point in her life at which the Superwoman myth had to be laid to rest. But she had not yet conquered the fear that dependence on others might compromise her own autonomy.

Linkages, Connections, and the Bonding Power of Dream Life

This dream helped Paula realize that the problems she faced could be resolved only through intermingling her own resources with the resources of others. She had known this intellectually, but the dream pointed out the fears she had of acting on it emotionally. When her father made an offer to help her buy a car she experienced it as both a promise (of financial support) and a threat (you'll have to become daddy's little girl again). In recoiling from this she doesn't fall back on the "I can do it myself " myth but feels that her task is now to reorient herself realistically to the fact that there *are* people who can be in touch with her needs and whom she can call upon for help. Feeling this way she can accept her own wish to get back to her family—but not until she is ready, not until she can do it without fear of losing any of her independence. The dream did not solve the problem for her but it did help her decide in which direction to move.

The tendency to focus on relationships with others is, as noted before, an important feature of dreams. When we are awake we devote much of our energy toward maintaining our individuality, defining our autonomy, and protecting our own borders. We experience ourselves as discrete individuals. We reach out to other discrete individuals and they reach out to us across what might be called emotional space—the extent of which is determined by the closeness or distance we feel in relation to others.

But when we go to sleep and start to dream, we begin to focus, not on our separateness, but on shortening this emotional space. Our concern is with the state of our connections to significant others and what has happened to these connections in the course of the day or two prior to the dream. To what extent has an encounter with the world hurt, impaired, corrupted, or threatened these connections? Conversely, to what extent has it touched off rich, unknown, and enhancing aspects of our relationship with others? It is as if our dreaming self is still concerned with certain fundamental facts that we seem to have neglected down through the course of human history: that we are all members of a single species; that the essence of being human is being connected with other humans; and that the schisms we have set up have kept us from realizing that vision when we are awake, a vision that has never been lost while we dream.

Self-confrontation

Paula's dream can be taken as an example of the way a dream expresses us to ourselves. Let us look at it more closely.

The images of a dream are, by their very nature, confrontational and expressive. We dream in images because of the natural way they convey metaphorical meanings. Appropriate images are selected and arranged to depict, explore, and deal with the issue at hand. In the opening scene of the piano contest we can feel the discomfort and dismay of the dreamer, the sense that the situation is awkward and strange for her, while her family seems oblivious to it. The image is a poignant, visual metaphor for the kind of distress that children feel when they are expected to perform for the benefit of their elders. A single image confronts her with the dilemma of her childhood, sums it all up powerfully and simply.

The black child who reacts so incredulously to the prize money offers another commentary, not only on the dreamer's childhood, but on the world of childhood in general. Children often do experience themselves as different and they can

met mother-
mother-
monster

be taken in by the prizes that adults dangle before them.

In the dream Paula begins to play the piano piece. We can feel her temptation to compete, to yield to the expectation of her parents, and the reluctance, then the pulling away, the recognition that she has outgrown that.

The dream ends on a note of uncertainty that expresses the fact that the conflict has not yet been set to rest. But the dream poses it more sharply and dramatically than Paula herself, consciously, ever had. She had made no choice: It is the very lack of resolution that is pointed out by the dream. Once Paula received that message, she became more aware of the extent and manner in which her past continues to exert its influence on the present. Enhanced self-awareness, rather than magical resolution of problems, is the end product of effective dream work. It is also the path to the healing of old emotional wounds.

6

Guidelines
to Dream Work

Dream work then, is essentially the effort to move into unexplored areas of our personality. But what strategy and tactics are needed to lay claim to the emotional territory covered by a dream? First of all it's necessary to realize that we are not out to hunt down an enemy, but to make a friend. We are not seeking any power or control over territory to be subjugated. Rather we are seeking to grow in depth by reorganizing our identity with the help of the images that inhabit this territory. To do that, we must start by increasing our awareness that there *is* territory to be explored. And that involves us in the problem of dream recall and recording.

Recalling Dreams

Obviously you must recall a dream in order to work with it. Working with dreams, therefore, often involves a self-conscious effort to recapture them. They seem to be intrinsically elusive, to dissolve soon after they are dreamt. Even if their presence intrudes insistently after we awaken, more often than not they fade shortly after. An intense dream may have a hauntingly extended life of its own, but such dreams seem to be the exception rather than the rule.

It is a good thing that we don't have anywhere near one-hundred-percent dream recall; otherwise we would carry into our waking life images and feelings associated with all our dreaming episodes of the night before—approximately one hundred minutes a night—and would be so inundated with our own dreams that we might not have time to cope with the realities of waking life.

The best way to start remembering your dreams is to tell yourself you are going to. If you want to badly enough, you can increase your own spontaneous yield of dreams. Ask those who enter into psychoanalysis. Even if they have not recalled their dreams since childhood, they will often start remembering them soon after they begin treatment. So the thing to do is to instruct yourself to remember just as you are about to drift off to sleep.

Some people can train themselves to wake up during dreaming periods. Most of us, however, have to start our dream recall efforts when we awaken in the morning. There is a three-part strategy that can be useful.

First, immediately upon awakening (either during the night or in the morning) train yourself to turn inward to allow any residual dream feelings or images to rise to the surface. To do this, lie quietly, minimize movement, and avoid distraction. Make a conscious and deliberate effort to avoid any act or gesture that would dispel the afterglow of the dream experience. Don't turn on the light, go to the bathroom, or even change position in bed. It does not matter whether what comes to you is from the beginning or the end of the dream. The main thing is to prevent anything from interfering with the state of quiet necessary for the dream's resurgence. Once you have pieces of the dream within your grasp, it is far easier to arrange it in proper order. If you can stay with the dream immediately upon awakening, your recall will be spontaneous and detailed. But if you lose it and try to recapture it you will have to pick it out scrap by scrap.

Second, particularly if you awaken during the night, write down whatever comes to you—an image, a fragment, or an entire dream. That means have a pencil and paper at your bedside. Some people find it easier to use a tape recorder. You can avoid turning on a light and disturbing your mate by having a small flashlight or flashlight pen nearby. Remember that if you don't write the dream immediately, it will probably have disappeared by morning. So don't just review the dream in your mind and reassure yourself that you will remember it. By morning all you are apt to recall is that you had a very important dream to remember.

Finally, while you are trying to outwit your dream demolition machinery, approach the task optimistically, even though you sense at the moment of awakening that the dream has already vanished. Perhaps it has, but all or part of it may still be salvageable. Don't focus on the fact that you have apparently drawn a blank. Instead, begin to see if by remaining quiet, you can make any residue, any image, any fragment or feeling find its way back into your consciousness. If so, you may be able to use it as a lever to pry some additional fragments loose. An entire dream can be recaptured this way.

Recording Dreams

It is important to record a dream as close to the time of its occurrence as possible. The longer the delay in getting it down on paper the greater the opportunity for taking liberties with it, for losing some of the detail, and even forgetting sections of it. The longer the delay the more chance for some of the content to be contaminated by waking thoughts. Put down every detail you can, every feeling you remember. Don't clean up a dream to make waking sense. Even though the peculiar aspects of a dream are often hard to put into words, get them there. Don't let yourself gloss over any aspect of the dream.

While you are recording your dream add any thoughts you can remember going through your mind just as you were about to drop off to sleep. What were you preoccupied with? These thoughts will often give important clues to the dream. Here is an example of such an instance, presented by a woman undergoing therapy:

> I woke with the image of myself impaled on top of a flagpole.

She had no associations and could do nothing with the dream. She was asked about her presleep thoughts.

> J. [her husband] wanted to have sex. I wasn't in the mood and offered some resistance. To my annoyance, he insisted and I ended up feeling both helpless and resentful.

Once her attention was drawn to these presleep thoughts, the connection to the dream immediately dawned upon her.

She felt as if she had been impaled at the end of a penis in an act which left her high and dry.

You may find the Dream Report Chart (Chart 9) useful in organizing your dream day-residue and presleep thoughts.

Simply keeping a dream journal can also be very useful. As a record of dreams alone, a journal can reveal much about your personal style of dreaming, the kinds of symbols you seem to favor, and the kinds of predicaments in which you seem to find yourself in your dreams. A word of caution, however. Unless you work on your dreams and keep some record of the work done, the dreams may seem obscure and lifeless when later reviewed. For a dream journal to be maximally useful requires a major commitment of time and energy—soon after the dream is first recalled. Yet there must be space left for later reflections; your initial work may set things going that don't surface clearly in your consciousness until some time has elapsed. So, if you decide to keep a dream journal, make sure to get the basic data down as soon as possible—especially your dominant emotion upon awakening. Record your feeling. Don't worry about arranging the entire dream in order unless you have so vivid a recollection of the total dream in its original sequence that you can simply write it from beginning to end. The important thing is not how you record your dream but that you preserve its mood, images, and scenes until you can do further work on it. When you begin to transcribe your nighttime rough notes into permanent form you'll often remember more details, even scenes that were omitted during the initial recall.

Sometimes we may have no recall of a dream on awakening—remember only that we did dream—and then the dream will flash back later in the day, triggered by something happening to us. The nature of the triggering experience, as

CHART 9

DREAM WORK SHEET

Name_____ Dream#_____
                                        Date _____

Dream:

Feelings:

Metaphors suggested by the imagery:

Personal Information: relating emotions of
dream to recent events, thoughts, and feelings

    Waking Context:

     Presleep thoughts:

Associations: integrating metaphors and
waking context

well as the dream, should be recorded. It may well be the clue
to the meaning of the dream.

Please remember one thing: No written record can recapture a dream in its entirety. It simply represents the best
reconnaissance photo we can make of the territory exposed
to view during the night.

And now we are ready to engage with the dream itself.

Repossessing a Dream

Before we can begin to identify with a dream we must
know something about our waking state, its limits and its
vulnerabilities. Our goal, after all, is to reclaim aspects of
ourselves that, up to that point, our waking self is either
unfamiliar with or has actively disowned. The imagery our
dream used in expressing these aspects strikes us as strange
since we look at it from the point of view of the waking state.
(See Chart 10.) And, unfortunately, we are culturally condi-
tioned to remain ignorant about our dream life. Throughout
human history people have focused much more on worldly
accomplishment than on the state of their inner life. Culturally we have made maximum use of our aptitude for language, logic, and order. As I have said, our linguistic abilities
are lodged in the left cerebral hemisphere (usually the dominant hemisphere), and we have become left-brain-oriented
people. In school we were taught to read and write, but not
how to relate to our rich imaginative dream life. The talents
of our right brain go relatively unacknowledged; for the most
part our emotional range and the problems posed by our
feelings are left to us to work out on our own, often in
devious and anarchic ways. Yet our dreams are as much a
part of our lives as is our waking state.

It takes work against resistance to transform the strange

TWO STATES OF CONSCIOUSNESS

Seeming Incongruities
Resolved by Dream Work

CHART 10

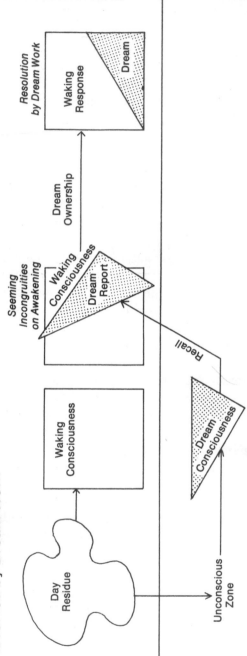

The diagram shows two different forms that consciousness takes. Waking consciousness (square shape) feels natural to us in the waking state. While we are dreaming, dream consciousness (triangular shape) also feels natural despite any strange and incredible events going on. When the dream is brought into the waking state, it seems incongruous and puzzling. Dream work creates a natural fit between the two forms.

scenario of a dream into something understandable and meaningful. When you remove a dream from its native, nocturnal habitat and present it to your waking self, it is surrounded by both friends and enemies. The friends of the dreaming self pursue the truth; the enemies seek to maintain the distance and sense of alienation, to aid that part of ourselves not ready or willing to look inward. The more you get into dream work the more aware you will become of roadblocks interposed by your waking self and the work needed to get around them. All you can do is to ally yourself with that part of you pushing to discover the hidden truths of the dream and hope this urge proves stronger than the tendency to let the dream drift gently away.

The best way to start is to focus on those feelings conveyed by the imagery and action of the dream. Can you feel your way back into it to pick up the mood and changes in tone as the dream progressed? Are there any feelings that persist into the waking state? Focus on the images of the dream and try to identify the points of connection between those images and your own life, past and present. Consider every person or object in the dream as a separate dream element and potentially important. Allow yourself to associate freely to each dream element, but remember that you are trying to shed light on the element itself; don't use the dream as a jumping-off point for an endless search into your own past. Just pry open the past to allow the thoughts and feelings aroused by the dream to rise to the surface.

Let us take a common type of dream: You find yourself back in a classroom, taking an examination and dreading the outcome. I have been out of medical school for forty years and yet I have dreams of this kind in which I find myself taking the final fourth year examination. Ask yourself what feelings predominated. Feelings of inadequacy, incompetence, fear of failure, concern with performance, feelings of competition, a need to excel, feelings of being judged, fear of exposure, excitement about the challenge? Do those specific feelings remind you of any recent happenings when you experienced the same feelings?

Sometimes it is the *absence* of feelings or the *inappropriateness* of feelings to the corresponding imagery that strikes us. In a dream you might find yourself on a battlefield, seemingly oblivious to the shells and bullets flying around you. Then ask yourself what connection you can make to past or present situations that others regarded as dangerous but you did not. Or perhaps the question should be, What situation of danger were you in that you were unaware of? The main thing is to examine the possibilities.

Once you have a glimmer of where the dream imagery is leading, you have to get closer to the dream by addressing the images and learning how to look at them metaphorically. In each instance the question to be raised is: What life circumstance is suggested by any of the attributes or qualities of the image? When you ask this of the images in your dreams you are apt to come up with a number of responses which do not register. But sooner or later one of the images will come alive with meaning. Our dreams are not a simple replay of the day's events, much as they may at times seem to be. There are metaphorical overtones that go beyond any literal meaning the events may have for us.

But now let's investigate some of the places our dreams go.

Sexual dreams

Sexual imagery is a prominent aspect of our dream life because of the important role that sex plays in our lives, the social constraints and conventions that govern it, and the problems that often arise around sexual needs. Furthermore, sex is the only significant bodily need for which actual rather than hallucinatory gratification can and does occur while dreaming. Sexual dream images can be dramatic and forceful metaphors to convey other feelings. After all, in everyday speech sexual epithets are often used to express aggressive or hostile intent.

By a sexual dream we mean one in which both the content and the feelings are sexual in character. Perhaps the dreamer was exposed to excessive sexual stimulation without consummation. Any unusual or enforced period of abstinence may result in a sexually tinged dream. Frank sexual dreams often occur during adolescence and not infrequently are associated with nocturnal emissions in the male and the experience of orgasm in the female. In this kind of dream there may be little if any departure from a realistic portrayal of the sex act.

In adults sexual needs and preoccupations are usually dealt with more indirectly. The visual scenes created by the dreamer and triggered by some recent life event are, in fact, metaphors intended to convey the dreamer's relationship to a particular problematic aspect of the dreamer's own sexuality. A male patient feeling driven in response to unsatisfied sexual urges, dreams of finding himself in a small boat being towed off the water by a giant airplane (the phallus erect). His sense of himself (i.e., the boat that he is in) is one of being pulled through life by the exaggerated importance of his penis (the giant airplane rising in the air).

Often there are both direct and indirect expressions of the sexual theme, the metaphors concerned with the context in which the act is carried out (at home or away from home, with the marital partner or a stranger) or how the outcome is depicted (gratification, frustration, failure, etc.).

Sometimes sexual imagery is a metaphor to express feelings of closeness and intimacy as well as the defensive maneuvers mobilized to ward off such feelings. Or a dreamer's preoccupation may be with questions of superiority and inferiority. Issues of control or loss of control may be expressed in sexual images. And strategies of aggression or retreat may be depicted as part of the dreamer's struggle against the intimacy and closeness of the sexual encounter.

The appearance of sexual imagery in a dream, therefore, may be the result of any current preoccupation of the dreamer—from that of explicit sexual needs to that of the need for closeness and intimacy with another.

Suppose, for example, a man had a dream hinting at latent homosexual tendencies. The dream may not mean at all that the dreamer *is* a latent homosexual, but rather that some kind of sexual feeling is emerging in him. He needs the freedom to recognize and confirm this. A person who has been excessively inhibited might initially have his sexuality expressed in his dreams in relation to someone of his own sex: someone more known and familiar. There is no need to accept a ready-made label prepackaged in an orthodox theory.

And so the dreamer should ask:

Is my dream the result of unmet sexual tensions?

Am I expressing a problem of my sexual life?

Am I expressing a problem of my life in sexual metaphors?

Lucid dreams

A lucid dream, as we have seen, is one in which you become aware of the fact that you are dreaming. Celia Green, in her excellent monograph, "Lucid Dreams," describes the conditions that lead to lucidity in dreams, the many forms such dreams take, and the way they end. She describes a "prelucid" dream as one in which a critical attitude causes the dreamer to ask: Am I dreaming? She also describes a phenomenon related to lucid dreaming called "false awakening." The dreamer is convinced that he has awakened only to discover that he is still dreaming, or, as in the following example, returns to sleep only to realize later that it was all a dream.

One dreamer about to attend a first dream group had this for a lucid dream:

> I was dreaming that I was dreaming and that I woke up and remembered the dream. I told myself in the dream that I could not possibly present such a tacky, inadequate, dull dream. I was disappointed so I told myself I had to go back to sleep to get a more interesting production going.

Many lucid dreams develop in the course of a nightmare and occur in connection with the dreamer's attempt to waken himself. When a dreamer feels threatened in a dream it is not uncommon for him to reassure himself by saying that "it is only a dream." The period of lucidity in these dreams is very brief and leads almost immediately to awakening.

Lucid dreams often tend to be more realistic in content than other dreams. The dreamer discovers or concludes that it is a dream when he is able to identify some incongruous element in the dream or become aware that some realistic details are missing. Once lucidity sets in the dreamer may attempt to control the future course of the dream.

Repetitive dreams

Dreams containing imagery similar to that of previous dreams and associated with similar feelings may occur sporadically or frequently. Such dreams deal with some recurrent issue in the life of the dreamer that has not been set to rest. Although the dreamer borrows images he has used in connection with this issue in the past he arranges them in ways that reflect where he is now and what changes, if any, have occurred. Once the issue is resolved, either in reality or through the successful working out of the dream, the repetitive dream ceases.

These dreams not infrequently go back to something that has been lost: a secure harbor, some source of excitement or pleasure. They may also concern the search for a lost relationship that had been fulfilling in some way.

A young woman had a repetitive dream in which a former boyfriend, from whom she had separated several years before, kept turning up and showering his affections on another girl. She was puzzled because she did not consciously regret the separation and had no desire to have him back. He had attracted her because of what she described as his "life force."

> This was a characteristic of him that I admire and wish to have in myself. I see him as alive, energetic, vital, into what he is doing and loving his life. By comparison I feel I am wasting time, unsure of who I am and with a blank feeling about the future.

The description of her former boyfriend led to the discovery of the hold this dream had over her. Actually she is also a vital, alive person who has not yet found herself. She is in the process of breaking with a conventional life-style and is actively trying to move into areas that she really wants to work in. Aware of this vitality and life force within herself, but unable to move toward its realization, her dream strategy was to connect with someone who did encompass these qualities.

Problem solving in dreams

There are many ways that dreams help solve problems we face in life. Actually all dreams are problem solving or are,

at least, attempts at solutions. Life is a series of learning
encounters in which we are called upon to make discoveries
about ourselves. Dreams register the tensions that are generated and explore the resources we have developed to cope
with them. Dreams are sometimes quite remarkable in the
way they enable us to make discoveries about the world.
There are many popular accounts of this kind of inventiveness leading to specific solutions. One was the invention of
the sewing machine. In a dream Elias Howe saw holes in the
spears held by threatening natives, and this suggested to him
the relative position of the hole in the needle that he needed
for perfecting the sewing machine.

Because dreams reflect back to us our own preoccupations,
they often seem to come as a response to our conscious need
to solve a particular problem. When we seem to reach some
sort of solution it is because our dreaming self takes a long
view of things and places the problem in its proper perspective against the backdrop of our lives. If, in fact, the problem
we address to our dreaming self is one which that dreaming
self judges of little consequence despite our concern, it is apt
to ignore the problem in favor of something else that it deems
more important.

When we speak of influencing our dreams, we are talking
about something both relative and unpredictable. When we
realize this we will not be deluded by the fantasy that we can
manipulate our dreams but will learn to count on them for
help with genuine, important concerns. The dreaming self
works with a larger version of our reality than is accessible
to our waking self and is therefore not manipulable by the
latter. However, our two selves are really one and try to work
in unison with each other.

I once was quite puzzled after an initial interview with a
young psychologist who had come to me for treatment. He
set a belligerent, skeptical, and challenging tone and dis-

played a degree of aggression that was not easy to deal with. I tried to listen respectfully to his view, but I felt uneasy about the session, unsure of the effectiveness of the position I took, and concerned about the severity of the pathology. I went to bed hoping consciously that a dream would shed some light on the dynamics of the situation. I had a dream that night in which I was gently leading a very tame and friendly ape down a path. This proved to be a truer picture of who my patient was than the wild and uncontrollable gorilla I had feared he might be!

Prophetic, prognostic, and warning dreams

While dreaming we are exquisitely sensitive to changes so subtle that they have not yet registered in our waking consciousness. We pick up psychological and physiological changes in their incipient stages, and if we are alert to the message of the dream we can be forewarned of their occurrence. There are many accounts of changes in one or another bodily organs that first registered in a dream. Psychological and emotional currents that we are unaware of may play out their trends first in a dream and only later in our waking life. Dreams that are truly precognitive, that is, those predicting events of which there are at present no indications, subtle or otherwise, are to be distinguished from the *apparently* precognitive dream. An example of the latter would be to dream of encountering a broken bannister while walking down a familiar flight of steps and then to have the bannister break the following day. The likelihood is that some subtle indication of the impending break registered in your mind and was an important enough event to be explored and recognized in the dream. But had you encountered a broken bannister in a building you had never been in before, yours might then have been a genuinely precognitive dream.

A woman in a dream group told us that every time water in any form appeared in a dream she would invariably experience a severe headache the next day. Two days later she reported a dream, one seemingly insignificant detail of which was the appearance of a small puddle of water. The following day she had one of her typical headaches.

Let's take a few more commonly experienced dreams and look at some of the metaphorical meanings that can be drawn from their imagery:

Dreams of flying

These may take different forms. You may find yourself walking, running or jumping, or remaining in the air for a long time. Or you may actually find yourself flying through the air. *Some* of the possible metaphorical implications might be:

I feel pleased, satisfied, high about something I have done.

I feel competent, effective, powerful in relation to a recent happening in my life.

I feel special, different, in some way superior to others.

I am surprised at the discovery of some unusual ability that I didn't know I had.

I am sexually potent, my penis is up.

Dreams of falling

These may take any number of forms from a simple sensation of falling to a specific scene, such as a fall off a cliff.

I have lost control.

I feel helpless.

I am in danger.

In case of a woman, I have sexual guilt—the metaphor of a fallen woman.

I have lost status in someone's eyes.

I have fallen from grace.

I am without support, have no foundation.

The number of metaphors that can be taken from even the simplest image is limited only by your imagination. The more you can think of, the more likely you are to hit on the right one.

Teeth falling out

This may be associated with various feelings:

Feelings of embarrassment and weakness.

Feelings of loss, particularly of something taken for granted.

Of passivity, impotence.

Of being at a loss for words.

Of concern with aging and with the general diminution of one's powers.

A dream in which baby teeth are lost may mean getting ready for whatever life has to offer.

Dreams of water

Water turns up frequently in dreams and in many different contexts. It may have broad, generalized references to the unconscious, to the womb and the security of intrauterine existence, to mothering, nurturing, and so on. It may represent something mysterious, threatening, dangerous. It may have more specific sexual references to the place where sperm (fish) swim around. It may represent our dream life (swimming around in a different medium).

The important question might be, What sort of water? A

swimming pool might convey leisure, competition, or
confinement of movement; a running river, the stream of life;
tides crashing on the shore, power outside our control, or
sexual surgings; a quiet deep pool, the existence of inner
resources.

Being naked in a public place

Have you found yourself in an embarrassing situation
lately? Have you felt exposed, ashamed, vulnerable? Has
your social facade been stripped away? Frequently in such a
dream the dreamer is the only one aware of the nudity. Are
you in possible danger of being seen for what you are? Are
you accepting the fact that you may be seen for what you are?
Are you trying to be seen for what you are?

Dreams of death

More often than not dreams of death, even of our own,
do not have an ominous meaning. They may, indeed, convey grief, despair, and loss. Or they may simply signify the
end of an episode in our life, even an anticipation of something new beginning. A dream of death may be connected
with aggressive, hostile thoughts toward the dead person:
Our dreams often resort to hyperbole to get their point
across.

Dreams of being chased

Are circumstances closing in on you? Are you at the mercy
of feelings that threaten to get out of control? Are you being
victimized by someone else's aggression? Do you have feelings of guilt and a fear of being caught? Are you trying to
get away with something? Are you in the same position you

were in as a child when you felt endangered by forces that were more powerful than you?

Color in Dreams

Color in dreams can convey many feelings and ideas. Green and red appear most often and both can elicit the full range of emotional response. For example, green can have life-enhancing, nurturing meanings, or it can have negative connotations of envy, jealousy, spite. Red can refer to passion, excitement, danger, or have more specific meanings such as a red stain referring to menses. Yellow, too, can have bright, idyllic, exciting references, or suggest fear or cowardice. Blue may refer to openness, expansiveness, or a "blue" depressed mood. It may have a specific reference to a male infant. Even the color black can have positive or negative connotations: it can refer to dire forebodings, a black mood, fear, danger—or it can have reference to comforting nocturnal images.

In our own dreams we often fall back on specific colors to depict particular moods or specific memories. For one dreamer yellow always referred to her mother because of a characteristic yellow apron she wore. The important thing is to think about what individual colors have meant in your life.

People in Dreams

People, as well as objects, lend themselves to metaphorical expression in our dreams. The people who appear in our dreams may be known or unknown, living or dead, famous or obscure. We may be currently involved with them or they may emerge from the past. They may be clearly in focus or appear as vague figures that are difficult to define.

The people in our dreams may be who they are in waking life, but not as we ordinarily experience them. They may be there because a new or heretofore unrecognized tension has surfaced in our relationship: something new we are experiencing from them or something new in ourselves. In other words the appearance of the character may imply some change in the relationship. Or we may have cast the character in the dream because of a quality in ourselves that we associate with this character but are only beginning to recognize in ourselves.

Then there are the dreams in which people who are important to us appear more or less as they do in waking life. In these instances it is the relationship that is important to us. We are preoccupied with that relationship and so if any emotional shift in it occurs, we are apt to dream about it.

When we resurrect people from our past with whom we have had little to do, or dream of people of little or no significance to us, it is likely that that person exemplifies something we are beginning to sense or feel about ourselves, or about someone currently close to us.

Figures who are vague, ambiguous, or shadowy often have some reference to ourselves. Maleness and femaleness may be juxtaposed so as to highlight another side of ourselves.

Important relationships don't end with death, so that the same possibilities hold when we dream of someone who has died.

Characteristics of famous people often touch us in a personal way, and we may express this affinity by including some luminary in our dreams.

People appearing in great numbers may have reference to a particular scene or event: a party, a picnic, a threatening or supporting force.

Word Play

We do interesting things with language in our dreams. We are extremely talented punsters. We invent new words. We have fun with double meanings. We use old words in strange or seemingly inappropriate ways. We create novel arrangements of words. We do all this so as to get our feelings across to ourselves. This manipulation of language is a favorite metaphorical tactic. The names of people or places also provide rich opportunities for punning and double entendres.

A woman dreams of meeting her estranged lover in *Connect*icut: Are they connected or are the connections cut?

A woman dreams of a man named Israel. She seems to be asking: Is he for real?

A woman named Janice appears in a dream and it becomes apparent that the reference is to Janus, the two-faced Greek god.

Time and Space

An important aid in thinking metaphorically is to appreciate the liberties we take with time and space relations in order to express things that are emotionally related. Subtly or boldly we combine past and present. We may dream of ourselves or of others at a younger age or at various ages in the same dream. Time may move quickly or slowly. Events may seem to be happening outside of any logical time sequence. The point is that we are not concerned with the natural temporal order of things, but with a reordering of time that helps us represent our feelings in a visual way. Space is used in the same way. The size of objects or people, the distances depicted, orientation to the right, left, up, or down are all pointers to some metaphorical expression.

The Context of the Dream

The work we do with feelings, associations, and metaphors may or may not result in a satisfying sense of what the dream is saying. It is often necessary to define first the relevant waking-life experiences that served as the organizing focus of the dream. This is the day residue that Freud suggested might take any of five forms:

1. Recent experiences which have not been carried to a conclusion during the day because of chance interference.
2. Experiences we have not had the resources to cope with at the time—what is unsolved.
3. Experiences which we have rejected or suppressed during the day.
4. Material that is set in motion in our unconscious by the activity of the preconscious in the course of the day.
5. Daytime impressions which are indifferent and, for that reason, have not been dealt with.

I prefer to speak of these significant events as *the present context of the dream*. Something in this context registers within us as new, unfamiliar, or challenging. Our awareness may be slight, incidental, and peripheral, but it doesn't go away. It touches on some unfinished bit of emotional business in a vulnerable area in our makeup. It acts as a kind of emotional time bomb which ticks away so quietly during the day that we don't hear it. It goes off when we begin to dream.

Presleep thoughts frequently provide an important clue to the context of the dream. It is as if, in the quietness of bedtime, we set the stage for the dreams to come. Make a conscious effort to recall your thoughts and feelings just before falling asleep. If this doesn't provide a clue to the imagery, then go over in detail all that you did on the day preceding the dream.

Unless we are successful in building the bridge between the imagery and our present life-context the likelihood is that we will not experience a real sense of certainty and excitement about the meaning of the dream. If a dream is suspended in a temporal vacuum, divorced from its immediate context, it may be stimulating intellectually but will be a pale and abstract replica of what it could be. If you can relate the context to the imagery, you are well on your way to appreciating the dream.

Often, though not always, we can trace references in a dream to past experiences. Such memories can enrich and extend our understanding of the significance of the present context, just as clarity about the present context can help our understanding of the significance of certain past experiences. In this sense dreams can be looked on as multidimensional encounters with particular issues.

A study of the sequences within a dream, as well as of the sequence of dreams occurring the same night, can help in tracking images. If we recall two or more dreams in a night, work with any one of them may shed light on the rest. If an issue is of great importance it is apt to surface in each of the dreams even though there may be no obvious connections. The sequence may show a succession of different ways of coping with the issue, each succeeding way evolving out of the efforts of the prior sequence.

Digging out the knowledge about ourselves that dreams hold, calls for using our creative facilities. We must let our imagination go. We must play with the metaphorical possibilities of the imagery, even if it takes us into places we would rather not go.

A Dream Glossary

If you keep records of your dreams, you will be able to note the real events that seem to be associated with particular imagery. In this way you can begin to build up a personal dream glossary for yourself. Certain colors may point to certain kinds of experiences or feelings every time they appear in your dreams. Certain objects may serve as useful self-images. One dreamer consistently sees himself as a captain of a ship, a general, a conductor of an orchestra. Another may use the image of an old, beat-up but indestructible Volkswagen as a self-image. An older woman summoned up in her dreams the image of a young lover long since dead every time she felt frustrated and dissatisfied sexually. Scenes of Rome appeared to a young man of Italian extraction whenever he found the atmosphere in his American home too oppressive. Any reference to food or cooking in a young suburban housewife's dreams had very negative associations. Her mother had put too much stress on food.

You will find that your own images serve as markers to specific tensions or problem areas. Write them down, and you will have the only kind of dream dictionary that can work for you: one based on your own dreams.

Even then, be careful not to let any external interpretation dictate the meanings you give your images. Update your glossary periodically. Metaphors may change their meaning for you as you expand your range of experience and learn more satisfying ways of solving problems.

7

Picturing Our Predicaments

Up to now our emphasis has been on the imagery of dreams and on how to respond to that imagery. Let's look now at the predicaments we are apt to dream about: the situations containing varying degrees of tension that cannot be resolved immediately. All of us have to learn to come to terms with authority figures, with the need to establish our own identity, and, eventually, with the need to adapt to loss or separation. Predicaments in our lives may arise in any of these areas.

Do encounters with authority evoke compliance and conformity, or resistiveness and defiance? Is the impulse toward independence and self-assertiveness strong enough to cope with whatever situation is involved? Other tensions appear in the struggle to establish and maintain our own identity. Can we define and respect our uniqueness or do we retreat into the security of anonymity?

Are we caught up in issues involving sexual identity? Are we involved in the war between the sexes? Do we embrace

authenticity and avoid sham? Is achievement or possession
a cover for being and feeling? Do conventional pressures
crowd out our individuality? Do we relate more to a sense
of our own value as a person or do we settle for material
acquisitions? Will the selfish or the selfless side of our nature
emerge? In situations that demand decisions do we procrasti-
nate? Do we feel threatened in the face of loss? Are we
subject to unreal expectations, or can we accept realistic
limits?

What characterizes a predicament are the opposing pulls
we feel when we are in one. Although such predicaments are
infinitely variable in form and appearance they can generally
be resolved into such polarities as:

Independence ———————	Dependence
Self-assertion ———————	Compliance
Self-definition ———————	Anonymity
Activity ———————————	Passivity
Authenticity ———————	Sham
Essence ———————————	Appearance
Being —————————————	Having or Achieving
Accepting ———————————	Denying

Our vulnerability is shaped by our past; individually we
are inclined to encounter certain predicaments more than
others. One of the best ways to get to know something about
them is through dream work, for it can teach us how our past
helps or hinders our way of coping with the predicament. We
get to know where our emotional sore spots are and how they
came to be. We get to know who we are and who we were.
The learning involves effort. It may even be painful. But it
need not be mysterious or beyond our reach.

We have been dealing with dream imagery and its relation
to the concrete realities of everyday life. Now we are con-

cerned with the categories of *waking* life that have importance for our dream life. We thus have a two-way approach
to dreams: One takes into account the way we talk to ourselves while dreaming, and the other the kinds of actual
situations we get into that arise from a faulty dialogue with
our past. Dreams provide us with the opportunity to get this
dialogue on the right track; our struggle to get it there makes
up the content of the dream.

The predicaments vary in their importance and so in the
feelings evoked by the dream imagery that portrays them.
Our dreams can frighten, amuse, inspire, and shame us. We
often are shocked by the intensity of whatever feelings do
emerge. Dreams can make their point effectively by carica-
turing our frailties, taking us down a peg when needed. At
the same time they bring out our resources.

Let's look at some of the more common human predicaments and see how they were dealt with in some dreams
reported to me.

Facing Change

The prospect of change evokes hopes, wishes, and fears.
Robert, a young astronomer, busily pursuing a successful
career, had put off thoughts of marriage. By the time he
reached the age of thirty-five his mother had given up all
hope of his marrying and so had sent him a plate bearing the
inscription: "A bachelor is a rolling stone that gathers no
boss." But shortly after he got it, he met a young woman and
decided to marry her. The night that decision was made he
went to sleep wondering what effect this major step would
have on his dream life and what anxieties would surface as
a consequence of it. As he told it: "I awoke with an image

of myself tossing the plate my mother had given to me into the garbage."

Robert is a tall, powerfully built man. On the next night he had the following dream:

> I found myself in New York City, looking up at the Empire State Building and wondering why they were adding twenty-six stories to the height of the building.

His fiancée was twenty-six years old.

Robert was understandably concerned with the impact of his decision and the changes it would make in his life. His predicament was one of either welcoming or resisting change. His dreams came to his rescue with directness and humor: He will easily toss his old lifestyle away and his life will be made larger, not diminished, by the change.

Another dream involving change:

Grace, a middle-aged woman attending a dream group held at a spiritual retreat, presented the following dream:

> Someone is in my bedroom and will not leave. I am still awake, curled up in bed, playing possum, waiting for the person and other guests to leave. In a courtyard my friend Helen and her spouse point to a flat terracelike arrangement of stones and say, "Aren't those stones lovely!" I lie down and set the stones out so that they follow the outline of my body. An eighty-six-year-old artist friend says I directed them to do it this way. The person who is waiting outside our window, watching us sleep, leaves. I get up and there is a very large garden flat of tall, well-grown but overripe broccoli plants that the visitor has left for us.

Work on Grace's dream brought out her preoccupation with whether or not she should continue in what she has been doing professionally, or make a change. She feels that, in many ways, she has been playing possum. She has drifted passively into many pursuits without being passionately committed to any one. The stones are seen by her friends as lovely (which is the way others view her life), but she experiences them as rigid, limiting containers of her life. The old artist is someone who spends much time sitting immobile in a zen posture. He seems to point to the family roots of her own passivity. The blossoms on the broccoli plants were lovely but overripe, reflecting her feelings of having gone to seed.

Her predicament, as depicted in the dream, is whether or not to move from a passive position (outlining her body in stone) to an active one (getting up and seeing the plant); whether or not she can see her life as it is, both the positive (the tall, well-grown, lovely blossoms) and the negative (the overripe plants), so as to be better able to make the choice. The person waiting for her to wake up is that side of herself identified with the unused potential in her, ready for her to make changes in her life.

The Search for Identity

Rose, another participant in the same workshop, presented the following dream:

I was at a crossroads. It was not a superhighway, but more like a back road, unimproved, with a dirt surface rather than blacktop. There were small puddles as if it had rained. I looked across the intersection and saw a store. It was Sears. How nice! They put a

store way out here where they never had a store
before, out here in a country setting where I can
enjoy it and feel happy about it. I looked closely at
the sign. It said *Sale.* I thought to myself, I hope they
have that sale table I was looking for with all the nice
items.

Rose had felt very much as if she had been at a crossroads
in her search for spiritual support. Retreats, such as the one
she was attending, gave her something her church at home
failed to do. In her own words: "For six years coming here
filled a basic need I didn't feel was being met in my own
church. But now I've gotten something going in my church
and I just realized I don't need this anymore. There is that
store in the dream, back in that rural area, where I live, with
all the things there to choose from and the choice is mine."
The dream seemed related to a song that went through her
mind as she was meditating: "Eyes have not seen, ears have
not heard."

In addition to its obvious reference—Sears is a place where
you can find almost anything—the name was also linked
metaphorically to seers in the spiritual sense. "I think I had
this dream because last night I was weighing whether or not
to cut off the source, that is, skip coming to these retreats,
whether I was ready to take that step."

Her predicament: was she or was she not ready to move
from a passive, disciplelike identity to her true identity as a
leader and innovator.

In a dream group of mine in which psychotherapists participated, Lena, a young woman, mother of two small children, presented the following dream:

I came to a swimming pool with Eva (age six), Billy (age four). It's the pool used by the day center where I leave the children when my husband and I work. Eva likes bathing and she goes off to swim with the other children. I know that I won't be bathing. Billy, who is thin and small, goes into the big swimming pool and is in water up to his chin. I know it's too high. At first I'm annoyed that I have to take care of him. Then, suddenly, he is in a small swimming pool to the left. I see him under the surface of the water, looking up at me. I get afraid. I must pick him up. He looks up at me smiling, expectant and trustful. I feel warm and affectionate and then have no fear of his drowning.

The pieces came together in Lena's mind when someone in the group saw the last image of Billy in the small pool as a fetus in utero. After much work had been done on the dream, this is how Lena saw it:

Last week my daughter went away with other children for three days. I felt sad about her being away and at the thought that someday she will be away for good. When she came back she began acting more independent and this too made me feel some conflict. She is ready for more freedom and in the dream she goes off to the other children.

Billy still likes to be a baby. The image of him in the water makes me think of my conflict over getting pregnant again. I don't plan to have any more children for the next few years and up to now I took it for granted that if I got pregnant I would have an abortion. I don't want another child and yet I'm strongly tempted to have one. There was

something joyful about that womb image of Billy.
They asked me at the day center if I could help out
with a picnic for the children. I told them I didn't
have time because of my job. I felt sad, but also
relieved, because I had my job to justify it. These two
things were on my mind last night—feeling sad about
Eva outgrowing her babyhood and feeling torn about
not assuming more of the parental role.

Lena's predicament grew out of the two pulls she was
experiencing: to be for herself and pursue her professional
career, or to be for others and fulfill her yearnings for more
children. Her daughter's reaction and Lena's reaction to the
three-day holiday was the context that exposed the conflict.
The dream made Lena much more aware of the pull of her
own maternal instincts and she ended the session by saying,
"I'm not at all sure now that, were I to become pregnant, I
would have an abortion."

Sarah, an eighty-three-year-old member of a dream group,
continued to enjoy an active career as a painter. The theme
of many of her paintings was young children at play. Her
husband, although living at home, was quite senile and required a good deal of care. She told this dream:

I suddenly found myself three months pregnant. I
didn't give it any thought. I was calm and unworried.
I had arranged to go to a certain private hospital in
six months. The woman in charge there was a strong
motherly type. Her husband came to my house and
told my family that his wife would no longer be
connected with the hospital. I knew I would still go
there but felt confused. I was sorry, worried, and

disappointed. I'll just have to go there anyway. I was
my present age in the dream. I knew I was going to
give birth. I didn't think of having an abortion.

The day before the dream was a difficult one for Sarah. She
worked late into the night in her studio and for the first time
became aware of an oppressive feeling; she was burdened by
the responsibilities of preparing paintings for shipment, the
financial transactions involved, and so on. She came home
feeling confused and discouraged. But the following morning
after the dream she felt completely different. "The dream
cleared my head. I walked into the studio and decided I
could manage if I did just one thing at a time. My mind was
clear and I was able to organize my work."
   Either the dream or the night's rest had caused this effect.
If it was the dream, she was responding to it purely at an
emotional level because she hadn't worked out any meaning.
She associated the dream with her husband: "I do feel he is
a child. There are times he thinks I am his mother. He sleeps
a great deal. It's as if he withdraws into a cocoon. . . ."
   When asked about her presleep thoughts Sarah commented: "I went to bed angry with myself. I had taken on
too much and made myself frustrated. I did say to myself
before falling off to sleep: "Do I need to do all this? Can I
learn how to eliminate what is unnecessary?"
   Sarah now felt that her sense of relief was directly related
to the dream and its message that the Superwoman image
(the strong, motherly person in charge) had disappeared. In
the dream the strong maternal image was split. She had no
wish to be saddled with a helpless child at her age. But she
would put up with her burden (her husband-baby) and come
to terms with what she could and could not do.
   The predicament here was that despite her urge to go on
as she had always done, she was no longer able to deny the

limitations imposed by age and circumstances, and therefore had to surrender the Superwoman image of herself. Her ruminations about this before going to sleep and the events of the day that led to the feeling of discouragement were the context for the dream. She felt better in the morning for having faced the reality and having accepted it as part of the human condition.

Reactions to Loss

Ellen, a young psychiatric nurse, received a letter from her grandmother. The letter evoked feelings of sadness and guilt; sadness because it rekindled the poignant sense of loss she still felt following the death of her grandfather six months earlier, and guilt because she had been meaning to write to her grandmother and hadn't gotten around to it. That night she had the following dream:

> I was in a hospital as a nurse and taking care of my grandfather. I was involved with all kinds of technical procedures—his intravenous, monitoring his respirations, etc. I was telling him not to move and not to massage his legs, as this could dislodge a clot and he could have another heart attack. The scene shifted and it felt like a film or a movie. There were huge cartons of Campbell's soup and these were being sent to different countries like South America. I awoke sobbing and crying.

In associating to the dream, Ellen spoke of how very close she had felt to her grandfather. In his lifetime he had performed many good deeds, and following his death a number of projects were launched to memorialize him.

Seemingly out of the blue she mentioned that she had an artificial leg, and it soon became clear that the dream was a response to the rekindled sense of a dual loss: the loss of her grandfather and the loss of her leg. In both instances skilled technical help was of no avail in averting the final catastrophe. The warning in the dream about not massaging the legs lest a heart attack ensue might have reference to her keeping her own limbs as unobtrusive as possible lest what is wrong down there damage her aspirations as a woman (her heart).

The final scene involving the cartons of Campbell's soup refers both to her grandfather and herself. The huge cartons of soup being shipped to the needy is a reference to the projects undertaken in connection with her grandfather's death. There is also a subtle reference to a change in her own life. She has changed from medical nursing (symbolized in the dream by the emphasis on technical skills) to psychiatric nursing in a community setting where the emphasis is more on relating and giving to large groups of people. The sobbing and crying on awakening is understandable. Her grandfather and her leg are permanent losses and nothing can restore them. This capacity to release feeling based on the development of an emotional analogy is quite characteristic of a dream.

At age four Marion was in an accident. She awoke in a hospital after a period of unconsciousness. One of her eyes had been injured. She recalls the hospitalization as a frightening, devastating experience. She found herself alone in a room. Her parents were not allowed in and she was left unattended most of the time, as she recalls it. Only one young doctor showed her any kindness. She had to wear glasses from childhood on, something she resented as she felt it detracted from her looks. She had been increasingly unhappy about the need for glasses and had been exploring other possibilities, including a new variety of contact lens, the soft plastic lens. She had worn contact lenses before but resented being dependent on them. She had acquired new glasses on the day of the dream. The night before the dream she was with a male friend and removed her glasses. His immediate reaction was, "Your eyes are really beautiful and I never noticed them before."

Her dream that night had a nightmarish quality:

I am put away in a sanitarium or hospital. At first I am told it is because I am ill and have to be isolated and that I will be out in a week. The rooms are cold and gray and there are bars on the windows. Somewhere I realize the awful truth. I have been put away.

Looking down, I see my feet wrapped in gray plastic Saran Wrap or gray metal or both, but I can still walk. Because they are all wrapped, it makes them look wide and larger and undefined in shape.

I'm in a hospital gown throughout. The atmosphere is definitely one of a police state. There have to be very definite reasons for anyone to be allowed into the room. Contact with men is forbidden. All moves are monitored.

A woman in a police uniform comes to my door. It's a stone door. I open only enough to reveal my face and upper torso as there are other people in the room and we are planning ways to get out of there. She says, "There's no one in there with you, right? I say, "Right." Then something happens that reveals the presence of others. I'm chided for this. It has something to do with having a compact, mirror, and lipstick in the room, which I wasn't supposed to have.

At this point I'm taken to a round brick anteroom. I think this may be when I find out I am going to be there for good. It is the place where visitors come, the only place where you can meet the outside world.

There are many elements in this dream, but the dominant theme is the difficulty she's had all her life coming to terms with the problem of her eyes, initiated by her traumatic experience as a child of four. She feels deceived, trapped, helpless, and hopeless. The dream is a response to loss in the sense of physical impairment. It depicts her as still involved in a desperate struggle for freedom (planning to escape, still having some freedom to move despite the impairment to her feet) and the cold, imprisoning, and unyielding reality she is up against (experiencing her eye problem as limiting her contact with the outside world). The immediate context, of course, was the visit to the doctor, the fact that the new glasses did little to relieve her distress, and the comment of her friend which had the effect both of making her feel good and of validating her sense of her handicap.

The situation had rekindled the old anxieties about her eyes, the effect that glasses had on her appearance, and the helplessness she felt in trying to dispose of the problem. Her concern with her appearance was out of all proportion to the actual effect of the glasses. Her failure to come to terms with the handicap resulted in an oversensitivity to her appearance and an underestimation of her true attractiveness and worth. These were the ingredients of the predicament that led to the dream.

Incidentally, Marion has done something that is quite common in dreams. She has displaced the focus of attention from the real source of difficulty, her eyes, to her feet. Such displacements have a metaphorical intent. In the dream she is not concerned with the fact that the actual reason she was brought to the hospital was because of her eyes. Her concern is with being able to move and escape. The plastic and metal which would be connected with the "crutches" (her expression) she needs for her eyes are now associated with her feet, both making them more visible and limiting her ability to escape.

This dream also points up in a dramatic way the powerful resonating impact of a traumatic experience that happened almost a quarter of a century ago. The dream helped Marion become aware of the hold her past has on her and of her need to escape from any limiting circumstances in her life.

Wishes can play a role in dreams and they often do when a loss is involved.

Mary's cat was nineteen years of age and suffering. She had grown blind, deaf, and, more recently, acutely dehydrated and weak. Sadly and reluctantly Mary realized that the time had come to put an end to the suffering. She wrapped her pet carefully and took a taxi to the veterinary hospital. Just as they entered the hospital, the cat had a seizure during which she bit Mary on the breast, which meant that Mary later had to go to the hospital for a tetanus injection. The whole episode was upsetting, messy, and heartbreaking. What a way to end a nineteen-year-old loving relationship.

Three days later Mary had the following dream:

I was in the hallway of my apartment and there was Snowflake (the cat). She looked healthy and was as affectionate as ever.

I thought to myself, That's great but what happened? I called the hospital and the vet told me that several of them tried to do something to save her but in the end they gave up and just left the doors open (the implication being that she just got up and walked out).

I felt so good to see her. As soon as I awoke I realized that what I had done was to replace an ugly image with this comforting one.

I think an interesting thing happened here. At one level this may be a wish-fulfilling fantasy to take the edge off the pain of Mary's grief. But a kind of healing seems to be taking place that goes beyond wish fulfillment. Feeling miserable about the cat's last moments, she summons earlier and positive memories as being more characteristic of her experience with Snowflake and feels better about terminating the relationship on that note. Perhaps, also, her dream was partly a feeling that her cat was now free from its suffering and so now she was free to have happy memories. The predicament was one of struggling to accept the loss but not being able to accept it on the terms under which it occurred.

The dreams presented thus far give some idea of the way our dreaming self responds to situations we face while awake. Sometimes our dream points the way to new and better solutions: Rose realizing that all she needed was in her own backyard. Dreams can mobilize unused resources and help us discover new answers. What they cannot do is create answers when answers do not exist. There was no way Sarah could carry on with the Superwoman image. The dream could only reconcile her to a more limited reality.

When there are no answers and the reality situation is a frightening one (as in a soldier's exposure to combat) or an entrapping one, as it was for Marion, the result is an anxiety dream or even a nightmare. It is as if all our dreaming self can do is wake us up and confront us with the fact that there is some kind of danger around in the hope that we can come to better terms with that danger while awake. After all, awareness of danger is the necessary first step to doing something about it.

8

Dispelling Self-Deception

Since dreams seem to use a current pretext to remind us of some unfinished emotional business from our past, we need to know more about this emotional heritage. Why is it so difficult to dispose of it? How do we manage not to see what is there to be seen?

The answer lies in the human tendency to create myths in the face of disturbing mysteries. When we are small we encounter more powerful, sometimes threatening, sometimes constraining forces about us. We do not yet have the conceptual tools to understand them, but we must protect ourselves and somehow manage to live with them. We use our imagination to provide us with homemade evasions that take the place of the puzzling or threatening situations we face. These evasions take the form of personal myths—myths that create a surface harmony between ourselves and the demands of a more powerful world.

We pay a price, however, for this temporary peace. For

once a personal myth comes into being, it becomes a tena-
cious part of our makeup and we see ourselves more and
more in terms of it. And so we reinforce the myth and what
was started in our childhood continues to color our lives as
adults. For it isn't enough to create a personal myth. Each
of us must learn how to maintain it as well. For this purpose
we develop a repertoire of self-deceptive strategies. These
enable us not to see anything about ourselves or the world
that would be incompatible with the myth, or else to distort
what we see to make it compatible.

Part of ourselves—the part that is in the dream-making
business—knows this and takes advantage of every opportunity to tell us so. Our dreaming self exposes and explores the
hold that these personal myths still have over our lives. It has
its own agenda and timetable which can lead us into a richer
and sounder involvement with ourselves and the world—*if*
we use our capacity for understanding to dispel the very
important misunderstandings we grew up with.

To the extent that personal myths pervade our lives we are
living on margin. All goes well only as long as the myths go
unchallenged, but there is always the danger that an unpredictable event will puncture the myth and catapult us into
the kind of predicament we are apt to dream about. The
event and the impact shape the dream. It is as if our dreaming self sent a camera crew to record the event and the
emotional rumble that followed it for later replay during a
REM period.

A common myth is that of personal invulnerability—"I
can take anything the world throws my way." We saw this
at play with Sarah who for so long was able to be wife, nurse,
career woman, and to deny the toll this and the aging process
was taking.

Another not uncommon situation that can give rise to a
crippling personal myth is that of the mother who is overly

concerned with the question of controlling her child. Take
the case of a woman with a bright, inquisitive daughter. All
children need limits set, but not at the expense of their
spontaneity, curiosity, and inventiveness. Yet if this child
follows her natural curiosity she will get into some kind of
mischief. Her mother harbors the myth that a good or even
perfect parent equates protectiveness with concern. She
feels threatened and overreacts with anger when her child's
impulses escape her control. The child is then made to feel
that curiosity is bad and obedience is good. A myth begins
to take shape in her which replaces the capacity for growing self-reliance with a belief in the sanctity of an external
authority.

Since the daughter's curiosity will persist, she must find
some other way of coping that will allow her to live in peace
with her mother. She learns to deny her own impulses or else
so distort her perception of them that they are no longer
invitations to new and exciting experiences but are, rather,
signals of something dangerous and threatening. She also
learns how to deny and distort her perception of her mother.
She continues to think that her mother is acting out of the
daughter's best interest when, in fact, the mother is driven
by her own anxieties. These misperceptions reinforce each
other in the limited setting of the family. But when the child
moves beyond the family, they become burdensome, constraining influences in her life. She then begins a lifelong
struggle to come to terms with them.

When a personal myth operates in this fashion, gaps open
up in our psyche: distances between the way things are and
the way we think they are. We grow up with emotional blind
spots. Our myths maintain the distance for reasons of security. The most treacherous aspect of all this, and what makes
dream work difficult, is that the myth obscures the fact that
the gaps exist.

Once we rescue a dream from oblivion we bring it into enemy territory to the extent that, in the waking state, the myth reigns supreme. So the question becomes: How do we allow that small voice in ourselves to tell the emperor that he is wearing no clothes? It's a delicate situation. We are called upon to match honesty and courage against the dead weight of denial and distortion.

The gap between the true and the false, the known and the unknown, forms the subject matter of our dreams. An aspect of ourselves that we have taken for granted is up for critical scrutiny. A part of our personality that, consciously or unconsciously, we consider invulnerable and inviolate, is now revealed as flawed. A personal myth has been punctured.

Let Nan describe a confrontation she had in a dream with one of her personal myths:

"For several days prior to the dream I had been struggling with some of the professional literature on dreams. Much of it was so technical that it seemed like a foreign language to me. I spent hours studying with pad and pencil on the right, text in front, and a medical dictionary on the left. Enthusiasm and interest in the subject kept me at it, digging away, and allowing some painful but exciting mind stretching to occur. It was exhausting and stimulating at the same time. By the fourth night I had become aware of a growing anxiety. I had this dream:

> We joined some others to watch a play that was to be a very interesting production. I began reading the script and grew concerned with how difficult it was to understand. There were many words that repeated syllables, such as "furfurfur tantantanerer." It was English, yet not English. I thought, "Mother will never make it through this."

"The dream made it obvious to me that something other than just the strain of hard work was beginning to register with me. It made me aware of the extent to which I was pushing myself in directions I didn't feel comfortable with. Old feelings of inferiority and fear of failure were being awakened. The dream shed some light on the myths that kept feeding these feelings.

"I tried to analyze it in terms of the dream images and their meaning to me:

Dream Image	**Image as a Metaphor**
We joined some others to watch a play that was to be a very interesting production.	I have joined with Monte in an interesting production—writing a book about dreams. Yet in the dream I feel that I'm a member of an audience witnessing a play written by someone else. There is a passive, detached quality.
I began reading the script	The passive audience role has given way to a more active one—that of an actor given a script to read. Is this a reference to my effort to become familiar with the professional literature on dreams?
and grew concerned with how difficult it was to understand.	Being a right-brain person (intuitive, musical, grasping things in their wholeness) I have never gotten over feelings of inferiority in a world being managed by left-brain competence. I am beginning to feel insecure, as I did as a child in coping with math and science. The feeling of being tested evokes a dread of failure.

Dream Image	**Image as Metaphor**
There were many words that repeated syllables such as "furfurfur tantantanerer." It was English yet not English.	I was dealing with and trying to master the technical literature. What my dream seems to be saying is that much of it strikes me as repetitious nonsensical jargon.
I thought, "Mother will never make it through this."	The part of me that is struggling through this is not the real me and it won't succeed. That is the part of me represented by my mother's influence: tending to be self-effacing and passive in the presence of authority.

"The myth here is that I have to live up to the expectations of others regardless of the cost to myself. I approached the task with a 'come hell or high water' attitude. Though I was uncompromising in the hours I put in, part of me remained detached from the effort. This aspect of the job did not absorb me as it might have, had I a more scientific turn of mind. It evoked old anxieties about failing. The fact that the task dealt with nonsensical jargon and that it was my mother who was apt to fail was my dream's way of suggesting that I stop putting authorities on a pedestal and stop knocking myself out, forcing myself into a mold that wasn't made for me."

The issue in Nan's case is that of maintaining her own identity. The predicament posed the dilemma of authenticity versus sham (the sham of less than wholehearted involvement). Her dream was the culmination of many hours spent with difficult technical material and the beginning of a reaction to the stress. And the myth, as she said, was the importance of living up to the expectations of others.

Her dream points up the strategy of self-deception, the way emotional residues from our past are triggered by a present situation and then shape our response to that situation. She had allowed herself to be aware only of the excitement and emotional stimulation of the effort. She had not allowed herself to see how some of the old problems were asserting themselves: denial of her own feelings, her concern with performance, her fear of failure, and her own passive compliant trends.

But now for a dream of mine. After all, dream work thrives best in an egalitarian atmosphere. So, if I am to use the dreams of others, I should be prepared to share one of my own. Here goes:

> I was in a room with an older man and with someone who was supposed to be my father. My father seemed young, even younger than I. He didn't look like my father and seemed dissatisfied or critical of me. In a vehement, angry outburst, I stood up for myself and told him of all the things I've done and my accomplishments—including the fact that I won a two-thousand-dollar writing prize. I felt a little abashed, as if I were boasting, but it felt good to express myself.

As I started to gather the associations, my initial reaction to the dream was puzzlement. Why a dream of my father? He had died many years ago and I couldn't remember the last time I had dreamed of him.

A sum of money is mentioned in the dream. My father was an extremely generous man but was subject to violent, angry moods. Once I was the target of one of his moods. When I was a small boy, he sent me to buy a newspaper. Something possessed him to test my alertness. He handed me a crumpled ten-dollar bill which I didn't bother to look at—nor did the news vender. So I returned with change for one dollar, which triggered my father's rage.

The dream made me think sadly of what a distant figure he was in my life and how much he was feared as well as loved by others as well as myself.

What set off the dream? I had moved to Sweden two weeks before the dream to begin a clinical training program for young psychology students. Two reactions were taking shape in me. One was relief at being away from the pressures of New York City and the complex administrative responsibilities that had been my professional life there. The other was a growing sense of exhilaration and enjoyment for the teaching work I was undertaking. My students were eager and responsive. There was easy contact between us across the generation gap. It was this latter point that I was thinking about before falling asleep. It made me reflect on my experience with my father and all subsequent authority figures in my life—how different was the attitude of these students toward me as an authority. This thought and my own growing sense of emotional liberation set the stage for the dream. But let's analyze my dream as Nan did hers:

Dream-Image	**Image as a Metaphor**
I was in a room with an older man and with someone who was supposed to be my father.	My concern is with the issue of authority figures and the source of these feelings in my relationship with my father. The older man may be myself.

Dream Image	**Image of Metaphor**
My father seemed young, even younger than I.	My father died in his early forties and I had this dream in my late fifties, so, in a sense, I am and have been for some time, older than my father. From my position now as the older of the two I can renew our relationship.
He didn't look like my father	He appears to me very differently now than when I was a child.
and seemed dissatisfied or critical of me.	Looking back at the incident of the crumpled ten-dollar bill I felt how unfair and even sneaky a thing it was to do to a child. All it did was make me feel guilty, stupid, and frightened of this otherwise generous man. His disapproval, while very rare, was also very devastating. I had no way then of coping with it.
In a vehement, angry outburst, I stood up for myself	Something connected with my teaching experience in Sweden, perhaps my success as an "authority," helped me, after all these years, to experience and express the anger I must have felt then.
and told him of all the things I've done and my accomplishments —including the fact that I won a two-thousand-dollar writing prize.	In turning the tables I seem to be using his own tactics against him by flaunting my superiority. I did actually win a two-thousand-dollar prize (shared by a colleague): Someone who can win that much doesn't have to be concerned with cheap tricks involving ten-dollar bills.

Dream Image	**Image as Metaphor**
I felt a little abashed, as if I were boasting, but it felt good to express myself.	I feel good about defending myself but also uncomfortable about the way that I go about it.

New and very positive emotional currents were sweeping over me at the time I had the dream. I was experiencing the change I had made as a healing, a renewing one. But change is still never easy or simple; to move from one position meant to reexperience whatever it was that led me to that position in the first place. There are two ways of growing. One is through accretion—adding to yourself through possessions, achievements, and the like—and the other is from within: being, giving, and enjoying. The first is a kind of social garment that gives status, respectability, power; the second is a natural, internal process. The emotional reverberations of my new situation were of new-found feelings of inner strength and a clearer awareness of the extent to which I had previously lived a life of "achievement" rather than of "being."

In a narrow sense, I was in the dream settling an old score with my father. In a more significant sense I was struggling against an old value system, realizing I was still very much enmeshed in it.

The issue was one of identity, as can be seen from the notes I wrote at the time of the dream:

> I had been thinking of the emotionally liberating and therapeutic effect this whole experience is having on me. I have a sense of my ego growing from within rather than through the accretion of degrees, titles,

papers to my credit, etc., as if I were rather belatedly carving out the realistic dimensions of my personal identity and, in the process, overdoing it to some extent.

The polarity of being versus having was sharpened by the new feelings and opportunities in Sweden and the loosening of Establishment ties back home.

My dream laid open a not uncommon myth, and one that I had never quite set to rest. Our parents are our first authorities. They are more powerful and knowing than their children. When these realities are mishandled or misused in relation to a child, a confusion begins to arise in the mind of the child that the combination of superior power and knowledge also means being right and being good. For a man to occupy so high a position, to be so important, to have so many credentials, he must be right, good, and well-intentioned. This sets the stage for the later tendency to place blind trust in authority and to struggle with self-doubt and guilt whenever our own feelings run counter to authority.

We can begin to see through this myth quite early, but to rewire our emotional circuitry is a more difficult matter. It involves getting close to and recognizing anger when it is present and feeling secure enough in ourselves to be assertive even at the risk of standing alone. For anyone with a heavy authoritarian influence in childhood, this is not at all easy. What happens all too often is that we recognize the myth and the accompanying strategies of self-deception only after we have reacted to the situation according to habit. For me it was Sweden that brought into focus a freer, more relaxed version of authority relationships.

Sometimes dreams stay with us for many years, coming back to puzzle us until some new insight lays them to rest.

What follows is one such example, also rooted in the personal myth of the sanctity of authority.

Thomas, a young psychiatrist, had this dream while preparing for a medical examination. It had occurred four years prior to the time he reported it but it was still very vivid to him. He had felt under heavy pressure at the time, working late and drinking a great deal of coffee. The night before the exam he experienced a momentary aphasia: For a short time he was unable to form any words. He felt confused and uncertain, but still determined to take it. That night he had the following dream:

> I was undergoing a medical examination about this aphasia. I was immediately taken to angiography. They came to the conclusion it might be a tumor. I saw the pictures. There were no positive signs. They decided to operate. I saw myself being opened up. I died during the operation. I came to the autopsy. There was my brain all nicely sliced. There were two fluorescent photographs of it in very bright colors. I discussed the operation with the pathologist. It had come out successfully. Everyone was relieved. It was good I had not survived the operation.

Although this is more than just an examination dream, it is a good example of one. It depicts the discomfort and distress of cramming one's head full of new facts (the growth of new tumor cells in the cranial cavity). This is followed by the feelings of helplessness and victimization the student feels at the hands of the examining authorities. (In the dream the passivity becomes more and more dramatically displayed as he moves through the stages of being examined, operated on, dying—the ultimate in passivity—and then the penultimate of passivity: having an autopsy performed upon himself.)

So let's look at the dream in the context of the dreamer's concern over the possible implication of his aphasia and over his degree of preparedness for the examination.

Dream Image	**Image as Metaphor**
I was undergoing a medical examination about this aphasia. I was immediately taken to angiography.	Express his anxiety with regard to his physical intactness (undergoing a medical examination) and his ability to speak out, to perform intellectually (aphasia). The images reflect the fact that it is the authorities who take the initiative and that he is cast in the passive role. They are testing him and he complies. They are taking him someplace where the outline of his newly acquired learning can come into view (the angiography room). The imagery reflects both the status quo—his awaiting the examination—and the intrusive novelty that interferes, namely, the unpredictable effects of the physical and emotional state he was in.
They came to the conclusion it might be a tumor. I saw the pictures. There were no positive signs.	The way he crowded his brain with new knowledge may have had a detrimental effect. The "tumor" is invisible, just as are facts crammed into one's head.
They decided to operate. I saw myself being opened up.	The teacher operates on the pupil, opens up his brain to see what he knows. The dreamer, or part of him, passively watches this go on. The teachers will get the information out.

Dream Image	Image as Metaphor
I died during the operation.	In relation to this, his role is one of total passivity (analagous to that of an anesthetized patient on an operating table). He is the complete and total victim, his own sense of ego and autonomy having been completely obliterated. It is this part of him, identified with the "I" or "individual," which dies during the operation. This is the price he is forced to pay in submitting to the system.
I came to the autopsy. There was my brain all nicely sliced.	Once he accepts the role of total victimization, killing off his own ego, an ego that groaned under the excessive stress he was subjected to, he can now coldly and with detachment view his psyche and identify with the pathologist in seeing the brain neatly sliced up (his psyche now dismembered for efficient and detached handling).
There were two fluorescent photographs of it in very bright colors.	There is a kind of advertising or public relation quality to this image. The concrete results of what he had gone through and accomplished are now on public display in a way that calls attention to them (fluorescent lighting, bright colors). This is the result of the examination, compensation in the form of recognition. He has surmounted his anxiety about his body (the aphasia) and his intellect (the examination) and ended up with two records (photographs) of his success, available for anyone who might wish to see them.

Dream Image	Image as Metaphor
I discussed the operation with the pathologist.	Having resolved his anxieties in this way, having his "success" visible to the public, he now moves into a peer relationship with someone who is a professional manipulator of dead tissue, a pathologist.
It had come out successfully.	Success as defined by the Establishment and achieved at the expense of destroying something in himself.
Everyone was relieved. It was good I had not survived the operation.	By virtue of these developments he has shaped himself into an acceptable form. Everyone belonging to the System is relieved. Only by surrendering his own autonomy by dying can he achieve success as defined by the System. In this sense it was good that he had not survived the operation. In philosophical terms he had disappeared as subject and reappeared transformed and identified as object.

The insistent, tragic quality of the dream lies in the final dialogue with the pathologist. Compliance and passivity, and the subjugation of his own needs, individuality, and subjectivity force the dreamer into an identification with a physician who deals not with live specimens but with those remains of the human being that are available for impersonal analysis. An important message conveyed through powerful imagery indeed.

The issue for the dreamer was one of identity. How could he maintain a sense of his own identity in the face of the physical and psychological tensions he was under at the time? The conflict he found himself in was that between being self-assertive and self-protective, or of complying with authority at any cost. He chose the latter course, and old self-deceptive strategies took over the situation: a near-dangerous denial of his own needs and an overestimation of both the power and rigidity of authority. Had he been able to deal with the situation in a more self-protective way, there is the likelihood that some allowance might have been made for his physical state at the time. At least he could have asked for it. The dream lays bare the hold which the myth of inviolate authority had over him.

In the four years since the occurrence of the dream Thomas had sensed its importance but had never penetrated its mystery. The work we did on it brought him in touch with the important trends in his character—his passivity and his attitude toward an authority that made him so vulnerable at the time of the examination.

Dreams like this are critical in terms of the message they are trying to convey. Their mystery haunts us, as it did Thomas, and the emotional shadow they cast over our lives is not dispelled until we finally come to terms with the meaning they contain.

9

A Family That Dreamed Together

The natural setting for dream appreciation is the family. After all, the sore spots and unresolved feelings pictured so extravagantly in our dreams are most frequently linked to the family. The support of the family can be very valuable to a dreamer struggling to get closer to a dream. And yet sustained dream work within the family unit is relatively rare.

Those who have tried it give evidence that new possibilities for expressing distress and desire, for confirming the rights of every person within the family, begin to emerge through such shared dream appreciation. Tensions which are normally not acknowledged, but which disturb our daily life, are nudged into the light of recognition and thereby help us to challenge old ways of viewing ourselves.

Families have a certain continuity based on the roles we allow each member to assume. But if originality and independence are to flower, that continuity should be based on the genuine abilities and needs of each member. Working together with our dreams can help us dissolve the false ideas we have about one another by making visible what each of us feels is truly important.

We invest a great deal of emotional energy in holding onto our opinions about each other, and we tend to rationalize these false investments. Any dreams that assault these patterns may be written off as ridiculous. Our instinct tells us to resist assault, and so working with dreams may appear to threaten the cohesiveness of the family. But the truth more often is that we are unclear about why each of us acts the way he does. We may be jealous, frightened, or angered by another. Our attempt to cope with our feelings molds our responses.

When we allow them to, dream metaphors help us to objectify our unacceptable emotions so that they can be talked about and even laughed about as absurdly human, and thereby help create deeper, more loving relationships.

One morning at breakfast Nan's four-year-old daughter, Kerry, told her she had dreamed about a baby bear, a daddy bear, and a *great big* mommy bear. That was all she could remember, but it was enough. As Nan thought back over the past few weeks, and especially that last week, she realized she was becoming overbearing, the heavy, the constant disciplinarian. She was spending as much energy nagging (to no avail) as teaching. Her husband, Howard, was not cast in this role. He and she talked about the dream and Nan realized she had been angry with Howard for not automatically assuming an equal share in the grittier aspects of parenting. Rather than working this responsibility out directly with him she was bearing down harder on Kerry.

Now they've developed ways of getting the mommy bear down to life size. Whenever Nan begins to feel like the victim of too little support she thinks, "I'm a *great big* mommy bear." That's her cue for calling a family conference.

Through her work with the Andersons, Nan got a
firsthand look at the kinds of issues which arise when dreams
are dealt with by a family over an extended period. Howard
and Nan had been friends of Cliff and Karen Anderson for
several years. Because of their close association, the Andersons knew of Nan's interest in dreams and grew interested
themselves in some of her dream experiences. But they could
not seem to get a handle on how the meaning of their own
dreams could be understood and used for self-healing. So
they asked her to teach them the techniques. And here are
some of the dreams they shared.

But first a bit of background about the Andersons.

Cliff was thirty-six and Karen thirty when they were married, seven years before the time of these dreams.

Karen taught in elementary school. She was one of those
sought-after teachers who are as concerned about the special
interests and personal needs of her students as with the aca-
demic curriculum. With her natural warmth and intuition
Karen had many friends. It was not surprising that Cliff, who
was rather reserved, responded to her initiative and her genuine appreciation of his talents.

Cliff had suffered from loneliness most of his life. He had
worked his way through college, a step no one in his family
had cared about or expected him to take. He lived at home,
for financial reasons, until after graduation, and then left for
Washington, D.C., with hopes of bettering the world. Instead the years that followed were desolate. He was successful in his field of public relations, but he felt little sense of
meaningful direction in his life.

Then he met Karen and through her his fog of self-doubt
slowly lifted. She appreciated the attributes his family had
ignored: his great talent as a cook, his feeling for music, art,
sailing.

Karen was from a socially conscious New England family:

titles, name, education, and status were criteria for success. But she recalls her family as loving, and feels all her needs were met by her mother. She attended a private girl's high school and, as was expected of her, went on to college. Karen felt she did not grow up until her parents died, within two years of each other. When she met Cliff, three years after that, she was teaching but eager to "find the right man" and have her own family.

Both Cliff and Karen were delighted that at last they had each other, could make a home together. But, of course, their life was no fairy tale with ever-after happiness. Karen fell into the footsteps of her mother: meeting everyone's needs at all times, not admitting her own needs. The lack of communication that had characterized Cliff's earlier life carried over into his relationship with his wife and two daughters, Thyra and Heather. Karen found herself resenting the children for their dependence on her and was baffled by her reaction because she loved them.

Involvement in a church had become very important, especially for Karen. Eventually both Cliff and Karen joined a "nurturing" group which had organized a small ecumenical school for spiritual growth. Within this intimate setting, they dared to open up and risk growing. It was at this point that the Andersons asked Nan for help with their dreams.

Several weeks later the work began. Cliff and Karen reported dreams one night apart.

Dream Number One: Cliff's

The group was gathered at our house and it was time to go home. I told them that I wanted to play a recording of my banjo solo. This is a recorded solo of the time I forgot where I was with the music and it is rather amusing. I found the record and started playing it. We sat around listening but it was not a recording of the banjo solo and the amusing part never came. Finally it came to me that I had not put on the correct record. I selected the right one and put it on the record changer only to have orchestra music come out of the speakers. By this time people were standing and milling around.

I selected the "correct" record again, but again it was different music. By this time people were getting anxious to go home and I was feeling very frustrated because I kept thinking I was selecting the banjo solo only to have different music played.

I apologized, but I was positive I had read the label correctly. The dream ended with the banjo solo music in my head but I don't think it was being played. . . . I was only remembering how the tune went. The dream ended there, before the group left, and I was feeling frustrated.

Cliff explained the context of the dream:

The night before the dream I was in a group discussing "calls" or gifts of individuals. What was said by Gordon [retreat leader] was very meaningful to me. What I considered my gift was jelling in my mind, but I didn't share it with the group because I didn't think it was the time.

Cliff had just come through a period of great dissatisfaction with his work and had changed to a job he found stimulating and fulfilling. He was experiencing an inner surge of newness and worth, which he was still reluctant to communicate. The dream seemed to be saying that although he enjoyed this new level of performance (the funny solo), he feared it would not carry the same impact for others, and so he was caught between his desire to share and his fear of rejection. If the music was not heard, it could not be criticized or ignored. Others could talk about themselves (in the dream, the orchestra music), but his gift (the banjo solo) remained a reality only in his head.

The next night Karen dreamed:

Dream Number Two: Karen's

Cliff had a sailboat, a large yacht, sitting in the harbor all ready to set sail. I was amazed, excited, and rather surprised that he was going to take the boat out since he had never sailed before. I was the sailor, having grown up on the ocean, and had in the past told him how he would love it if he ever had the opportunity. His boat was vivid in detail and very colorful. The sky was very blue and crystal clear. . . . There was an air of happy anticipation which I shared as I told my people that Cliff was about to go out.

My boat was nowhere to be seen! Every once in a while I would catch foggy glimpses of it in the distance, but it was so hard to make out—sort of like an impressionist painting!

Karen's thoughts about the backdrop of the dream:

We had just had a retreat during which Cliff felt aware of a specific direction related to his gifts . . . a way he could make a personal impact on the world's need. We were both excited about it. It was something I had prayed for and wanted for years.

I felt frustrated by my own lack of a clear direction or vehicle in which to use my talents. In the past I had been the one to feel the direction, and I felt a bit envious now that the shoe was on the other foot!

Karen's dream expressed her feeling that Cliff's boat had come in and allowed her to deal openly with her own doubts and frustrations (she only catches foggy glimpses of hers). She was both responsive to and envious of what Cliff, in his own dream, was fearful would not be appreciated or accepted. Cliff's and Karen's dreams show a magnificently supportive dovetailing.

The next dream was reported by seven-year-old Thyra, the older of their two daughters. Cliff tended to become upset with her when she expressed strong emotion, and so she had learned, in order to receive her father's approval, to put her feelings in the deep freeze. Despite her adherence to the personal myth that it was wrong to be angry, an increasingly unhappy situation at school exposed some of her anger and she had the following dream:

Dream Number Three: Thyra's

There was an oil can in front of the school. . . . Someone had put oil and gas in it. It started to explode. I ran home . . . it was going to explode all over the country, so we had to go all the way to the North Pole. Then we met someone, my teacher . . . and my dad said, "They have dumb curtains." Someone snatched him because he said this about the curtains. He was put in jail. My mom let him go. Then we all went to the North Pole . . . and when it exploded, it spreaded all over, but only in Virginia. It was a scary dream. I was surprised when I woke up because when I was asleep I thought it was real.

Thyra and her parents worked together on the dream, and all three began to realize the necessity for Thyra to accept her anger as an essential part of herself. It wasn't easy because it involved rearranging the emotional position of the family members. Cliff had to be willing to look more closely at his own unexpressed anger before he could be helpful with Thyra's.

In an unexpected completion of the family dream circle, Heather, the five-year-old Anderson, was the next to report a dream.

Dream Number Four: Heather's

I was playing "follow-the-leader" with friends in our back yard. Thyra was in the front yard playing with her friends. My friends were supposed to follow me, but they wouldn't. I was crying and my mother put me and Thyra in the car and locked it. I got mad and kicked a hole in the windshield and stepped on Mary's toes.

Heather tended to vacillate between bossiness and baby tactics. She was dependent on Thyra to clear the way for her (in the front yard) and the day before the dream had alienated a group of her friends by ordering them about and becoming upset when they did not obey her (would not follow her). The metaphor of being locked in the car is a seeming reaction to Karen's attempt to talk with Heather about the necessity of acting more grown-up (the car is a symbol of the way adults move). Unable to take the step into a more mature approach to conflict, she reverts to infantile kicking. Her last act expressed the way she's been experiencing the world. Her friend Mary is also a younger sister. Heather, through identification with her, gets her toes stepped on.

The dream alerted Heather's parents to the intensity of her conflicts.

During this period Karen had a dream which was the prelude to a painful basic change that initiated a new era in her relationship with Cliff. At the time of the dream, she was very disturbed by the minister of her church who was unable to relinquish his control and allow other people to take over the areas of responsibility they had agreed to assume. She felt he was afraid to let people make their own mistakes because of his need for perfection. His attitude was hobbling the work of the church and exhausting himself.

Dream Number Five: Karen's

I looked out to the cottoneaster [ground-cover plant] in our front yard. My mother had just finished cutting and pruning it back so far that it almost ceased to exist. I was *furious* and gave her all my anger verbally. Cliff and I had just discussed that I would prune the plant where it extended into the lawn. I mentioned this to my mother and the next thing I knew it was severely cut back.

Karen made these additional associations:

It reminds me of the time in our back yard when mother went out with her shears and pruned back our beautiful red rambler roses to the point where they died.

Karen had been raised to maintain peace at all costs, a process that had severely cropped her emotional display. Anger had always been forbidden in her family. As she gained the confidence of maturity, her feelings of anger demanded equal time. The experience of being boxed in by her clerical friend triggered the memory of older psychic mutilations, and though her socially "proper" waking consciousness was not ready to admit it, she was furious.

A few days later Karen was able to confront her minister and, in an extraordinary demonstration of openness, he dealt with the issues she raised and told her she had helped him to break his own sense of isolation. They were both enriched by the encounter.

With this encouragement, Karen confronted a neighbor whom she felt was adversely affecting Thyra and Heather. And finally, most threatening of all, she confronted Cliff. Surprisingly she found herself feeling freer with and closer to the people she confronted.

That night she dreamed:

Dream Number Six: Karen's

I was in some kind of complex transportation system with tunnels and stairways, and landings . . . something like the Boston subway system I took to school as a child. There was a vehicle waiting for a great crowd of us to get on . . . couldn't tell whether it was a train or a ship. I had a feeling of excitement and anticipation. I was going somewhere. I had a small red suitcase with me and I was pleased that I didn't need a lot of luggage . . . just one piece for the long journey.

I can't remember whether I was going up or down steps but we, Thyra and I, were on a landing. Thyra had my suitcase and I suggested, "Just leave it there, that's fine." I was involved with somebody or something and I left. I didn't feel bad about leaving Thyra. She was going somewhere, too. She was very mature.

At that point she left my dream. It was getting time to get on the vehicle. I went back to get the suitcase, but it wasn't there. I spent a lot of time looking for the suitcase. Up and down, and all around. I rechecked everywhere I had been because I knew it must be there. It was time to get on the vehicle. If I was going to go I had to get on without it. I just hoped someone had picked it up and put it on for me.

I chose to get on. All of a sudden it was like a party atmosphere and everyone was having a good time. Then I saw that everything that had been in the suitcase was laid out for me—I think clothes and things like that. Everything was in the right place.

Karen associated the complex transportation system with the trip she was taking into her inner self. Her commitment to the journey had given her a sense of adventure and inner excitement.

The red suitcase she identified as her anger that contained within it all that she needed . . . that which was essential to her well-being. It was her adult self that must be responsible for the anger. The child within her was growing up and would no longer attempt to handle the anger (suitcase) in the old ways.

She felt the dream was saying that she could lose her temper, but she must not disown it. If she were willing to admit it was hers, then it could be opened up and everything else would fall into proper perspective. She would be able to function affectively . . . even enjoy herself! (Contents of the case laid out; everything in its right place; the party on the vehicle.)

Five-year-olds tend to have a great many bad dreams and nightmares. Heather was no exception. Several days after a family outing to nearby caverns, she had the following dreams:

Dream Number Seven: Heather's

We went in a car to a cave. I was on this ledge looking at the ten-foot pool of water. I slipped off the ledge and went into the deep part. Mommy reached over and pulled me up and out. I learned my lesson though . . . not to go out on the ledge. Daniel was there playing with blocks.

Dream Number Eight: Heather's

A woman in the cave . . . she was our guide in the cave we went to . . . had a thing on her head that made a caveman voice come out. Mommy and me were scared and we ran home.

The day before the dream Heather's best friend had come to play and Heather had had trouble sharing her bike. Karen used a timer to structure sharing periods. Earlier Heather had had to defend her bike from a neighbor boy who would borrow it and then ride off without thought of returning it. Trying to grasp this complex difference in regard to property rights, sharing, and protecting was apparently more than Heather could handle (she was over her head). She had to depend on her mother to straighten out the situation (pull her out of the water). There was in the dream an element of courageous risk taking, but a failure to appreciate the possible consequences.

By the end of the dream Heather seems to decide temporarily that it is better not to get into situations she cannot control (as with the sharing and protecting of her bike). Being a little child (Daniel), whose only concern is playing by himself with his blocks, is comforting.

In the second dream the conflict she is attempting to escape is personified by the scary woman in authority who says things that make her run away . . . but not without her mother as security.

Dream recalling and reporting was picking up, at least for Heather and Karen. Most of their work with Nan was done over the telephone; they recounted each dream to her, describing the sorts of experiences of the previous day that had disturbed them in any way and then discussed the metaphors and personal associations. Often Karen had to supply the context for Heather as it was difficult for the child to identify her feelings. Sometimes she seemed to be responding genuinely and sometimes trying simply to please Nan with her answers. But Heather was enthusiastic and meticulous in describing her dreams to Nan.

Karen was in the process of trying to accept and appreciate new and intense feelings. Because she was sharing her dreams with Nan on a regular basis through this turbulent period, it was not surprising that she had the following dream:

Dream Number Nine: Karen's

I was talking to Mag, my college roommate, on the phone. She began talking on and on about a conference with national leaders and I think she wanted me

to send something via our representative to the conference although she wasn't going. I felt physically
trapped in a very tight jersey which I was trying to
take off. I finally and slowly stopped panicking and
first took out one arm, then the other, and then
slipped it over my head very easily. No big deal or
effort, and I was free of it. While my friend was
talking, I left the phone for something, figuring she
wouldn't even know I had gone, but when I returned,
there was no one on the line. I ended the dream
halfheartedly trying to call her back.

Dream Number Ten: Karen's

I was in some kind of gallery or school with lots of
people. A fire alarm went off and we all walked in an
orderly way down the fire escape on the outside of
the building. We were very chatty and casual.

Karen made the following comment:

My roommate was a very directed, sure person
... involved with trying to open up staid institutions.
Nan's the same way—very channeled. I think some
of the things we have been coming up with are too
close to home. I want to get away from the phone
... away from Nan ... away from whatever it is I'm
dealing with.

It appeared the dream was reflecting both her anxiety over
dream work and also her need to handle the problem (too-
tight jersey) in her own fashion. She couldn't be pressed or
forced to take off what was constricting her, else she would
panic. Karen felt the jersey represented her anger and how

to get rid of it, i.e., easily separate it from her head. If she took it one step at a time, at her own pace, she could manage. Her ambivalence over returning to the phone probably represented fear of manipulation, the anxiety of self-revelation, and a genuine desire, despite her fears, to examine her dreams honestly and learn from them.

Dream number ten is another look at the "jersey." A gallery is a place where creativity is on display. At this point Karen felt her own creativity was involving her in confrontations with others. She said, "This is a new aspect of relationships for me. I don't want to go around spouting all my negative feelings all over people, but I want to be free to express myself when it's good. Very tricky. Perhaps when that is freed, I can direct my creativity toward art, toward stitchery."

The dream seems to be asking, "Is it safe (hence, the fire alarm) to display my true self—my anger—in public?" The danger is distinct enough to force her to leave the gallery, but not so threatening as to cause panic. As with the jersey, she is, in coping with the problem in her dream, deliberate and persistent.

Our momentum when awake—the rate at which we are able to absorb, adapt, discard new material, our capacity for welcoming challenges—is as personally monogrammed as our metaphors. Just as if we were to attempt to understand the images in our dreams in a universal way (that is, devoid of the precise meaning etched out of our past and current experiences), we would strip away their specific emotional import and hence lose the compelling force that enables us to change; so, if we pace ourselves to the expectations of others, or push ourselves because of fear and self-doubt, we may find ourselves stranded on the beach or drawn out into a turbulent sea. Learning to gauge our momentum and trusting our individual pace means learning to differentiate between the ebb and flow of creative movement and blocks and hesitations due to anxiety. Some trial and error is necessary. We discover that being marooned is not permanent isolation, that there are ways back to our inner balance. Help of some kind seems to be available. And more importantly we come to know that the help derives from something within us, beyond our conscious manipulations, something that is constantly sending us clues as to what issues are most significant for our present growth, and how deeply these issues should be probed.

Dream work went underground for about two weeks after the above reports, as Karen and Cliff began experiencing the vague and then more acutely painful repercussions of Karen's having expressed her previously mute longings and anger. Then in one night she recalled two dreams:

Dream Number Eleven: Karen's

Cliff and I were going to visit some friends in a building. They're people we don't have much in common with.

There was a smoke bomb or something in the building and we all had to vacate. Sue (a friend) was there . . . all elegantly dressed. It was cold and snowing and icy. Sue was running and I knew she was going to slip because she wasn't dressed right for running. And she did.

Dream Number Twelve: Karen's

Jerry (a friend) was writing a movie script. I was just "around." Two friends arrived from far off. It was like a scene from a movie for a while . . . on a beach with war going on out in the water. Battleships, bombing, etc. I watched as a spectator and then realized I could get hurt . . . I moved over to the side against a breakwater.

Then back in Jerry's office two gals came in talking about school in Africa. I announced perhaps I would go with them as I was a teacher. They were pleased. Then I heard all the problems involved. There were kids whose parents didn't care . . . problem kids . . . very hard to deal with . . . and I kind of decided I wouldn't go . . . although I still pretended I would.

Karen's initial associations were:

I had been thinking of Sue and how she was becoming more and more like her parents. Her husband was falling into the same pattern. Jerry's ideas were always crazy but fun. Risk is like that . . . irrational but fun. Perhaps I was feeling the need of an adventure.

Nan pressed her to go more deeply into what had happened the night before the dreams. Karen admitted she had been very unhappy. She had wanted to go out and do something "really fun" but she hadn't been able to put her finger on what it was she wanted. Later she realized that Cliff was withdrawing and rejecting her, and thus she wasn't experiencing *anything* as fun.

The setting of dream eleven visualizes the problem. Karen and Cliff are physically together in the same building (some aspect of their marriage) but remain nonparticipants, aloof, as when not enjoying a situation, or not wanting to get involved.

Next they abandon the attempt to be together at this point. The ramifications of working out what is causing Cliff's withdrawal and her own feelings of rejection become threatening. (The smoldering problem forces them to vacate the building.)

What is Karen's response to the threat and retreat? Act cool. (Snow and ice.) Put up the best possible front. (Elegantly dressed.)

But now she has another problem because it's hard to deal with danger if you are trying at the same time to project a smooth, placidly elegant serenity. She could fall flat on her face. Which she does!

Then she realized she was saying to herself, "I'm getting more and more like *my* mother." (As she had accused Sue of being.) "I'm pretending everything is beautiful. I don't want to ruffle the waters again."

In dream twelve, again, the observer maintains her distance. This time Karen is alone, as in the end of dream eleven, and the situation appears potentially more ominous (a movie war scene). Although she tries to assure herself that whatever she and Cliff are going through is just pretend (a movie), the reality of the battle becomes stronger and she retreats.

Dissatisfied with her solution of flight, Karen constructs another solution for dealing with the problem: get involved in some primitive way (the school in Africa). If she were a teacher she could be a part of the scene, but superior to it, maintaining a separateness, not totally admitting her own basic needs, desires, and expectations.

Again the solution raises more problems. If she takes the risk of involvement, she is immediately thrown into an anxiety-producing situation. She is forced to deal with someone who has to some extent been damaged by insensitive parents. (These were the roots of Cliff's withdrawal tactics.) She reverses her decision and decides not to go where her natural native impulses can be seen or used.

Nan was becoming concerned that Cliff was experiencing the family dream work as an intrusion on their private lives. Although he had indicated enthusiasm at the prospect of this rather experimental approach to growth, the issues were becoming more sharply personal. He had put only one of his dreams into the corporate hopper. Without the genuine consent of all the members, Nan felt she did not want to persist. They talked together, and he expressed a willingness to have them continue. Nan remained unconvinced, until two days later when Cliff handed her a written account of a dream. Afterwards they titled it "A Sticky Situation."

Dream Number Thirteen: Cliff's

Someone (unknown male) came to my house (which was unfamiliar to me) to help me plant some plants which I had previously dug up, and the plants were sitting in the yard in a very dried condition. They resembled large cacti, but were supposed to be evergreens. I made some comment about the fact that I should have been watering them while they were sitting in the yard with almost bare roots. The "someone" was also going to take some of these plants to his house. While we were working in my unfamiliar yard we noted a beautiful vegetable garden in my back yard which I explained was Karen's. The garden had beautiful full plants bearing bountiful fruit. Next to this garden we had planted three of the dried unattractive plants and I thought perhaps I had taken too many and not left enough for my helping friend.

Cliff felt that the dream had two themes:

1. Karen is flowering and somehow I'm not. I was not jealous of her garden. I admired it and was surprised to find this in my own back yard. The night before my dream Karen said she felt I needed to work on recognizing my positive qualities.
2. Sex.

Until recently Cliff and Karen had experienced a basic compatibility in their physical relationship. Now strained reactions were becoming evident in their sexual relationship, as in other areas of their lives.

Nan and Cliff reflected on the various metaphors in his dream and came up with these comments and connections:

In the setting there is a mixture of the known and the unknown, familiar and yet unfamiliar, and in the midst of this is presented the task of getting something back into an environment where it can grow, mature, develop, flourish. It had previously had such an environment, or at least a more favorable one, but now was cut off from a sustaining source. Had dried up. What had dried up? A cactus. A masculine, fundamental sort of plant which contains a life-giving fluid. Obviously a sexual image.

These cacti had not only been uprooted, but were being judged for failing to be what they were "supposed" to be, evergreens: perhaps the unrealistic Superman expectations of sexual adroitness.

Cliff was not nurturing the plants. A part of him knew how to help them, but he could not or did not look after their needs. Now their roots are exposed. Cliff has not been attending to the problems that have been causing him to feel inadequate.

The "someone" helping Cliff was never fully recognizable,

but may have been the part of himself that is the helpful person, the person who has always been attuned to the needs of others, the supporter; now at last available to help himself.

They both spy Karen's garden, which appears to be flourishing, flowering, and bearing fruit. And though he is happily amazed at finding such lush growth in his own back yard and accepts his place next to her (plants his cacti), he nevertheless feels diminished in contrast.

The questions raised for Cliff to consider were:

Why demean the nature and beauty of a cactus?

Why is a cactus inferior to a vegetable?

Why can't differences be pleasant contrasts rather than springboards for guilt and self-doubt?

A cactus is capable of surviving in the harshest environment. It can sustain life by its juice when nothing else is available. A cactus *is* evergreen, though it doesn't look like other evergreens. A cactus is good! What is not good is not giving it soil to grow in.

After such a large leap into the dream circle, it was not surprising that Cliff's next dream reflected a move toward reevaluating his position. Three days later Cliff called Nan with the following dream:

Dream Number Fourteen: Cliff's

Karen and I were invited to the Pendletons' for dinner at six P.M. We had a drink at home because we knew we wouldn't have anything to drink there. We arrived promptly at six and ate at six.

There were the four of us. After dinner Lynn, Jerry (Lynn's husband), and Karen left the room. I was at the table by myself. Outside a high window to my left was a lookout tower, next to the house. I could look into the tower room from where I was.

A boy child opened the tower-room door and I could see him . . . the light coming in from the outside allowed me to see him. He was looking into the room where I was and I couldn't tell whether he could see me because the lighting was rather dim in the living room. Then other boys appeared, and I didn't know whether they could see me either. I was fascinated by them but didn't want them to think I was staring at them. It was awkward.

I got up and walked to the front of the house, in the same room, and looked out. Several hundred yards from the house was the ocean. It was a misty day. There were large swells in the ocean but they didn't break. Even though it was the ocean, it didn't look like the ocean because there were no breakers. It was strange.

Lynn came in as I was looking and we had a conversation about the ocean. She turned on the outside lights. One on the ocean and one on the tower. Immediately the tower light went out.

She said, "How did that happen? Oh, the children over there—they must have turned it out."

I thought, "How could they have turned out the lights when the switch is here by the door?"

As we were standing there, the tides and waves began coming in. The waves were no longer at a distance but were lapping at the front of the house. I looked at the waves and asked, "Is this normal?" I decided I wanted to get out. It seemed abnormal to me.

Cliff had had a very pleasant weekend. In fact his relationship with Karen was opening up again in deeper and enjoyable ways. What was causing the sense of danger?

Nan offered the suggestion that the Pendletons might be a metaphor for the Zimmermans, as she and Howard did not serve cocktails before dinner. Cliff said, "It's true. We *do* have a drink at home before coming to your house!" The setting of the dream then was Cliff coming into Nan's home, seeing something (dreams) from her perspective.

After eating where both couples could see him (exposing his inner desires and needs), he was left alone with the consequences. His instincts told him to be careful: Be sure you keep an eye on what is happening (thus, the watchtower). He was fascinated by the parts of himself he was discovering in his dreams, but wanted to keep his distance from these immaturities (represented by the boys in the tower).

The watchtower has a view of not only the house, but of the ocean beyond. Cliff associated the ocean with his own life energy, but this ocean was not acting in its normal, spontaneous manner. It was containing its energy, not allowing its swells to break: his controlling his actions so that others are not aware of the surging energies beneath his calm exterior.

Nan (Lynn) joins him as she did when discussing the dream and they have a conversation about the ocean. This turns light on two areas: his strategy of withholding himself from public view (the swells that don't break) and his watchdog techniques (his watchtower manned by childhood defenses).

Cliff protects his tower by having the boys (psyche-guards) turn off the light, but the ocean plunges out of his control, acting like a real ocean, with periods of turbulence.

Frightened by the wildness, strength, and closeness of the ocean, Cliff reverses his original observation that the bound breakers were strange. He now labels the *new* situation as abnormal, which makes reasonable his decision to leave.

Cliff was acknowledging the reality that if he decided to continue with his dream work, old safeguards would lose their capacity to limit his reactions and feelings. Although this would seem beneficial, there was the danger these powers within him would not appreciate his limits and he would be engulfed. He was saying: Perhaps we are not supposed to delve into our unconscious. Maybe dream work isn't a good idea after all!

Despite the enormity of his doubt Cliff risked the consequences of exposure by telling Nan his dream and working on its further implications with Karen. In fact, much of his anxiety abated after he analyzed it so graphically. Karen saw more clearly that his periods of withdrawal were not so much a personal denial of her as an attempt to control some turbulent inner material. And he began to see that so much control was no longer needed.

This marked another step in the gradual downplaying of control within the Anderson family and the greater sharing of responsibilities and support.

The serious commitment to dream work caused waves of tension and unrest to ripple through the family. Any experiment in change tends to produce anxiety. But by staying with the task and searching for new answers the family arrived at a more open and honest level of problem solving.

In Heather's dreams the inner conflict between the safety of babyhood and the freedom and joy of growing up was ever present. Cliff not only saw her development, but became aware of places where he, as a child, had not been encouraged to emerge.

Dream Number Fifteen: Heather's

Daddy and I went to a picnic. Then I crossed the street without Daddy when he took a shortcut. (I got kind of lost from him and thought he had gone home without me but I looked around and saw him picking daisies in someone's yard.) Then I ran across the traffic line . . . a man quickly got out of his own lane into the free lane (like Daddy does). I got on the wheel and climbed up on the car and the man took a stick and pushed me off and said, "You'd better be careful!" I saw it wasn't Daddy. I went over and got Daddy, who was picking daisies, and then we went to the swimming pool.

The dream mirrors the push-pull of growing up. Heather wants greater freedom for fun (picnic) and mobility (swimming). She checks out the safety of her ventures against the reactions of her father.

There is the approving Daddy, of whom she is not quite certain (he disappears and is found indifferently though benignly picking daisies). The approving Daddy is somewhat elusive, but she is able to relocate him in the end and they go off together to the desired location—the swimming pool, where she can both enjoy herself and demonstrate her physical independence in public. Heather was learning to swim in waking life.

There is also a disapproving Daddy. As she boldly crosses the street alone she becomes threatened by his reactions (his car enters the free lane where she is standing). Next he verbally cautions her against spontaneous movement ("You'd better be careful!").

Heather then takes the initiative in getting back to the approving Daddy and the two of them make it to the swimming pool.

A few nights before, Cliff had read a Dr. Seuss book to the children. The last line read, "Having fun is good!" He said he had grown up with a feeling of guilt about anything that was fun, and even now rarely truly enjoyed himself. Somehow it wasn't "right." Cliff could see that Heather was trying to establish, within her increasingly separate self, whether or not "fun is good." Perhaps they could teach each other how to get a kick out of life.

Heather's struggle with the issues in her dream images was helpful to Karen. Karen now knew that what she said to Heather was not falling on deaf ears, but that within Heather private ordeals were being waged for the winning of her girlhood.

Dream Number Sixteen: Heather's

I was walking home from the swimming pool with my yellow badge. [At her pool, when you have gained a certain degree of swimming expertise, you qualify for a yellow badge. This allows you to go to the pool unaccompanied by an adult.] I was ten years old.

There was a man on horseback with a hat with a fringe all around the edges. I had to hide. I came in the house and hid behind the couch, but he was on the deck and he could see all of me. He saw me through the windows. He put me in prison and shot me through the openings (of the bars) and killed me.

The day before the dream had been a good one for her. There were no big scenes and she had demonstrated a great deal of independence in creative ways. After having the dream, Heather tiptoed into Karen's bedroom and quietly tapped her on the shoulder. She reported her dream seriously and calmly, but afterwards she said she was scared and wanted Karen to sleep with her. Karen said she couldn't do that, but she would go down to her room and give her a back rub for a while. Within about ten minutes Heather announced she was all right and would go back to sleep—which she did.

In this dream, as Heather gets stronger (wins her yellow badge, attains the age of ten), her adversary also gets stronger (he's on horseback and he kills her).

Karen then had a dream that vividly portrayed her attempt to find her proper role as protector and stimulator.

Dream Number Seventeen: Karen's

Peg (a friend from home, very cool under pressure—not easily upset) and I were sitting on the rocks by the ocean. It was a very powerful section of the coast. Huge waves lapping over the rocks and barnacles.

Peg's daughter (same age as Heather) was playing on the rocks, going down toward the ocean. I was afraid she would slip and hurt herself on a barnacle or fall into the water over the cliff. It was the wrong place to let a child play . . . a little child toddling around in diapers. Peg took my advice and went down and got her daughter. No one was harmed.

Karen's reflections on the dream:

I think this is about the amount of freedom I should give Heather, and Thyra, too. I have trouble knowing where I stop and Heather starts in terms of creative internal and external structure.

I've been thinking a lot about Heather's bad dreams, wondering what I can do to help her.

Summer arrived. The Andersons packed up enough belongings for a three-week vacation and flew to Utah. A hastily written postcard from Karen said she and Cliff had taken a side trip, leaving the children with friends. It was great to move about without responsibilities and with stretches of silence.

When the Andersons returned, Nan was out of town, and almost six weeks passed before she received a somewhat reluctant phone call from Karen. Thyra, the older child, whose position of independence and at-homeness in the family was envied by Heather, had had a high-anxiety dream during Karen and Cliff's minihoneymoon. Thyra reported the dream to them, then adamantly refused to talk further about it and flew into a rage over any intimation that her parents wanted to understand what she was feeling during that time.

She screamed, "I'm not going to talk about it, ever! I'm never telling another dream!" It was as if her feelings were so personal that she was afraid to admit they were there.

Now Thyra's single dream report during the period of family commitment to dream work began to have new meaning. She had agreed to the plan but had maintained a secret and undetected negative response by her silence. However, the pain of separation from her parents during their trip had triggered a compelling need to communicate, a response which she furiously regretted when the immediacy of the pain subsided and she was at home with everyone back in place.

Obviously Thyra's claim to the privacy of her dreams must be respected, but her family worried about the cause of her passionate protectiveness. What within her appeared to her so fragile as to demand unquestioned distance?

Heather emerged as occasional comforter to her older sister. It was as if this revelation that her reserved and artistic sister was not necessarily the personification of Perfect Daughter had unrolled a new section of Heather's own script. She became much more gregarious, entertaining and visiting friends with increased poise and eagerness.

Thyra did not regain her outward confidence. Later the family was to learn that there were physical and developmental lags (fortunately reversible) that were undermining her enjoyment of self-worth.

It was time for a new tempo to be established between Nan and the Andersons. They now knew the basic dream-work techniques; they had their own tools. They were free to use them or put them aside for other approaches to growth, or for the very understandable need for rest from introspection. So Nan's role had changed. The Andersons talked about their dreams among themselves as they did their other private affairs.

Months later, reflecting on this lap of their dream trip, Karen said, "At one point, just before vacation, I felt I had had enough. You can do it that intensively for a period of time and then it's not healthy anymore. You become *too* self-observant. It wasn't until I got away on my vacation that I realized that it had gotten to be too much. Dreams are a tool for growth and you can't be growing every minute of every day. There are times when you're waiting before you go on to the next spurt. . . . and when I reached that point, *then* I wanted to really listen to my dreams again."

Nan had had a similar reaction to their work together. During this same conversation with Karen she recalled, "I had gotten to the point where I knew I couldn't keep on with the steadiness of the intensity, either . . . but I think that's the way it is when we're all being real with each other. I don't think I would have wanted to keep on when you were ready to slow down or change. Yet almost up to the moment of recognition of this feeling I had wanted every minute of it, and was myself stimulated by it. When you came back it was obvious that we were all ready to rearrange things a bit . . . and we did!"

After Christmas, Karen called Nan to say that Thyra had spontaneously shared a dream, the first since her angry summer closure. Very cautiously Karen had asked one or two questions for clarification. Thyra was neither effusive nor reluctant and expressed no ambivalence over sharing the dream with Nan.

Dream Number Eighteen: Thyra's

Daddy and I were driving in the car. We came to a red light and Daddy didn't stop and we ran through the red light and crashed. All of a sudden the car became an airplane. We went flying through the air and it didn't cost any money. A nice lady stewardess gave us a dinner and that didn't cost any money either.

In the first part of this dream Thyra and her Daddy violate the rules (run through a red light), and they survive. In the second part of the dream the regulations are withdrawn (no charge for air travel) and they enjoy the gift. Part two seems to be saying it's all right to do what we did in part one. The question was then, what was the danger (red) or authority (red light) that Thyra felt had been challenged and conquered. Without more specifics from Thyra it was almost impossible to come to a conclusion, and the Andersons considered it imperative not to press Thyra after her long dream-recall hiatus. But two possibilities surfaced from a careful consideration of recent family life.

After seven years of physical reserve, Thyra was allowing her winsome feminine seductiveness to show in her relationship with her father. She would lean against his chair and twirl his hair around her fingers, and in other acts of affection express her attraction to Cliff. Previously Cliff had tried to encourage her closeness, but when she would not respond, his reaction would be, "She's too much like me," and the distance would remain. Perhaps as Cliff had become less rigid in the expression of his anger and expectations, Thyra let go a little as well, dropping her myth of self-sufficiency. She and her father together crashed through her conventional rules for survival—physical and psychic distance, metaphorically expressed by the red light. Some cues from him had put her in the car and together they survived the impact of their new encounter. Suddenly they were flying high, with conventional demands (paying for air fare) temporarily lifted.

The second speculation as to what specifically might have triggered Thyra's dream had to do with Cliff's mother. Thyra's grandmother had stayed with them for four weeks during the Christmas holidays. During the last week of her visit relationships began to wear a bit thin. She became critical of Thyra with undercutting comments such as, "Thyra used to be a good eater, but now Heather's the good eater." Cliff confronted her with the inappropriateness of such remarks. That was an innovative move on his part: was this the daring crash through the red light?

Either way, one thing is certain: Thyra and Cliff in the dream act as allies, first countermanding an order by an assumed authority (traffic regulations) at the risk of annihilating something as critical as life itself. There is indeed an impact, but it culminates in a new freedom.

Karen said of Thyra:

She is worldly-wise in strange ways. I think she could be very much aware, without having anyone verbalize to her directly, that Cliff withdraws from his mother. She must know he is not relaxed with her, and also must sense the recent changes in their relationship. I couldn't say that about Heather . . . she just gets angry and talks back. But Thyra watches and listens and reacts deep inside herself.

The dream seems to be saying, "My Daddy and I see the danger, but it's all right because he's with me."

Karen and Cliff also recalled dreams the week following his mother's visit. Karen told Nan her dream, but it was obvious that she and Cliff had already come to appreciate its meaning; Nan had one notion about a metaphor, Karen thought for a moment, then said it just didn't fit. She had become her own dream guru.

Cliff had decided to work on some unresolved areas of conflict with a psychiatrist and Nan asked him whether or not he might want to discontinue sharing dreams with her during this period. After talking it over with his psychiatrist he decided he would like to tell her this dream. It seemed to him that this dream rounded off something they had all come through together.

Dream Number Nineteen: Cliff's

Our whole family, all four of us, were in Africa. We were walking through Africa and in my dream I could see the entire continent—like looking at a map. We had been walking a long, long distance on a very deserted desertlike road. Thyra said, "We've come a long way. How large is Africa?" I could respond quickly because I (in waking life) had just recently found out that "It's three times as large as the United States." That's a long walk!

We seemed to be going in a southeasterly fashion, and then we wanted to go northeast. On our way up the continent we got off on the wrong dirt road. Again I could see the whole continent . . . very definitely, the roads. The road we were looking for was a superhighway-type road, but we were on this little dirt road. This led us to a wealthy resort area with well-dressed people, all white American types. We were on a hill looking down to this plush outdoor, palm-treed veranda. I was aware that we were sitting on the roof of the building. I pointed this out to Karen and the girls. We couldn't stay there because we didn't belong there; besides, this was not getting us to where we wanted to be.

We went into the kitchen area where food was being prepared. We asked directions. A lady, a servant, had a map on the wall and was showing us where we had gone wrong and where we could get back on the main road. We left there, walked down the dirt road, and got on the main road.

The dream occurred at the end of his mother's visit. Cliff sensed the necessity for the four of them to be alone again, to explore all that they had in common and to go forward together—even if the prospects appeared vast and the support sparse. Had he to some extent experienced his mother's visit, despite the difficulties, as an oasis, a surcease from the focused commitment to movement and growth that had characterized the months before her arrival? The family had taken a side road, been in a protective compound—a closed, plush society. In some ways his mother's visit was a comfortable time for him because while she was there he and Karen could not work as openly with the issues between them. The mother acted as a buffer, for they attempted to protect her from the pulsations of their family life. For Cliff, life was less intense—at least on the top layer—while his mother was there. But underneath something was pressing for freedom. He kept his distance in the dream, did not allow himself to settle for the comfortable and superficial status quo.

In his dream Cliff did not ask help from the guests (social contacts or his mother), but went to the kitchen where the cook gave him directions out of the villa—exactly what Cliff had done in waking life when he started sessions with a psychiatrist. He was asking in essence, "How can I get back into life (the main road)?" and he was asking this of someone paid (the servant in the kitchen) to respond to basic needs— his psychiatrist.

The servant did not put him in a car and drive him to his destination, did not do the work for him, but she did suggest the proper route. Cliff recognized he had a long way to go; it was going to be a hard trip in a big country, but he was off. He left the tempting haven and headed for the open road —with Karen, Thyra, and Heather.

There is no conclusion to the Andersons' story because they continue to use their dreams as a vehicle for growth. On occasion they ask Nan to listen to one of their dreams, and she shares hers with them. Cliff is no longer in therapy. He and Karen are both seeking ways to help others get in touch with the inner springs of healing. Karen was coteacher with Nan in a recent dream workshop. Her sensitivity to the predicaments that often block our growth, coupled with her appreciation of the variety of meanings available in any image, has helped many people get in touch with their dreams.

Every so often Heather rushes up to Nan and pours out a dream. She rarely wants to consider it past the telling, but she is obviously fascinated by, and proud of, what she has produced.

Thyra reserves her dreams for her family, but both children are at home with their dreams.

Whether or not the Andersons are a typical American family isn't of great importance. Certain trends from their experience can be applied to family dream work in general.

Dream work reveals the strengths and weaknesses of all family members. No one person can be the authority on every issue. Once that idea is accepted, the position of each member within the family structure becomes more flexible.

As preconceived notions about the family give way to new perspectives, there is conflict and anxiety. The more openly these tensions can be dealt with, the higher the value of the family's dream work. At best the sharing and change proceed unevenly. Each member of the family has his own pace. Respecting these differences is a necessary safeguard against destructive pressure and manipulation.

Family dream work is a hard but warmly rewarding process. And it is a natural method, for it uses our distinct personalities to recognize, repair, and extend the emotions that are woven into the fabric of family life.

10

The Dream
and Society

Do our dreams come to terms with social myths in the same
way that they help us see through personal myths? Can they
be a source of social as well as personal knowledge? Can we
learn to look at dreams from this perspective? Should we?

A myth, as we've been using the term, is a self-deception
that we embrace unquestioningly because it provides us with
a degree of security and comfort. It is an assumption about
our own nature or about the nature of others that is not valid
but is, nevertheless, taken for granted. It is so much a part
of us that we are unaware of its operation and the price we
pay for maintaining it. Its existence signifies a gap between
our real and our spurious knowledge of ourselves and others.
As we have seen, that gap leaves us vulnerable when actual
events expose the sensitive area and confront us with the fact
that our habitual responses are no longer adequate to the
situation. We are left puzzled, anxious, and generally at a
loss as to how to respond. Our dream images reflect this

dilemma and make it possible for us to look at the particular false belief that has helped create the difficulty. Once we allow ourselves to become aware of the existence of a gap and its particular nature we are in a position to do something about it. This, of course, is what dream work is all about.

The misuse of power in human affairs is one of the sources of personal and social myths.

Personal myths arise in childhood because of the many opportunities for parental power to be abused. Parents continue to be seen as good, strong, all-knowing, even when they do silly, foolish, and even destructive things to children. The child needs the parent so desperately that he will often experience himself in the wrong and build up myths about his own inadequacy and unworthiness.

Reality has a way of jolting us out of complacency. It brings us face to face with parts of ourselves that we have disowned or denied. If we expand our vision and examine the misuse of power on a larger social scale, the origin and nature of social myths comes into view and all that we have said about the personal myth applies on this larger scale.

There are segments of society in a position to misuse power and to deny that any such misuse exists. Rationalizations buttress the denial. These deeply ingrained, taken-for-granted rationalizations form the social myths at work in a given society. Such myths are apt to operate to the disadvantage of minorities, women, children, older people, and the poor. These are the groups that, in the past and to a continuing extent in the present, have been deprived of power. It is axiomatic that the abuse of power involves power deprivation.

The jolt to a social order may come in the form of an intrusive event such as a riot or mass protest that calls attention to problems that had heretofore been swept under the rug. A social myth is then on the verge of being punctured,

exposing the gap between the supposed intent of certain
social institutions and their actual impact on the lives of
people. The crisis creates the possibility for a deepening understanding of the forces at play but doesn't ensure a successful resolution. The opportunity may be dissipated if all that
results is the patching up of old strategies. If, however, the
expanded awareness spearheads a movement for genuine
change, the myth may be laid to rest. Each such tension,
then, is an invitation to growth, whether the tension is experienced by the individual or by the society.

What does the analogy we have drawn between personal
and social myth have to do with dreams? And of what importance is the connection to anyone engaging in dream work?

Dream images are borrowed from the almost infinite repertoire of images available to the human race from its early
beginnings. They come from our social heritage and from our
current social existence. We rearrange and rework them to
suit our own ends. Although the end result may be our own
creation, the components of the image are borrowed from
"out there." The meaning that we give them is influenced by
the meaning given to them out there. An example of this
might be a woman who dreams of a cow as an aspect of her
own self-image. The image of a cow has certain social connotations; domestication, contentment, passivity, nurturing,
etc. The dreamer borrows the image of a cow because one or
more of these meanings represents exactly what it is she is
trying to say about herself. If you were to dream of a Rolls-
Royce (and if you weren't in the income bracket where Rolls-
Royces were commonplace) you would be making use of
another social image, one suggestive of status, prestige, and
privilege. When images like these begin to acquire a fixed
social meaning they become social stereotypes.

In Sweden, where the woman's movement started early
and resulted in many apparent social changes, passive images

of cows continue to appear in dreams. This reflects not only
the hold that earlier personal experiences have but also the
fact that social change comes slowly. Here are dreams of two
Swedish women, both of whom lead independent lives and
would be considered good examples of liberated women.

A's Dream:

A girl came down a hill in the country leading a cow.
A boy ran in front of her, wanting to tease and hurt
her. When they came down the hill the boy lay down
on the ground and pretended that he was giving birth
to a child. He parted his legs and pretended to kick
the child away. He seemed intentionally malevolent
toward the girl. A voice in the background said,
"Now it is all up with the milkmaid and the cow."

B's First Dream:

In the dream I see a picture hanging over a little
chest of drawers that was in the nursery when I was
a child. It is a picture of Dutch farmers' wives with
wooden shoes on their feet and cows grazing in the
meadow. I come to a woodland lake where the cows
are standing and drinking water. One of them lifts
her head and looks at me with her beautiful cow eyes.
Suddenly she winks with one of her eyes; a wink of
understanding. I want to be big, a big cow and be
together with them, wise and clever as they are.

B's Second Dream:

I see a house in the country. I enter with my mother
and my little daughter. We hear groaning from the

barn. I remember I have heard that something terrible has happened to a cow in this place. I go to the barn. The cows are lying on mattresses in beds. Somebody has skinned them alive! It looks terrible. They are groaning. Blood, flesh, and skin are mixed.[1]

These dreams reveal various meanings the cow image can have. In B's first dream it is associated with nurturing, beauty, wisdom. In the other two dreams the helpless and vulnerable aspects emerge.

Stereotypic images of this kind betray the existence of a social myth. They arise because they capture something about a sore spot in the social organism. They are shorthand references to certain unpleasant truths, such as racial prejudice, male chauvinism, and the unequal distribution of the good things in life. They exist as stereotypes as long as these blemishes are somehow rationalized and accepted. All of us are contaminated by these stereotypes but some, like Archie Bunker, embrace them consciously.

To the extent that our dreams incorporate such stereotypes they may be said to point in two directions: inwardly, to some unfinished bit of emotional business that is unique to ourselves; and outwardly, to some unsolved problems in the society of which we are a part. And they are a reminder that a connection exists between the outside problem and the inside one. The woman who dreams of herself as a cow lives in a society in which, in many respects, those features that make women second-class citizens still endure. Even in Sweden the seats of power are largely occupied by men.

That a relationship exists between personal and social issues is not all that surprising. The problems we face are not altogether homemade in the sense of being just a private family affair. There are institutional arrangements and attitudes that stimulate the emotional turmoil set into motion early in our lives. The limiting or destructive emotional fall-out from social myths is as real for society as a whole as it is for those whose lives are governed by the myths.

The oppression of blacks in this country has led to a number of stereotypes, many of which have fortunately faded into oblivion. But one which endures in the dreams of white females is the stereotype of the black man as personifying both the excitement and danger of sex. Its occurrence has no relationship to the sophistication or egalitarian-mindedness of the dreamer.

Dorothy, a talented young therapist, had one such dream:

Dorothy's Dream:

I was in a school cafeteria, sitting at a table with other people. The only person I recognized was my friend, Hilda. I went on line to get food. It was self-service. There were two kinds of soup, neither of which looked good to me. I suggested to Hilda that she take one and I take the other and we could share them. Nothing in the soup looked appetizing. I went back to the line. While there a black man came behind me, opening up my bra. I didn't know what to do. I was standing there letting this thing happen. He disappeared before we went back to the table. No one knew about the man but me.

Concentrating only on the appearance of the stereotypic image of the black man engaged in a sexual approach, the following comments of the dreamer are relevant:

Before falling asleep I was reading an article by Karen Horney on women's fear of men. I know I'm preoccupied with the woman issue and my identity as a woman. I'm in a relationship now that I know won't last. I choose men who are nurturing but not satisfying. I am concerned with how I will get my needs satisfied and what will happen to my sexuality.

The dream depicts two responses to her sexual need, one bland, uninteresting, but nourishing, the other sneaking up on her from behind, exciting, frightening, and potentially dangerous all at the same time. Her own passivity is implicit in both situations and perhaps accounts for her need to see the man in some kind of overpowering role. The stereotype was conveniently at hand—the aggressive black male and the passive victim.

In the current generation of young women, dreams of protest are prevalent. Again, they represent a search for personal identity as well as a struggle against the stereotyped acceptance of the woman as a second-class citizen.

Jill's Dream:

It was a sunny day. I was in a field where there was nothing but grass. I was carrying a small child and walking along the base of a big hill. Then I was halfway up and in the midst of a group of people who were progressing along and also carrying children. Suddenly a large tractor trailer started across the hill as though to go through the people. This was the first of more to come. The people were there to stop the trucks. I yelled to them to go get in front of the trucks and that the driver wouldn't hurt them. I seemed to know this. I put the child down. There was a loud noise as if someone had thrown an explosive. I threw myself over the child but we were OK.

I began to sit down with a five-year-old blond boy.

I felt as if I knew who he was. I said to him, "You know my name." He said no, but teasingly. I said, "Yes you do." He said, "That's right," and he repeated my name. I sat down and awoke with a great feeling of calm.

These were the events of the day before that had a bearing on the dream: Jill had been examined by a male gynecologist that afternoon and had come away feeling upset and ill. She'd gone to her mother's for a visit and unexpectedly ended up having dinner and staying there overnight in her old bed. She spent several hours that evening working on a paper on the Equal Rights Amendment (ERA) for a course she was taking. Before going to sleep she watched a movie showing female law students protesting against the discriminatory practices of one of the male professors.

I will not go into the personal dynamics of Jill's dream because I want to highlight the social facts that have a bearing on it. Jill felt drawn to the woman's movement but also felt conflict about what her role as a woman should be. She identified the huge tractor trailer in the dream as male power and saw herself as assuming a leadership role in mobilizing the protest of the group.

She was aware of very contrasting feelings the night of the dream. She felt the warmth of home and hearth, the sense of nurturing and support, and the desire to have a family of her own. Although deeply committed to a career, she welcomed the surcease from the struggle she was going through at work as the leader of a feminist protest group and at school where she was also preoccupied with the feminist issue. She felt the dream was trying to place that struggle in truer perspective in relation to what she really felt her values were. As she said, "The truck couldn't stop me but the kid did." The child's acceptance meant more to her than did the leadership role she'd played earlier. It was more important for her to be an adequate woman in the eyes of a child than to her peers in the movement. It was the response of the child at the end that led to the feeling of calm. The dream didn't deny the existence of the struggle or the role she could play, but it did highlight other values she holds dear.

When one is young, female, and hopes to make a living through art, there are many difficult social realities to overcome. Dora is a young artist trying to establish her independence and finding it rough going. She has a strong sense of her own artistic integrity and a strong resistance against compromising it. She resists the idea that, in order to make money, she may have to commercialize her talent. She feels further handicapped by her ignorance about money matters. To remedy this she recently took a course in economics.

Dora's Dream:

I'm in the living room with wealthy older people. My mother is there. I don't participate in the conversation until the subject of money comes up. I begin to express my view. I am very enthusiastic. I'm aware that almost everyone is becoming increasingly uncomfortable but I don't care. I am curious about their different reactions. No one seems to want to deal with the point I bring up about the Gross National Product and how the international debt is never paid, but is simply traded and extended. People divide up, talking among themselves and not dealing with my points at all, just waiting for me to finish. I grab a woman's arm and I say, "But money! No one can even agree on what it is." She replies, "It's just about everything and we certainly know about it and how to use it."

The night before the dream Dora had been talking with two
of her friends about the problems of women in our society
and the problems artists face in making things that will sell.
Living at home in a well-to-do milieu she is in contact with
a generation that "certainly knew about it (money) and how
to use it." She felt the dream exposed two self-images.

> As an artist I was silent, feeling separate, inept, and
> disapproved of by these wealthy people. I had my
> own ideas about money which I couldn't get across
> to them. They just tuned me out. But this also shows
> another side of me, a presumptuous and superficial
> side, trying to lecture them on money from a theoret-
> ical point of view when they knew far more about it
> from a practical point of view. With regard to the
> Gross National Product, I really think that most of
> the *products* we produce and sell as a *nation* are
> lacking in aesthetic quality, are indeed *gross.*

Without going any further into the personal meaning, the
dream does offer a commentary on the plight of the young
artist in our society.

The following dream reveals the interplay of a personal
dilemma with a prevailing social tension. It is the dream of
an ambitious young black lawyer working hard to advance
himself. At the same time he feels strongly committed to
"being of help to my people."

Edwin's Dream:

I was playing baseball with a childhood friend in a
wooded area. There were two out for the home team.

> I looked and assessed the situation. I realized that the
> better team was the one that was out on the field. I
> felt conflicted. I wanted to be on the winning team
> but my friend, who was on that team, said that I
> would have to play in the outfield. This didn't appeal
> to me. I wanted to be at bat and the center of the
> action.
> I wound up coaching a rundown between first base
> and home plate. I finally saw the first baseman was
> going to miss the ball. I encouraged the batter to go.
> He rounded first and was going to second.

The night before the dream Edwin had been at a meeting
where he was called upon to act as a mediator between a
group of black workers and their higher-ups. He realized
that, as an educated black professional, he was facing choices
that would test his resolve to be a leader to his people when
such choices might compromise his own ambitions. He read
the connections of this event to his dream in the following
way:

> In the dream I was torn. I wanted to be part of the
> winning team but I knew what would happen if I did.
> I would find myself out in left field, socially success-
> ful perhaps but unimportant, unrecognized, and un-
> fulfilled. This is what happens to upwardly mobile
> blacks. They are co-opted and give up the struggle.
> The other choice was to do what I could for my own
> home team. I would have liked to be a hero and save
> the game by my performance at bat. This is the part
> of me that wants to make a grandstand play and gain
> recognition. In the dream I seem to have worked
> through to a role that will take into account my need

to further develop my professional skills and, at the
same time, direct those skills toward helping my
team.

The kind of rundown is, of course, impossible in
a real game but it does point up another aspect. Any
winning play is fraught with danger. To be a real
leader like Martin Luther King or Malcolm X can be
fatal.

The baseball field and the Great American Game had
become the metaphor for the struggle between two opposing
teams—those who had made it in the Establishment and
blacks who remained disenfranchised and who were, as in
the dream, on the losing side.

There were a number of more personal associations to the
dream, but one in particular opened the dream up for the
dreamer. He became aware that the friend in the dream who
warned him about being in the outfield if he joined the winning team was a composite image of two childhood friends.
One tended to play it safe and went on to a successful career
in the business world. The other took risks, became alcoholic, and died quite young. He could identify with both. The
dream seems to be saying that both images would have to be
transformed if he was to work toward his ideals and still
survive. It also points to a strategy that seems to work. Being
on the losing side he has to take advantage of the errors of
his opponent. He does this in the dream even at the risk of
being "run down."

Awareness of this social dimension to our dreams can be
useful to us as dreamers. Through the social stereotypes that
appear in our dreams, we can learn more about the role that
stereotypes play in our life, the social myths from which they

are derived, and the way our own life is connected to that social myth.

We are social beings and by gaining a more honest perspective about society and our role in it, we can become better social beings. So there is social knowledge to be mastered as well as personal knowledge if we are to realize our potential for a wholesome sense of connectedness to ourselves as well as to others. As social beings we are carriers of embedded kinds of ignorance that resist recognition and are difficult to root out. These are the areas that are likely to become visible in dreams. Therein lies the special importance that dreams have for us.

There are, of course, many important differences between personal and social myth. Perhaps the most important one is that individuals dream, societies do not. The dream is the individual's way of getting out of the embedded system and taking the much-needed outside view. In the case of society it is up to an individual or group of individuals to acquire that outside perspective. The dream doesn't take the place of such a person, but it can help us each become more of the kind of person who *can* see society from a fresher and more honest perspective.

Let me use a dream to illustrate in greater detail the reflection in dream of a social myth and the relationship of social to personal myth. The dreamer, Monica, is a young Swedish woman who recently returned to her country after a brief vacation with her husband in Cyprus. She had the dream the morning of her return. It was presented to the group shortly thereafter. Three recent events were identified as relevant to the dream:

> 1. Sunday, the day before the dream, we were out in the sun for two hours and I was badly burned. I had to stay inside the rest of the day. It made me think

about the sun not only as a source of pleasure but also as something that can torture. It can turn pleasure into its opposite.

2. We were taken to see beautiful and ancient mosaics in the home of a wealthy Greek. Something about the luxury and splendor and his smug attitude repelled me. The thought occurred to me that evil lay behind all this splendor. How many people had to die for it? How many people were kept in poverty?

3. Last night my husband and I were discussing some of Freud's writings on the death instinct. We felt critical of modern psychoanalysts who we thought did not take into account the potential for evil in every man.

Monica thought the dream had to do with her own connection with evil.

Monica's Dream:

I am an adopted son to a grim despot named Amin. He has another adopted son. That son is more on Amin's side than I am. Amin loves these two adopted sons even though he is very cruel and dislikes everyone else. He loves us but doesn't trust us. Whoever opposes him—it's off with his head. We live in a stone castle. I want to escape but there is no one I can trust, not even my adopted brother. I have to get permission to go for a walk in the woods, but have to go with this brother. When he turns his back I say I'm going to pick certain mushrooms. I start to run. He knows I'm trying to escape. I have to go back.

Since I chose this dream because of what it can tell us about social myth, I will deal primarily now with its social implications.

Dream Image	Image as Metaphor
I am an adopted son to a grim despot named Amin.	Amin is evil. I am related to evil through a process of adoption. Evil has a controlling hold over me. The son here is the more active side of myself. I think of men that way, the side more capable of fighting back.
He has another adopted son. That son is more on Amin's side than I am.	The duality here represents two aspects of myself—one siding with Amin, the other one not.
Amin loves these two adopted sons even though he is very cruel and dislikes everyone else.	No one is completely evil. There is love there, too.
Whoever opposes him—it's off with his head.	Evil must not allow itself to be seen; therefore the head has to be removed.
We live in a stone castle.	Living with evil is cold and imprisoning, but at the same time connected with royalty, splendor, etc.
I want to escape but there is no one I can trust, not even my adopted brother.	I feel alone in my protest. There is a part of me I cannot trust because it is drawn to this evil.
I have to get permission to go for a walk in the woods, but have to go with this brother.	Something in me wants to risk freedom.

Dream Image	Image as Metaphor
When he turns his back I say I'm going to pick certain mushrooms.	I'm trying to outwit a part of my own self.
I start to run. He knows I'm trying to escape. I have to go back.	I fail in my effort to get away from the other side of myself and its attachment to evil.

Monica herself had sensed the connection of the dream to good and evil. What all three events before the dream had in common was their paradox of encompassing good and evil at the same time. The sun which was the source of life and pleasure could also be destructive and painful. The home with the mosaic treasures was beautiful but built at the expense of others less fortunate. Psychoanalysis as a theory can be a positive good, but according to Monica many analysts don't take into account the potential for evil in every man. When one goes by appearances, only the good is seen. One has to go deeper into the situation before the bad emerges.

It is interesting that Amin is not seen in the dream. The face of evil never makes a direct appearance. There is not a sense of Amin as a particular individual in the dream, and as the dreamer remarked, "It could have been any country in which this was taking place."

The personal myth that has been punctured is that Monica is not connected with the evil that exists. The connection emerges in the image of the other adopted son, his allegiance to Amin, and the power he still has to prevent her escape. It is not the existence of the despot that we have to worry about. It is the existence of the despot in us that should be the real cause of our concern. The choices we make as individuals influence the level and power of the evil that exists about us.

Here is someone struggling to come to grips with the problem of evil that pervades the social structure, an evil that is not seen but that exists and makes its presence felt from time to time. The social myth, then, is that evil can be personified and thereby lets us escape the burden of our own responsibility for it. The name Amin emerges in the dream as a social stereotype for this personification of evil.

There are two ways of dealing with social evil. One is to see it as external and unconnected with ourselves. The other is to admit and explore our connection with it. In the first instance the cause of evil exists outside of ourselves in the person of a Hitler, an Amin, or a crooked politician. In the second we own up to our responsibility and the way our own self-seeking impulses allow for the appearance of social evil, even sustain it. The dream reflects the dreamer's very personal sense of connection to evil. It's part of her upbringing, her heritage. Part of herself is loyal and committed to it. There is a certain seductiveness to the love and security offered by Amin.

The three events alluded to in Monica's life made her realize how easy it is to be taken in by the appearance of things, to be seduced surreptitiously and unknowingly into an alliance with evil. The only safeguard that exists for her and for everyone is that there is choice. Every moment presents us with a choice. Only if we choose evil will it endure.

If dreams reveal how social and personal myth interpenetrate, they can be of importance to anyone seeking to dispel social as well as personal ignorance. Their value lies in our ability to view the system we are examining from a point outside the system. At night we not only experience ourselves differently from the way we do when we are awake, but we also separate ourselves temporarily from the social system and have the opportunity to see it from a different perspective. Our dream images are like pictures sent back to earth from a camera located on a satellite in space. The broader scene emerges. If we think of a dream as a psychic satellite located outside of time and space, then the information it sends back encompasses a temporal span as well as a spatial one. In other words it presents us with an expanded view of the past as well as the present and a more comprehensively-based projection into the future. (See Charts 11 and 12.)

Dream work should be of interest to investigators of the social and political scene, who have a hard time grasping current realities from a base within those realities. A fresh perspective in the social sciences occurs when a social investigator somehow manages to gain a perspective from outside the system he is examining. This is not easy to do while awake and involved in the system, and probably no more than a handful of social theoreticians have succeeded. It is something we all do when we sleep. And we do it quite effortlessly.

Social myth and personal myth serve the same function. Both seek to preserve the existing arrangement. But life is not static, and so myths are challenged from time to time. The individual experiences these challenges as a tension of some sort. Society experiences them as social crises in acute or chronic form. To resolve the tension in the direction of healthy growth requires a degree of demythologizing. The rigorously honest reflections of personal and social truths that appear in our dreams present us with the opportunity to reexamine both personal and social myths and to begin the process of dismantling them and moving forward.

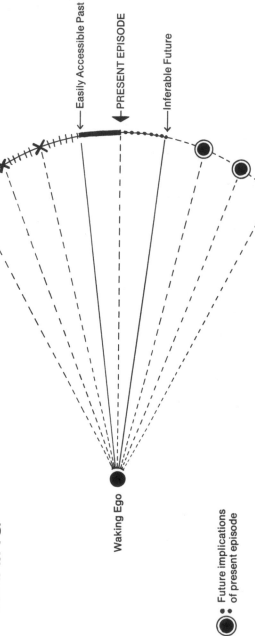

WAKING MEMORY: Limited Access to the Past

CHART 11

BIRTH

Easily Accessible Past

PRESENT EPISODE

Inferable Future

WAKING

Waking Ego

Future implications of present episode

Remote past experiences related to present episodes

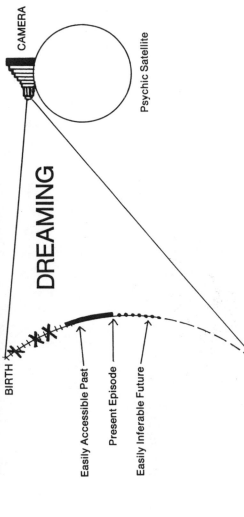

CHART 12

THE EXTENDED RANGE OF THE DREAM

CAMERA

DREAMING

Psychic Satellite

BIRTH

Easily Accessible Past

Present Episode

Easily Inferable Future

Dream consciousness offers a different and larger perspective on our lives than is available to us while we are awake. Since the images derive from a point outside the waking system, the view they encompass of that system is a more inclusive one. The diagram shows the range of the camera extending into the future. This is meant to suggest that we can make a more reliable projection into our future if we have a more comprehensive grasp of our past.

11

Dream Appreciation in Public

In the early seventies consciousness expansion was the password and growth centers were flourishing. An invitation from Esalen was my introduction to this scene and it came at a propitious moment in my life. I was ready to test something that had long been incubating in my mind: my feeling that not only could serious dream work be pursued by anyone so interested, but that it *should* be so pursued, and that I would like to try a group approach. As I said in the introduction, my work as a psychotherapist had convinced me that there was nothing esoteric about dream work and that it was something a nonprofessional could master. And my work as a community psychiatrist had convinced me that all communities seriously interested in the question of mental health should take a great deal more responsibility for learning about their own psychological health and how to maintain it. It seemed to me that dream work represented a readily available and remarkably powerful means to do just that.

I took advantage of other opportunities to explore dream-group work, so that by the time I left for Sweden in 1974 I had some notion of how a group might help a dreamer connect with his dream. My year and a half in Sweden gave me the opportunity to test these ideas with a captive audience of therapists in training. When I returned to the States in 1976 it was with the conviction that group work with dreams was to become the central focus of my professional life.

Yet, you might easily ask, what sense does it make to bring other people into the world of our dreams? Dreams are, after all, a personal expression and if we are not going to discuss them with a specialist, why bring anyone else into the picture?

As we have seen, when it came to dream interpretation, there have always been others involved. The other was cast in the role of the expert, the priest or shaman of old, the psychoanalyst of today. Freud shaped the role of the other along therapeutically helpful lines recognizing the important fact that others do not bring the same protective biases to the imagery that the dream does. The clinical emphasis unfortunately, however, reinforced the concept of the expert. The dreamer came to accept an authority outside of himself who could offer an interpretation or who could validate any interpretation of the dreamer's. In greater or lesser degree this involved the surrender of the dreamer's authority over the dream.

But the question is: Can a group function in such a way as to be helpful and at the same time respect the dreamer's authority over his dream? Ideally, therapists try to function this way, but their own authority and their theoretical allegiances often interfere. What can a group do?

We have stressed the dream's propensity for telling the truth, emotionally speaking. The images reflect the way things are at a feeling level. While we are asleep and dreaming, our self-healing machinery propels us into a realm where feelings are displayed honestly. They shape images that may frighten or delight us, but that is not their intent. Their intent is simply to tell it like it is. All this changes again when we open our eyes and reengage with the world about us. Subtly and often unconsciously, values other than truth and honesty tend to come into play. We seek to maintain a certain social image and play down any feelings that may be at odds with it. We hold onto certain attitudes toward others and ignore or suppress feelings that are at variance with these attitudes. The change from dreaming to waking effects a radical transformation. We move from a realm of honesty to one in which honesty becomes mixed with expediency. While dreaming we have been given a clear lens with which to examine ourself. When awake we often look at the same situation through rose-colored glasses. And to make matters worse, we have no way of knowing that our vision is now colored. We may be aware consciously that the dream holds the key to some mystery about us, but, like a blind detective, we are not aware of what that mystery is nor how to look for clues.

Obviously such a handicapped creature could use some help. This is where the group comes in. As I envisage it, the task of the group is to define that help in a way that works in harmony with the nature of the dream, respects the intimate relationship of the dreamer to his dream, and preserves the dreamer's authority over his dream.

Before a dream group gets started it must be clear about a number of issues. Presumably the members have joined together because they are interested in sharing their dreams with others in order to get some help with them. But working with dreams involves dealing with the most private and intimate form of communication we are capable of experiencing, and so there must be safeguards:

The group must understand the need for confidentiality, must respect intimate disclosures, and must not divulge the identity of the dreamer. Tape recorders, for example, should be used only with the permission of everyone in the group.

The decision whether or not to share a dream and make public the kind of information contained in it should always be up to the dreamer. It should be the result of a genuine desire to share and explore, not an act of compliance.

Work on a dream is open ended in the sense that we never quite know in advance where it will lead. It is important to impress on the dreamer that he has the option of stopping the process at any point that he wishes without offering any reason. He is then free to work on it alone or, if he is in treatment, explore it further with his therapist. Or he may simply table it until he feels better able to cope with the issues it raises.

In my groups I explain the nature of the process briefly in advance; it is a process that unfolds in three stages. Let me illustrate by giving excerpts from the very first session of one of my dream groups: Helen, Iris, Ann, Della, Irwin, Bess, and myself. As the leader I was more active with this group than I would be in later sessions when the members had worked together longer.

Stage I

MONTE: Is there anyone who would like to share a recent dream, preferably one from this morning and one that is not too long? I ask for a recent one because I think it is important to link the imagery of the dream to the specific recent events that are implicated in it. The further back in time your dream occurred, the more elusive those events become. But there's nothing inflexible about this. If a past dream is of particular importance to you we'll take our chances with it. If a dream is important enough something about the context will stand out and be remembered.

A short dream has several advantages. It is often easier to work with a dream that is not too complex. Shorter dreams are easier to remember and need less time to work through. So we may be able to consider more than one dream in a session.

If you have brought notes, try to tell your dream and then fill in from your notes. The rest of us will listen intently and take notes. It's important to have every detail recorded exactly as the dreamer tells it. Seemingly insignificant details may turn out to be important.

Bess, you have a dream for us?

Bess's Dream:

At the beginning my son and I were on a dark street at night. The streets were wet and shining as if after a rain. It was not a residential area. There were warehouses and tenement buildings. It was definitely in the city. I don't know what we were doing there.

All of a sudden five or six guys jumped out of a car with guns and masks over their heads. They grabbed us and pulled us into the car and drove us away.

Then the scene changed to one of brilliant sunlight. We were in a very arid, chilly, mountainous area. I'd escaped from the men. I was panting going up this steep hillside. There was a tremendous sense of urgency and rushing. There was no breeze. Everything was in brown, rust, or tan—earth colors. Nothing was growing.

I got to the top of the ridge when I suddenly realized, What good is it to escape and get help if I don't find my son again? They will disappear and no one will find them. I turned around on the ridge and decided to go back. I didn't seem that upset about it.

When I was coming up the slope it was like a desert. There was nothing there. Now there was a lot of activity. There were men in hardhats working on an enormous ramp of earth as if they were building a ten-lane highway. A great slash across the ground had been dug up. It was a deeper brown and a different color from the surrounding earth. They had a giant earthmoving machine about twenty to thirty feet high.

I felt a little surprised at myself going back to the kidnappers. It was as though I had accepted it and that we were all going to do something constructive and positive, some kind of mission. We were all going to be living together. The kidnappers were among the men working and no longer seemed like criminals at the end. I could have gotten away by myself but without my son.

MONTE: You may ask Bess any questions you like to clarify any of the content you may have missed, but don't ask her for any interpretation. This is only the first stage and we want to stay with the dream just as we heard it. (There was some attempt at identification of the dream characters.)

Stage II

MONTE: No more questions? Okay, we are ready for the next stage. Bess, you can sit back and listen now and take notes if you like. It's time for the rest of us to work. Knowing only Bess's dream, we are in no position to know where it came from or what it means. But there is something we can do to be of help. We can each try to make the dream our own, respond to it as if it were our own. Tell us any feelings you had as you listened to the dream. Don't try to rationalize or

defend them—just share them with us as they occur to you.
The point of this exercise is to make you sensitive to the fact
that dreams originate in feelings and express feelings. We are
not asking for objective comments on Bess's dream or on
Bess. We are asking how the dream affects you. Later we will
check your feelings with Bess and you will probably be surprised how often you will pick up feelings that she had.
Sometimes you will even pick up feelings she had but was
unaware of.

ANN: I felt terror, horror, and then passive and apathetic.

DELLA: I was afraid at first and then resigned.

IRIS: I had a feeling of panic and urgency.

IRWIN: I felt caught in a situation which at first seemed
hopeless and then there was hope.

ANN: At first I felt selfish and then remorseful and regretful.
There was a feeling of submission and self-sacrifice.

IRWIN: I felt I had the opportunity to live a new life.

HELEN: I felt out of control and impotent in the beginning
but then got renewed strength and felt comfortable going
back.

MONTE: I was struck by the feeling of contrast—the dark and
the light, the barren and the growing, the men being criminals and the good guys, giving up my son and going back to
him, the drabness when I'm alone and the colorful scene
when I go back.

IRWIN: I feel as if I'm taking a gamble and there is a risk.

MONTE: Now begin to work with the images as if they were
your own. Look at them, not as literal statements, but as
metaphorical ways of saying something about your lives. If
you had created this image what might it suggest about your
feelings, your aspirations, your tensions, and your conflicts?
Just project your own meanings into the imagery as freely
and as honestly as possible. It isn't a question of being right
or wrong, so anything goes. Use your own speculative, imagi-

native responses to create for Bess a reservoir of possible meanings for the imagery in her dream. Share whatever occurs to you without worrying about its relevance for Bess. We will check all that out later. We all swim about in the same social sea, so that there is some likelihood we may use the same image in the same way. You will probably be surprised to see how much of your input will resonate with Bess. Please remember that no matter how convinced you may be in your own mind that the meaning you are giving to the image applies to Bess and not yourself, everything you come up with in this stage is to be considered your own projection until and if it is validated later by Bess.

IRWIN: If this were my dream it would seem to imply a change of life-style.

IRIS: I have the feeling of cutting the umbilical cord in reverse. It's as if I've been too fused with my son and it's time that outsiders had an influence on him. I'm making progress in my own independence without him. I want to dig into myself.

ANN: I respond to the panting and urgency with a masturbationlike image of doing everything on my own.

HELEN: I realize that what I left behind wasn't so bad. I just hadn't looked at it in the right perspective. There are new aspects to it.

MONTE: Being on the ridge suggests I can get two different views—one forward, the other backward.

IRIS: Progression and independence without my son is arid.

IRWIN: I feel as if I'm looking for a direction.

ANN: The dream has sexual overtones to me. I feel as if I've escaped from entrapment and am running toward freedom.

DELLA: In order for me to go ahead I'm going to have to work out my past.

MONTE: The colors suggest Mother Earth and the birth of something new.

IRIS: The huge machinery reminded me of the movie *Close Encounters* where the aliens were smaller men.

IRWIN: The ten-lane highway suggests a path with many possibilities.

HELEN: The ramp means I'm going onward and upward.

ANN: There is an almost religious quality to the dream where people seemed insignificant and were living for big causes.

It is important that this part of the discussion be allowed to run its course without any sense of time pressure. Important, too, that if there are any details in the dream not taken up by anyone, the leader should raise them. But, as you have seen, the leader is very much a part of the group and gives his own responses all along.

The group worked on this dream for over an hour. They came up with much more than I had presented. Some of these projections were wide of the mark. Some were very much on target and oriented Bess to the dream's general area of concern.

Stage III

MONTE: Now we are ready to bring Bess back into the picture. Everything we've done so far has been with the hope that some of it may be helpful to her. But she is the final judge over what is, or is not, helpful. She is the final authority over her dream. So Bess, you take over now and you can respond in any way you wish. You can tell us if any of the feelings and meanings we offered struck a responsive chord or you can begin with your own ideas about the dream. Take all the time you need. And along the way, try to identify the recent specific events in your life that can account for why this dream occurred now.

BESS: I could identify with a number of things that came out. The feelings were very strong, especially the feeling that, when I could see both sides, I could decide. I want to feel free. I don't want to feel pressured. Many of the feelings expressed matched my own. They made me feel the contrast between the empty landscape and the focused concerted work. There are things I want to think about, like what the dream says about my relation to my son. Why didn't I think of him while escaping? I was upset about leaving my son with these terrible people, but at the same time I had the feeling it was for consistency. It was the same way I felt about his getting into sports. I knew he was at a stage when he should but, at the same time, I don't respect the macho image. I have mixed feelings about it.

The comments about the change in landscape seemed right but not about the feeling of being anxious and trapped. I knew my son was not in danger. The feeling of having to give up control in relation to him struck me.

At this point Bess had a beginning but still vague sense of the dream. A dialogue was then initiated between her and the group to explore further the meaning the images had for her. I explained that at this stage anyone can put questions to Bess, provided they are rhetorical and intended to stimulate her into further explorations.

IRIS: What was your feeling about the ten-lane high-way?
BESS: There was a rush of feeling. I could feel the adrenalin in my system. It was a tremendous feeling of change, as if I were taking off into the unknown. Maybe I was getting into more than I bargained for. There was excitement and anticipation and perhaps a fear of not being up to it.

DELLA: How did you feel when you saw the men digging up the earth?

BESS: I wanted to be part of it, to join with them.

The dreamer sometimes needs assistance from the group in building the bridge between the imagery of the dream and the actual events that led to it. Only when this is achieved is there a full sense of identification with the dream: ownership of the dream would be another way of putting it.

MONTE: Does the dismal setting of the dream connect with any feelings you had recently?

BESS: I missed a class I wanted to attend last night because I had to take my son to a cub scout meeting. I suppose there was some resentment there. Also last night my boyfriend was with me. He kept talking about marriage. I wasn't feeling too well so he made supper for all three of us. I felt pressured by him. I didn't respond and he left reluctantly. I have a slightly absurd feeling about the whole thing as if I'm being pushed into a relationship. There is a strong feeling of pressure.

At this point I began to orchestrate much of what had now come to light through the group work. In calling attention to the reflection of these events in the dream I engaged in purposeful exaggeration because the dream itself often uses hyperbole to emphasize feelings.

MONTE: Try this on for size, Bess. These thoughts occurred to me as you were describing the events of last night. You were eager to go to your class but were prevented from doing what you wanted by these horrible gangsters who kidnapped you and your son, who pressured you into a course of action other than what you wanted. You experienced two kinds of pressures last night, both from men—the men who ran the cub scout meeting and "kidnapped" not only your son but you, and your boyfriend, whose overtures were experienced as pressure. He came over for a fun time with you and ended up cooking dinner for you and your son and going away frustrated. You are, as indicated by the escape attempt, concerned with freedom; but, despite the limitations imposed on you by motherhood, you don't want freedom at the expense of abdicating your role as mother. That would only leave you arid, dry, barren. So you find a way of going back to get your son and also to arrange for building this superhighway of infinite possibilities. The men are then transformed from gangsters to men doing constructive work (construction workers).

Bess felt comfortable with this way of bringing the imagery and her life situation together. She said: "The one feeling I always have is that I do want to live my own life, but not at the expense of giving up my child and my family life. They are equally important to me."

By the time we had finished Bess had a clearer sense of the connection of the dream to the events of the night before, as well as to the more important struggle going on in her life: a struggle for a more emancipated and fulfilling role for herself than she had experienced in the past and particularly in her former marriage. She did feel at a point where she could go either forward or backward, but in this instance, going back meant going back to something new. That was more desirable than going forward in the sense of a complete break with her past and her family. There were other issues raised by the dream with regard to her feelings about men. Bess acknowledged this and felt there was more work on the dream she had to do on her own.

The Nature of the Process

The most important thing to remember is that the dreamer is in control of the process from beginning to end. The dreamer makes the decision to share the dream. The dreamer decides how much self-disclosure is comfortable. The dreamer can stop the process at any stage and does not need to continue as far as others in the group might wish to go. At no point should a dreamer feel under constraint about sharing a dream. There is never a question of rotation or taking turns. At no time should anyone be put on the spot or made to feel guilty. The only reason for the group to be there is to help the dreamer with the dream.

The flow of the process is illustrated in Chart Thirteen. Now let's examine the reasons for each stage.

Stage I

An interesting thing happens in the group when someone decides to go public with a dream. The group members seem to become aware that something special and delicate has been entrusted to them. The dreamer sets before them a most intimate part of his being. He lays bare a section of his soul. This seems to mobilize a special concern within the group. The dreamer feels this supportive response, and trust is quickly generated.

As the group becomes more experienced, they will begin to listen more carefully to the qualifying statements the dreamer uses in introducing a dream:

"I had the strangest (silliest, stupidest) dream last night."

Is the dreamer trying to create distance from the dream, avoid its message, discourage the group from working with it?

"I had a dream but if someone else would rather go first."

"I had a dream but I'm sure someone else has a better dream."

Does this suggest a tendency to hide and be self-effacing,

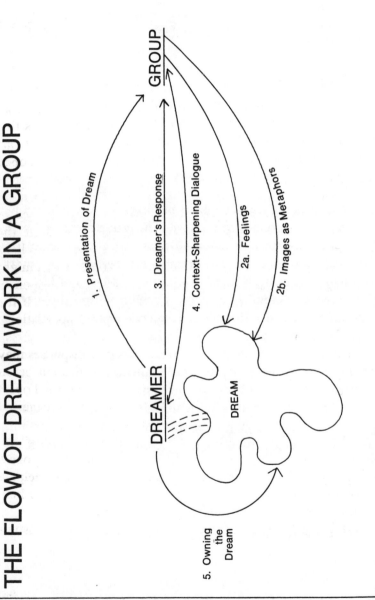

THE FLOW OF DREAM WORK IN A GROUP

CHART 13

1. Presentation of Dream

3. Dreamer's Response

4. Context-Sharpening Dialogue

2a. Feelings

2b. Images as Metaphors

GROUP

DREAMER

DREAM

5. Owning the Dream

to be inappropriately modest in a self-defeating way? These may be the very things dealt with in the dream.
"I don't know whether to share this dream or not. I guess I'll share it."
Again, the qualifying ambivalent statement may give a clue to the dream.

Stage II

Why do we wait until the group has had its say before we bring the dreamer back into the picture? The reason is tied to the issue of honesty and expediency we spoke about earlier. No matter how earnestly the dreamer may want to open up the dream, there is always the chance of some self-protective and defensive measures. They may take the form of unconscious distortion of what is shared or avoidance of certain areas of the dream. In either instance what the dreamer says is apt to track the group's responses into lines suggested by the dreamer's associations. Some of this might be helpful, but there is the danger that the group's responses may be limited by the waking biases of the dreamer. If the group members start without the dreamer's associations, their responses will be free and spontaneous, coming from where they are in relation to the dream. The responses may sometimes be wide of the mark, but they will often be on target—and those responses might have been screened out if the group members had been working along lines suggested by the dreamer.

We are not concerned with the number of "wrong" responses, because, paradoxical as it may seem, *all* responses are helpful for our purposes. A "wrong" response helps a dreamer define what the image is not and thereby may help the dreamer get closer to defining what it is.

In Stage II the group must be watchful of anyone assuming an authoritative stance vis-à-vis the dreamer. If a member starts by saying, "You must have felt so and so," he should be reminded that the subject is the member's feelings, not the dreamer's. This is also true when, working with the imagery, someone tries to impose a personal interpretation on the dreamer.

The dreamer is in a unique relationship to the group and to himself during this phase. He listens to others working with something he has created. The dreamer is aware that, at times, the group members say things that strike close to home. Gradually he is confronted with more and more possibilities in the dream which may be uncomfortable, even embarrassing. At the same time the dreamer realizes that he is in a position to examine these discoveries under circumstances in which he need not disclose them to anyone else nor defend himself against them. When someone is confronted by personal truths while free to accept or reject them and not be defensive about them, the natural response is to embrace the truth. There is something in most of us that senses the healing powers of truth.

Before leaving this stage it is important to be sure that the group has attended to every detail of the dream. It can be helpful to write down the contributions of the group and to rearrange them to follow the dream's structure. Special attention should be paid to the sequence of the images. When they are reexamined in their natural order, additional clues may become apparent. An image that may be puzzling out of context may assume meaning when related to preceding and succeeding imagery. Sometimes a recapitulation by the leader can help in this regard; this can serve not only to organize the dream in the group's mind but to pull in details that were overlooked before or not given sufficient attention. When the group has done its work thoroughly, little recapitulation is needed.

Stage III

In this stage it is important to sense and respect where and how far the dreamer wants to go. Despite the fact that he has shared the dream, it still remains the dreamer's own. With the support and help of the group he is trying to move into a position of greater honesty and responsibility toward the dream. Yet in the opinion of the group the dreamer may be blind to something obvious. And the group may be right about this. Long ago Freud pointed out that it is easier for others to read our unconscious than it is for ourselves. We may be able to be more honest about another's dream, but we don't have to live with the consequences of that honesty. Despite this possibility, however, a good working rule for this phase should be that only what is validated by the dreamer should be considered as related to the dream, regardless of how right anyone else feels about the ideas that are not accepted by the dreamer. In most instances such ideas turn out to be the group member's own projections.

It is actually in this third phase that the group has an opportunity to check out which responses were related to the dreamer and which were purely their own projections. During the second stage responses are often a mix of what the group members think may be going on with the dreamer and what they sense is coming from themselves. Now they can discover that what they thought was a perception of the dreamer's situation was in reality their own projection. This then becomes a learning experience for all of the group, an indication of where some of their own perceptions are biased.

During Stage III the important function of the group is to help the dreamer build the bridge between the dreamer's imagery and life situation. The connections will often appear spontaneously as the metaphors spring to life in the dreamer's mind. Sometimes the specific context remains obscure in spite of the dreamer's conscious effort to get at it. Two suggestions are often helpful: One is to encourage the dreamer to recall the thoughts he or she had just before falling asleep, since this is when the day residue often begins to surface. If this is not successful it may help to ask the dreamer to recapitulate the events of the day preceding the dream. What sometimes starts out as a recital of seemingly ordinary events is often interrupted by a flash of insight. The dreamer's face lights up with that "Eureka" feeling. The excitement of discovery outweighs any embarrassment or tension that may have been associated with the original incident.

In the dialogue that ensues between the dreamer and the group, it is important that the questions be put so that the dreamer experiences them as exploratory and open ended. Again, while group members have the freedom to ask any question, the dreamer has the freedom to handle responses any way he chooses. Usually those questions are about overlooked details or responses that need further elaboration.

Being sensitive to the dreamer includes sensing the proper moment to bring the process to a close. The group must be careful not to push a too compliant dreamer past the point that he wants to go or, conversely, to stop before a dreamer is ready to stop. Here the dreamer is the key. Only he can sense for sure when that moment arrives when he can, with confidence, competence, and openness continue the process privately. If the group members have been successful they have functioned as midwives; they have brought the dream out to public view and helped establish the dreamer's connection to it. When this happens their job is finished and the job of the one who gave birth to the dream begins in earnest.

12

Dreams People Share

I hope that this glimpse of group work shows how effectively a small group can help us appreciate our dreams—and ourselves as the creator of the dreams. The group not only stimulates interest in dream work but also becomes a powerful instrument in involving the dreamer in his own dreams. And it can help identify some of the artful maneuvers that stand in the way of dream appreciation. The listeners in a dream group are concerned only with what the dream is saying. The dreamer is struggling with two problems: What is there for me to see in the dream? What am I doing that may be preventing me from seeing what is to be seen? Put another way: What part of the dream will I find it easy to own, and what part will I be tempted to disown? The dreamer finds sitting on both sides of the table a difficult position, especially in the early stages of dream appreciation.

The outcome of shared dream work is often remarkable. It can be likened (except as to motive) to the experience of the two hungry men and the stone soup: Two men who were traveling had a pot but nothing to put into it. They came to a square in a tiny village and stopped by a well to rest. One of the men put water into the pot while the other gathered two stones to add to the water. They built a fire under the pot and began to stir it. After a while some villagers gathered at the well. An old woman asked: "What do you have there?"

"Stone soup," the hungry man answered.

"Never heard of it."

"It's very good but it could use a carrot," replied one of the men.

The old woman walked away and returned a few minutes later with some carrots which she added to the bubbling soup.

The next villager who asked about the soup was told how delicious it would be if it only had some onions. Off went the villager and returned to add his onions.

Again and again inquirers were assured that stone soup was a delicacy but needed only a bit of this and that to bring it to perfection. Intrigued by the making of stone soup, each villager contributed a vegetable, a bit of meat, some spices, and so on. At last the soup was finished. The two hungry men then invited all who had contributed to a fine feast from the great steaming pot of stone soup.

In dream work we start not with an empty pot but with a dream that really contains the ingredients for the soup. But sometimes we can't do much with it by ourselves. So we bring the dream into the square of the dream group and let the members drop their bits, their feelings, their reactions, their questions, into the pot. Then we have a mix that will enrich both dreamer and listeners.

Although there is nothing particularly technical or difficult about the process as we have described it, there are some aspects that warrant further discussion. Some people may have difficulty grasping what the term "visual metaphor" means. Since this is basic to dream work I try to make it clear at the beginning by using the following example:

A suburban housewife dreams of riding down Main Street on a unicycle with traffic all around her. The dreamer has never been on a unicycle and has no interest in trying one. Yet in terms of what she has been experiencing in her life, this is the image best suited to bring out the situation she is in. Her dream uses the image to make a comparison with her waking life in an expressive and dramatic way. It is a visual metaphor. What do you think it might be pointing to?

When it's put this way, the group catches on to the idea and comes up with all the possibilities that occur to them:

She is in a very precarious situation.
She is showing courage and daring.
She is very vulnerable.
She is being a show-off and exhibitionist.
She is concerned with her balance emotionally.
She is performing.

Other possibilities will probably occur to you. One of the above possibilities did connect with the dreamer. This, as we have seen, is one of the things that happens in a group.

But let's examine some of the other common phenomena of dream-group work.

First Dreams

Participation in a dream group is an unusual and demanding commitment. Dreams are, after all, private events and are not often shared with people we don't know well. Most of us have had nothing in our past experience to prepare us for sharing ourselves at such an intimate and revealing level. So, at a first session, a number of protective restraining mechanisms come into play. A part of us may consider this a rash step and be concerned with what carefully guarded secrets may be exposed. Initial dreams often touch on the tensions that arise when the impulse to share, trust, and reveal, conflicts with the equally strong impulse to hide, evade, and conceal:

> I dreamt that I was in bed and dreaming. The next thing I knew is I was startled by the fact that my bed flew right out the window with me in it. That's when I woke up.

This dream shows the dilemma quite clearly. The dreamer started out wanting to comply with his own expectations that he share a dream. His self-protective strategies came into play so that the dream he had was one in which he, the bed, and the dream all went flying out the window. We are extraordinarily clever about things when we are asleep and dreaming.

Here is an initial dream of a young woman:

> I was hanging wash, including underclothes, on a clothesline outdoors. Mau Mau warriors appeared as if ready to do battle. I suddenly draped myself over the clothesline and remained motionless, hoping to disappear. It worked. They never saw me.

This dream, too, seems to be a response to the implicit demand of the situation to share a private corner of one's self and to the anxiety that resulted. Things close to her personally, her underclothes, were being put on public display. The MauMaus conveyed to her a sense of threat from aggressive and alien sources. Her initial impulse to comply and display was replaced by the sense of an impending battle. Like the previous dreamer she managed a disappearance act. By merging with the clothes hanging on the line she, as the person exposed, disappeared and fooled the enemy.

Acting the Dream Out

We are all aware that the people we associate with have various personality styles. This person is passive and compliant, that one domineering and controlling, another too intellectual, still another too emotional, and so on. It can be helpful in a dream group to sharpen our observations along these lines, for these traits are apt to be the ones depicted in the dream. A dreamer who is depicted as responding passively in a dream may, during work on the dream, also be noticed as responding in a passive manner. When a group observation of this kind is validated by the dreamer, it adds to the impact of the relevant imagery in the dream.

Sometimes a more specific kind of behavior can be noted and correlated helpfully with the imagery of the dream. Lucy, a young woman, shared a dream that involved her mother and a mute boy of twelve whom Lucy had been counseling. The dream was rather involved. The group worked well with it and, knowing the dreamer's past enthusiastic responses to group work, expected it on this occasion as well. It was somewhat of a surprise when she had very little to say. It seemed almost as if she were deliberately clamming up. When one member of the group asked her if this behavior might be connected with the image in the dream, the floodgates opened. It seems that in the previous session the behavior of one of the group members had reminded her of her mother. That person had remained silent in a way that had troubled Lucy and brought her back to a struggle she had had with her own mother. She had experienced her mother as an ungiving person and had often felt an impotent silent rage toward her.

> My mother's message to me was to be quiet. Her silence was all pervasive. In the dream I was about to have fun until my mother entered the picture with her reproving silence. It was at that point that this silent little boy appeared.

For her the mute child symbolized her inability to speak out in a situation that was painful to her. Her own silence and withdrawal was her defense against what she had experienced as a hostile silence from others.

This is an example of how tension may arise between group members and be reflected in a dream. The answer to whether to deal with these tensions within the group or to allow them to be worked out between the individuals involved depends on the degree of discomfort the issue causes and on the skills of the group. In this instance the events of the previous session were explored and the tension relieved as everyone's perception of the incident came out into the open.

Emotional Torrents

Dream work will sometimes open up long-buried emotional sores and release torrents of feelings. The most effective way the group can deal with such a situation is to allow the dreamer to go with his or her feelings. Sometimes a well-meaning member will try to be reassuring but succeed only in cutting off the flow of feelings. The best thing the group can do is to make the dreamer feel that he can give full vent to his emotions within the group. Nothing much more than that is needed.

Lillian, a young woman recently returned from a skiing holiday, shared the following dream:

> I was at a ski lodge. I was in one room and decided to go into the room next door. It was a very large room. This room was very nice. It had lots of people in it who were having a good time. There were lots of goodies around and it was a big party. I thought to myself, "Why didn't I get to this room before?" I walked out the back door and decided to ski. There was a mountain right behind me. I was by myself.

Following are some of the group responses that built into an emotional crescendo for Lillian.

Group work with feelings

"I felt as if I were going off on my own and it took courage."

"I felt frightened about going into that large room."

"I wanted to be with the others but pulled away."

"I had a feeling of disappointment and envy as if it were too late."

Group work with the images

"The mountain suggests both struggle and accomplishment."

"Skiing is a lovely sport. I feel alone."

"The picture that comes to my mind is that of a sad waif, pressing her nose against a store window and looking sadly at all the goodies beyond her reach."

"Someone got there first and spoiled it, as if I have an older sibling who got there first. I felt left out."

These last contributions about the sad child and the issue of sibling rivalry precipitated a tearful reaction from Lillian that lasted for several minutes. The group remained quietly supportive as her feelings swept over her. When she regained her composure, she was eager to share with the group what she had been going through as the process evolved.

> When we started I had no idea what the dream was about, other than its connection to my recent ski vacation. When you began talking about sadness, deprivation, and then mentioned sibling rivalry, everything suddenly fell into place and this terrible sadness came over me. My brother was with us on this vacation. He is ten years older and he did get all the goodies. For the first time I felt the sadness of it all and the sense of loss. The other day a friend of mine who had just met my brother sized him up as a vulnerable guy. This shocked me. I had always idolized him. My reactions to this led to the dream. I began to realize my friend was right and if I had only known this before it would have saved me a lot of pain. That big room in the dream was his room. I could see only the goodies. It was too threatening to me to see the vulnerability. I had to walk away and embark upon my own lonely struggle. It's scary to go down the mountain alone.

These were some of her immediate reactions. The important thing was that she now felt connected with the dream in a feeling way. She could now begin to sort things out for herself.

Unusual Images and Words

When, in our dreams, we go to the trouble of creating strange and bizarre images, or when we make up what seem like meaningless words or phrases, our understanding of the dream may rest on our ability to discover how these images or words came into being. Often they are composite pictures. Two or more images may be condensed into a single image. Similarly, new words may be created out of the fusion of several components. Consider this fragment of a dream:

> Then I heard Willa (my godchild). I went to look for her and found her stuck, buried under the stone with just her head showing. I thought, "My God! I must get her out." Then I noticed her face was the face of a pig, with a big pig's snout. She was alive at first but then she became dead.

The dream was worked on in its entirety by the group. The dreamer responded positively to the suggestion that the child in the dream was a self-image. She then went on to develop this composite image:

> I've been working on the question of my extreme dependency on Dr. R. [the dreamer has been in therapy for several years]. Willa is a beautiful, angelic, and bright child. I do think she represents me as a child, although I thought of myself as ugly. I was the middle of two gorgeous sisters [the dreamer is an attractive middle-aged woman]. For me the pig stands for greediness and overdoing it and there was this side to my makeup. But I'm beginning to see that for me to get over my childish dependency I have to accept myself as I am, the greedy, ugly, and avari-

cious side as well as the generous, giving, and caring
side. For the adult to emerge I have to accept the
child, warts and all. I was never the ugly child I
thought I was. Having rescued that myth from oblivion I can now set it to rest.

In the following excerpt, also part of a longer dream, a
strange word appears:

John, one of the men I work for, was in the bathroom
with me. He was sitting yogalike in a sandbox.
. . . I heard the word *smanning* called. I asked what
that was. He said it was a word for opening a door
to a different consciousness.

The dream itself was long and complicated. The dreamer
was a young woman who was having problems in her marriage. For several days before the dream she had found herself preoccupied with sexual fantasies involving the men in
her office. Working on the dream made her realize that she
had been acting in a teasing way at the office. This seemed
related to the *manning* part of the word—going after men.
At the same time there was something good and uplifting
about the word that appeared in the dream. It was as if these
sexual feelings were connected to a newfound feeling of freedom and well-being that seemed to hold the key to a different
level of consciousness. The yoga position of the man suggested something spiritual, something that might be connected with a swami. At that point what clicked with her was
that the word in the dream was the combination of swami
and manning and that in the dream she recalled that she
wasn't sure if the word was *smanning* or *swamming*.

One of the lessons the dreamer has to learn is not to back away from any dream, no matter how bizarre or frightening it may seem. There is something there to be attended to. If the confrontation is allowed to take place, healing will occur. The following dream illustrates this. The dreamer, a man in his late thirties, introduced it as having a nightmarish quality. The dream was presented before a fairly large audience: some forty participants in an adult-education class. I was more active than I ordinarily would have been in a small group session, since I wanted to use the material to illustrate the process to the audience as we went along.

Here are excerpts from the session:

Roger's Dream:

I was going downstairs to the playroom at night. It was very dark. When I got there I turned on the light and saw my father hanging from the ceiling. I found myself flying up toward him. I felt fear. I said, "No, no." I was awakened by my wife. My father was white and blue like a dead person, talking, muttering. . . . nothing I could understand.

MONTE: Let's try to get a feeling of the dream that was shared with us. With what kind of feelings did it leave you?
STUDENT I: I mean, it's up and down. It's hectic, disturbing . . . agitation. . . .
STUDENT II: Fear.
STUDENT III: I get the feeling of guilt. The feeling that somehow he was responsible for this. It really shook him up. That's the gut feeling I get.
STUDENT IV: I also get a feeling of being frightened and scared.

STUDENT V: Going into the basement was like returning to the womb. It's dark. If we want to go into it more deeply, it's the death wish against the father. It made him feel guilt and terror in wishing that. If he does replace the father, he will be punished and killed off. Because his father motions him to come up [this part was not in the dream] and he feels he's getting his wish and his father is dead—then he will be punished and also be killed.

It was pointed out that this was an interpretive, theoretical summing up that was inappropriate at this point.

STUDENT II: I get a sense of desire to gain closeness with his father, but also a great deal of apprehension about doing it before it's too late, or realizing the father was closer to being dead. . . .

STUDENT VI: This going down into the darkness could be going deeper into his own unconscious. An examination of himself. Perhaps to find something very personal there. . . .

MONTE: O.K. Now we're beginning to talk about metaphors. Any other feelings?

STUDENT VII: Is it possible that this is really not his father? I don't get the feeling from what he says that the father, as such, is in the dream. I think that might not really be his father. . . .

Again, this was the tendency to think in terms of metaphors rather than stay with the feelings.

MONTE: Anything else by way of how the dream makes you feel? How the dream makes *you* feel? Doesn't it scare you a little bit?

ALL: Yes . . . yes!

MONTE: Right. It gives me a scary feeling. To have that stark and dramatic portrayal of a gruesome death scene—and that's what it is in the dream—is a somewhat overwhelming image. Now, let's try to take a closer look at the metaphors.

You began commenting on them. Can you do anything with the metaphors?*

STUDENT III: I don't know whether it would be a metaphor. I just have the feeling that it was an instinctive act to try to stop inevitable death. He says his father was muttering. Now there was an element of life, if you can mutter. Of course, the white and blue creates a horror picture.

MONTE: You're reacting to the picture in a very literal way. I'm trying to get you to react in a metaphorical way.

STUDENT IV: The father is unattainable. He talks and yet he doesn't understand.

STUDENT VI: I think he placed more importance on: I went down . . . that direction. . . .

MONTE: What's the importance you give this?

STUDENT VI: Despair.

MONTE: Anything else about down—going downstairs?

STUDENT VI: I just associate it with death too, I suppose. . . .

STUDENT VIII: There might be something in his business or personal life or whatever—going down—well, first of all, the thing that he's after, which he thought was right, he now suddenly realizes is wrong, and so he backs away. Going down is like he kind of knew already that it was wrong, but he was going down to it anyway.

STUDENT VII: Looking at the hanging itself like it was a metaphor, could it be like he represents a situation that's unresolved? A decision, maybe, or a conflict between him and his father, not necessarily his father—maybe a conflict within himself that is left hanging . . . ?

MONTE: Good. Yes?

STUDENT I: If we can accept the assumption that they're both

---

*This transcript is from one of my very early workshops. I had not yet insisted on their talking about the dream in personal tones as if it were their own.

him in two different stages, his going down might be into his subconscious or some fragments of the situation or other. And the fact that the words are unintelligible, would be that he himself is not telling himself possibly . . . I get the feeling that going down it was dark and then when he wanted to go up his subconscious said no.

STUDENT VII: Well, I think he's scared of losing his parents and dreading to face the day when he has to lose them.

MONTE: None of us, including myself, is able to say anything about this with any sense of conviction. All of these ideas as we hear them are possible. Going down might be going down into his subconscious. It might be rummaging around in his childhood, et cetera. We are in the dark and to really work on this dream I think we'd have to turn to you, Roger. Do you want to tell us what you think? Do you want to tell us or give us some of your associations or ideas about it?

ROGER: There are some things about conflicts. I do have some conflicts. Conflicts with work versus home. I don't know which parts I fantasized. I just know I was very glad to wake up.

MONTE: I can understand that.

ROGER: In fact, I was shuddering. I was glad to hear the various thoughts of the other people because they're looking at it without any kind of personal relationship, the way I might look at it. The one thing that struck me was I do have this conflict currently. Somebody said that I might be doing wrong and thinking about it. I might be trying to correct it or I might be fearing something. All of those things hit home. They're personal in one respect or another.

STUDENT X: In terms of conflict, could it be that his subconscious is saying that if he resolves it in a certain way the results could be so horrible that it could create this kind of horror for him, and then he's saying: "No, no . . . I don't want. . . ." [The student used these words to express his feelings. They were not in the dream.]

MONTE: That's a very insightful comment. What, in the dream, might make you think you're on the right track? What in the dream might substantiate that?

STUDENT X: Actually, what made me think of it was his saying that he was in conflict, but the fact that the whole dream is so horrible and that he was saying, "No, no. . . ." Do you mean what specific . . . ?

MONTE: He does mention that this horrible scene is taking place in a playroom, in imagination. . . . We play in our imagination. It's not for real. Nothing in the dream is incidental or irrelevant or unimportant. And if he says, "The scene I'm about to describe is taking place in a playroom . . ." then he's saying that for a reason. Perhaps in the dream he is playing out a drama. That's what children do. They play at the real world, but it's play, it's not the real thing. Is there anything else that you want to try to get out of this? Are you satisfied with where we are?

ROGER: Yeah. I really don't know how to delve any deeper into it or if there's anything more to it.

MONTE: Do you want to delve any deeper?

ROGER: Sure. Wherever it takes us it's all right with me.

MONTE: If you dream of doing away with your father and it's not really your father, what might it stand for?

ROGER: Authority figures.

MONTE: Right. Authority figures. A boss? Somebody with power over you? Bigger than you? More powerful? Does this have anything to do with your conflict situation?

ROGER: The conflict situation is one which I think every businessman faces. That is the sacrifice of having to go to work and dedicate yourself to the job versus coming home and spending time with your family and wife. And that's the conflict everybody faces but I never thought that at the age of forty, I'd face it the way I do today. I work for a rather large corporation. I'm very comfortable in my job but what I'm saying is that I think my ego forces me to go further in the job, while at the same time the sacrifice is too much. I don't feel I want to give up my family. That's the basic conflict that I find myself in. I thought that I'd resolved it in favor of my family . . . and yet . . . I'm not really sure.

MONTE: O.K., now does this make any more sense? Might the father in the dream represent *his role* as a father? That's the conflict. Am I going to be a good father or am I just going to be away and absent and involved and unfatherly? Now, I think we're looking at the dream metaphorically. In the beginning some of you jumped on him and accused him of thinking of patricide—killing his father.* He's not doing that at all! He's concerned and anxious about preserving his viability as a father because the life is being squeezed out of that part of himself. Something has a stranglehold on his ability to participate in as fatherly a way as he obviously wants to participate. A noose around your neck is a very powerful metaphor for something strangling the life out of you. You've got to learn to move away from the literal. You'd get the police in here if you looked at it so literally. . . .

Once the class was helped to look at the image as a metaphor for what was happening to the father in himself they were quick to see the nature of the conflict.

STUDENT X: Well, he said it was a struggle between his ego and what he thought he could do and wanted to do at work

---

*I'm exaggerating here to make a point. Although only one person voiced this explicitly I'm sure the same thought occurred to others, as it also did to myself. What seems obvious in terms of psychoanalytic theory is not always the most correct. The dreamer's father was long since dead and there was no indication that unresolved hostility toward the actual father was at play here.

as opposed to what he should be giving his family—the tearing between the two.

MONTE: That's the basic conflict out of which these images came. And, as he said, it's a very hard struggle because there's a tremendous pull. And if there are opportunities opening up in the job or you're involved, there is a natural tendency. . . .

ROGER: (interrupting) . . . I would really like to have the best of both. It's very difficult to balance an equation. It's very hard. It's almost like you have to choose. You really have to choose.

MONTE: I think that's what the dream is saying to you. Choose!

ROGER: (interrupting) . . . There is no more specific—I mean, we all rationalize one way or the other and I'm just saying that it appears right now that I have come to a crossroads, in effect, which I didn't believe I'd come to so early in life. It seems that we go blindly through life and maybe some people go through longer than this, not recognizing it—this kind of conflict—and really don't see it until maybe it's too late.

MONTE: I think that's true, but if you want to be a real father you've got to recognize it at your age; otherwise it's too late. By the time you realize it, it's time to be a grandfather . . . so, it was a crisis dream, you see, and that's why it was so powerful, so frightening, why it mobilized so much anxiety and why it actually ended up being a nightmare. The conflict developed to the point where the situation has infringed upon his paternal neck.

STUDENT X: How does our work help him?

MONTE: You have to ask Roger. Whether our efforts to work with the dream and frame it in a meaningful context are helping will depend on whether he himself feels anything in response to that effort. A dream is an attempt to confront ourselves with things that are going on. It's a reflection of something happening. We may not understand it but we feel it. What we try to do is help the dreamer understand it. Where Roger goes with his dream is a function of all the pressures and responses that he's subjected to in his life, including his intelligence, sense of reality, sense of responsibility, and everything else. Perhaps this understanding, this self-communication, may help him relate to the conflict a little more realistically than he might have, just working with it blindly.

ROGER: I'll just confirm that by saying I think the dream depicts the way I really am thinking. In other words, I think that I am opting for the family, obviously, but the conflict still exists because the habitual dedication exists or the habitual commitment is a very tough habit to break.

MONTE: What would you say it has over you? It has a stranglehold over you. Right? That's your metaphor. That's the most obvious metaphor in the dream. That something has a stranglehold over your role as a father and you're suffering as a consequence. If you cut off the oxygen supply you get desperate. If you cut off your food supply you can last for a week. But, if you cut off your oxygen supply, there's only a very short time.

STUDENT VII: Someone just asked how this dream might help him. Certainly it's an understanding or a projection of his own feelings. And if he can know that he can make his decision for himself.

STUDENT V: Don't professional men rationalize that about their career? That they're doing it for their children and wife, and they don't feel this guilt.

MONTE: Right. That's the difference between the waking self and the dreaming self. The waking self can indulge in the luxury of rationalization. It can hide the whole conflict; but the dreaming self is left with all that is swept under the rug during the day. It's left with the truth. I wish I had had that dream when I was forty. I think, in that sense, it's a very healthy dream. It's scary, frightening, nightmarish, but it's still a good dream to have—to be concerned about that kind of loss—because the unfortunate thing is that not enough people are concerned about that loss.

ROGER: I thank you all.

MONTE: All right . . . we'll lay off. . . . [*Laughter*]

We picked up the cue here that the dreamer was satisfied with the work that had been done. There was some further discussion that raised some general question about dreams that often come up.

STUDENT X: What occurs to me is the fact that what our subconscious is dreaming is so much smarter in terms of using metaphors. I mean, I can't think of metaphors to write in a letter to somebody as striking as the metaphors that come up in dreams. This is something that has always puzzled me.

MONTE: It's a fact that we are ingeniously creative while we sleep. If you were to take all the information that we have about this situation and try to paint a picture or create a movie—in other words, to create visual images about it—you probably couldn't create or say as much as he did in these few simple images. They convey so much in a succinct and compressed way, with no excess baggage, right to the point. Everything counts. Everything is meaningful. Going down . . . looking at what's below, in the dark, the playroom setting, and then this stark imagery of what's going on in this playroom where things are supposed to be light and gay and fun. Look at this dramatic struggle going on in that room! It's absolutely true that our dream life has not received enough recognition. In fact, it's been derogated. I think that dreams employ to the fullest our most precious potential—creativity. We're enormously creative when we use images to talk about our life. Translating life experience into visual imagery is creative, consistently so, intensely so, and we do it automatically!

STUDENT X: I'm not sure that really answers her question about the metaphor, does it?

MONTE: The reason I've spoken at length is that I don't really know why we are so much smarter in a creative sense when we dream. I have a hypothesis, which is that if we could be as honest and as related to our feelings when we are awake as when we are asleep, then I think we'd all be more creative. I think that's the way that artists are. They relate honestly to their feelings, come what may. It was very courageous of our dreamer to bring that dream to the group because of the honest picture of his feelings. If you look at it as you did at the start, you accuse him of all these goings on, making him out to be a horrible creature. But he's a very human person in a very human conflict and is very honest in depicting it. And I think that's all that creativity is: It's honesty and relatedness to feelings. Perhaps it's one other thing: the ability, through that degree of honesty, not to be fooled even by the familiar or surface appearance and therefore to look deeper and be able to see things that are otherwise overlooked.

STUDENT XII: I'm puzzled about this "honesty." Why do we disguise and symbolize things? Why can't we *be* honest and open and just simply say how we feel instead of using all kinds of metaphors and symbols?

MONTE: Well, there are many reasons for it. I haven't used the term "disguise," have I?

STUDENT XIII: But we do disguise. . . .

MONTE: Do we?

STUDENT XIII: Didn't he . . .?

MONTE: I don't think he disguised anything.

STUDENT XIII: The figure of authority. Why couldn't he just have himself hanging there?

MONTE: He was talking about the stranglehold that reality has on his aspirations to fatherhood. I don't think there's any disguise. It's a very dynamic, concrete portrayal of that feeling. I don't look at dreams in terms of disguise. I look at dreams rather as dramatic presentations of what we go through—what we feel, what we experience.

STUDENT II: The pictorial dimension piques my curiosity. The dream is visual, primarily. I don't know how you could verbalize all that is in the image—the picture is worth a thousand words. If he wanted to write out what he was feeling in words he would spend an hour. Just as we have in describing what's happening—what he described in a single image.

MONTE: If we cut off reality as we do when we're asleep we can't think the way we ordinarily do. We need input—public and social input, to be able to think in terms of language and abstract reasoning. As soon as we lose that, then we think very concretely and in terms of imagery: Our images express feelings that have never been conceptualized very clearly. Metaphor is a device that people have developed to express something they don't understand or to emphasize something that they can't put into language easily.

Let us trace the reactive process the group went through in response to this dream. It began with their profound feelings of distress and discomfort on hearing the dream. They then moved away emotionally by engaging in a paradoxical maneuver. By talking about the dream literally—implying, for example, that the dreamer was responsible for the death of his father—they were, in fact, not talking about it at all. It was only when the dreamer revealed certain facts about his current life situation that a real engagement with the dream became possible and a meaningful link was established between the dream and the waking-life situation of the dreamer.

That the dream may have deeper levels is certainly true. But these can be looked at by the dreamer, if he chooses to do so, once he has made the connections to his current life situation.

Attitudes toward dreams change profoundly during dream work. Dreamers find themselves responding positively no matter how disturbing the content or how upsetting the feelings are that stem from the dream. As one member of a group put it, "The most important discovery I've made is that there is nothing to be afraid of in dream work." And another added, "Even when I experience the dream as powerful I have no aversion to working with it, knowing that I am apt to find something positive or helpful in it. I have learned that dreams are more concerned with our resources than our limitations. If I succeed in articulating the dream with my life, it always shows me trying to move in a more human direction."

13

On the Practical and the Problematic

How do you start a dream group? Let's look at some of the practical issues involved.

Composition of the Group

Dream groups can come about in a number of different ways. Natural groups can spring up among friends, members of a family, people at work, or even among strangers who find they share a common interest in dreams. The first thing you have to decide is whether you prefer working with people you already know or whether you will accept anyone who indicates an interest. The advantage of knowing the group members beforehand is that there is a level of initial trust, a willingness to share. But there is a freedom in sharing dreams with strangers. In one of Nan's workshops there was a mother and daughter-in-law. The young woman felt hesitant to share the details of her personal life because, quite naturally, it involved intimate feelings toward her husband. She felt it was a violation of her husband's privacy to say certain things in the presence of his mother. Yet she was an open person, eager to receive the group's feedback. Another mother and daughter averted the possibility of a similar conflict by joining separate groups. It is important to consider that the foibles and strengths of each member will become known to the others through dream work.

Opening group membership to anyone who shows an interest takes some organizational effort. To recruit members, consider placing an announcement in a local newsletter (community, preschool, food co-op, church, PTA), or posting one at work, in your local college or university, in grocery stores, or on any other available bulletin boards. Be aware, however, that there is always the possibility that someone might join for personal aggrandizement, as a forum for broadcasting his own point of view, or for some other manipulative purpose.

Gearing into an existing organization, such as a YMCA, church, or school helps a group and gives it a common meeting place. This is an especially good procedure if more than one workshop is planned. Any oversubscription can be used as the starting membership of the next group.

What forming the membership amounts to really, then, is deciding what combination appeals to you—couples, friends, strangers, mothers, singles, whatever—and then spreading the word to them. It doesn't take long to locate six or eight people who are eager to give four or six evenings to exploring the meaning of their dreams.

In the dream groups I have conducted, most often the people start out as strangers. This works out well. They become known to each other through their dream work. In more natural groups, such as in a family, a school, or among people who work together, the participants start off with a wider array of common interest and more knowledge of each other. But this, as we have seen, can either facilitate or limit the work. The facilitating effect comes from the rapport and trust already built up; the limitations from the frequency with which tensions vis-à-vis other members of the group are apt to come up in the dreams.

I have been impressed with the diversity of people, both in background and age, that can work well together in dream groups. I have had in the same group people ranging in age from the early twenties to eighty. Some, however, particularly young people, prefer a more homogeneous age grouping and the commonality that goes with it.

Professionals (those practicing psychotherapy in one form or another) and nonprofessionals can do well together. In almost all of my groups there is a mix of the two. Credentials alone provide no particular status in experiential dream work. Many nonprofessionals work very effectively in a more intuitive way. On the basis of their experience some professionals can help the group move farther than it would otherwise. Occasionally problems have arisen from the tendency of therapists to adopt a therapeutic stance. They may use the dream as a jumping-off point for the investigation and revelation of personal hangups, whereas all the group is out to do is to help the dreamer feel the way back into that part of himself or herself that is being reflected in the dream and appreciate the artistry and healing power of that reflection.

The leader will need the group's assistance in making sure that one person does not monopolize the group or divert it from its desired purpose, even, if necessary, asking that person to leave. Remember that dream groups are not therapy groups, where interpersonal difficulties are explored and help offered. The goal of a dream group is to help a dreamer connect with his dream so that he is in a better position to work on his problems himself. The composition of the group can be any mixture of people which allows this to happen in a supportive way.

Should husbands and wives be in the same group? My experience so far has been mixed. When both are seriously interested in dream work it works out well for both. On the other hand, when one partner is dragooned into it or comes for reasons other than an interest in dreams (envy, possessiveness, exhibitionism, etc.), it has not worked out.

The Question of Leadership

Can a group be put together without an experienced professional to help it get under way? Yes, because, as I've tried to explain, *the leader does not stand in a special relation to the group because of any superior knowledge of dreams.* The basic qualification for the leader is a thorough understanding and mastery of the process that has been outlined, its rationale, and its safeguards. The role of the leader is to insure that the process evolves as it should and that the needs and rights of the dreamer and group members are respected. The leader is there to preserve the integrity of the process, not to display superior sophistication about dreams. Leadership skills and experience can result in more effective dream work, not because the leader becomes the authority on the dream but because he has learned to use the process to maximum advantage and is also aware of the limitations of the process. The more he knows about dreams, the better for the group, but no more so than if anyone else in the group had that knowledge. In other words, the absence of a professional should not deter you from forming a group.

Perhaps no one feels qualified to lead because the process is new to all. Then the group itself can assume the functions of leadership since, most likely, all the ingredients needed will be there among the various group members.

If you lack an experienced leader, try designating someone as a moderator who will help the group to bring each phase of the process to a close and to move on to the next phase. This responsibility could even be shared on a rotating basis.

There are three main areas over which the leader must assume responsibility:

Respecting the dreamer's privacy and his authority over the dream.

Keeping the group members honest.

Keeping the dreamer honest.

Respecting the dreamer's privacy and authority

This aspect of the process cannot be stressed too much. As leader, I will sometimes put it this way to a novice dreamer: "You may feel somewhat inhibited about offering a dream to public view. It is important to realize that you control the process and can blow the whistle at any time. You decide what to accept or reject of what the group has to offer, you give the signal for closure. The group is here to help but to go no farther than you are ready to go."

And I say to the group:

"You may encourage but not push. Stick to the content; that is, the metaphors in the dream. Do not try to manipulate the dreamer into going beyond the dream material itself. By presenting the dream the dreamer is saying that he is ready to work and be helped at this point to see the problem, the crisis, or the threat to his equilibrium. You do not determine how deeply the dreamer is to deal with the material. Remember, in dream work it is not your will but the will of the dreamer that is important. Each of us has a distinct pace and momentum for exploring the psyche. Spontaneity and strength cannot be coerced."

Keeping the group honest

Since the primary task of the group is to help the dreamer, the leader must see that no one is there to work out private feelings toward the dreamer or to validate private ideas about dream interpretation. The dreamer alone is the expert in regard to his dream. Again, a group member may feel certain that the dreamer is not seeing something that the dream is saying, but the group member may be wrong. There have been times when I, as an experienced worker with dreams, felt certain that I was correct about a particular perception only to be proven wrong. The group's job is to take the dreamer as far as he is ready to go with the dream in public, to be in tune with where he is, not to settle for less and not to push the dreamer beyond that point.

When the process is understood and adhered to, very few problems arise, though, as in other social situations when people come together in a group, there may be tensions. It takes skill and experience to recognize and deal with them. The dream work may have to be stopped for the moment so that the group can focus in on the issue. It is also the leader's responsibility to detect any unconscious manipulativeness on the part of the dreamer or other members of the group. Perhaps the most important responsibility of a leader is to maintain a sensitivity to the dreamer's reactions, to know when to keep the process going, when to check in with the dreamer, to help a more compliant or reticent dreamer to express himself for himself, and to sense when the question of closure should be raised with the group.

Leadership skill, training, and experience can bring another dimension to the process. When working on a dream the group approaches the imagery from any angle and in any order that the members wish. Although much that they come up with may be on target, a certain fragmentation does result. A good leader is aware of this and can, at the end of the second stage, reorganize the contributions both of the group and of the leader into their more logical relationship to the sequences of imagery in the dream. The leader can sometimes integrate and orchestrate the exchanges that occur in the third stage to help the dreamer put the dream together.

Lest you be discouraged by the seeming enormity of all these tasks, once again a reminder that the group is making a composite brew: Each member brings an ingredient into the pot of group maturity. Each is responsible for an honest contribution as dreamer and audience. No one is the master chef.

Keeping the dreamer honest

This may seem a contradiction to my earlier point about respecting the dreamer's authority. But it isn't when it is understood that in presenting a puzzling dream, the dreamer is asking that we help identify the source of the puzzlement. Dreams never lie, but the dreamer can lie.

No one in the group is under any obligation to reveal anything, but if a dreamer does choose to go forward and seek the group's help he is obligated to deal with the group honestly. A dreamer may, after sharing a dream, wish to back away without seeming to do so. Instead of invoking the option to terminate the process, the dreamer sabotages it through evasive tactics. When asked about events that led up to the dream he may give incomplete or misleading answers. He may be unwilling to offer any acknowledgment of the group's efforts or even deny that any of their suggestions rang true, because he is maneuvering to keep the myths about himself alive.

As I have said, the dreamer often gives clues that he is hedging by the way the dream is introduced: "I had the most meaningless dream last night." The leader must get across the idea that no dream is too short, too ridiculous, too boring, or too unimaginative to be worked with, and so none of these excuses should be acceptable to the group.

In the course of presenting a dream the dreamer may offer rationalizations for omitting sections: "This part is too complicated." It is important that no dream be tailored or tampered with. The dreamer must be encouraged to report the entire dream if he is to share the dream at all. If the dreamer seems overly anxious and defensive, someone in the group should attempt to raise this to the conscious level by asking, "Do you want us to continue with your dream?"

Time Arrangements

In general, time arrangements can be quite flexible. My preference is for weekly sessions, but some groups have carried on successfully on a once-a-month basis. Not too many people are apt to find the time to meet more than once a week on a sustained basis.

I have found two-hour sessions to be the best working arrangement. That leaves time to bring up unfinished business or additional information from the previous session, to deal with a dream that may be difficult or complex, and even, in some instances, to work on more than one dream. Dream work should proceed with no pressure of time. Frequently I have spent the entire two hours on a single dream. Anyone who shares a dream deserves the best of the group's effort, regardless of the length of time it takes.

Written Records

We have spoken of the advantages of keeping a dream journal. In group dream work it is advisable to jot down the dream as soon as possible, in order to have as accurate and detailed a record as possible. The dreamer should tell the dream slowly enough that members of the group can write it down. In this way they can have exact notes to refer to.

Some participants find it helpful to take notes throughout the process. Ideas can be jotted down as they occur in the course of discussion. Having a written record can help in later attempts to collate the contributions of the group against the unfolding sequence of the dream.

A further advantage to note taking is its use after a session. In their eagerness to work through the dream material and get as many things to fit as possible, the group and the dreamer will sometimes force-fit items or accept meanings without being sure of their suitability. If a little time is allowed to elapse and a dream is reviewed after a few days the forced fits and unsure meanings seem to melt away and truer notions surface. It is as if ideas are set off at the session that take a longer time to work their way to consciousness.

Nan has a special system for keeping the records of a dream session. She uses a coleader or recorder to help make visible and clarify the three-stage process used in our dream workshops. After the dreamer has told the dream the recorder writes *Negative* and *Positive* on a large piece of paper attached to an easel. As the group members express the feelings that were generated in them while they were listening to the dream, the recorder writes these feelings under the appropriate heading. Sometimes response to a dream is both negative and positive; ambivalent emotions are listed between the two poles. This system of writing down words and feelings keeps the group from working with images too soon; that's easy to do because the images exert a strong pull and can be fun to work with, more fun than trying to dig down into complex feelings in order to identify them in a lucid manner. Generally there is an initial spurt of feelings, followed by the group's assumption that all possibilities have been exhausted. The recorder encourages the group to wait and to continue to look for those subtle, more difficult-to-express feelings. When all of them have been noted, the sheet is taped to the wall, where it is accessible for additions and for connections between negative and positive feelings.

Then the recorder puts a fresh sheet of large paper on the easel. This time the images are written down, sometimes as subheadings of other images.

Let's see how it works: A mother of four reported that her dream began in an old house; within the old house were the dreamer's house, several apartments on various levels, and one lone bedroom.

First *Old house* was put on the paper and underlined. The responses of the members were printed beneath it—life, myself, my life, well built, having seen a lot of life, needing repair, etc. Next the recorder indented and wrote down the subheadings of the various living arrangements within the old house. *Dreamer's house:* exclusive, separate, permanent, and so on. *Apartment:* temporary, no return on the investment, no room for expansion, crowded, less responsibility, etc. *Lone bedroom:* isolation, rooming house, inner hiding place, private, reserved for intimacy, disconnected, and so forth. This sort of diagraming enhances non-linear thinking, where ideas and images may be moved about and connected in various ways to demonstrate the largest range of relationships between images.

The recorder translates onto paper all the varied responses

of the members. This requires condensing the responses, yet preserving the precise distinctions the members are making. It is the members' responsibility to be sure that the recorder does preserve the exact meaning of each comment.

Nan finds this a good exercise in training the mind to be sensitive to the extensive range of responses and the connections between these responses. What is printed on the charts represents the work of the group and can easily be reviewed by the members and the dreamer.

At the end of a session the dreamer is given the sheets to use as he mulls over additional aspects of the dream or as a reminder of the detailed work done by the group. As one dreamer put it after sharing her first dream with the group, "To have attentive listeners as interested as you are in exploring my dream is a tremendous experience."

Group Contract

Since our dreams mirror our deepest hopes and fears, there is usually some degree of discomfort at the exposure involved. Certain explicit contractual arrangements can provide some safeguards:

We will attend all sessions unless absolutely impossible.

Continuity of attendance enables trust to build more quickly and helps through periods when a feeling of dis-ease generated by dream work might tempt you to withdraw. In one group a member confided on the second night that she would not have returned had it not been for accepting this commitment. She developed into one of the most energetic and insightful members.

The sessions are closed to visitors.

Exceptions may be made if the entire group agrees *prior* to the visit. One new person changes the dynamic of the group and can easily keep dream work at a surface level. It is surprising how often the work of the evening can be ruined if this is not made explicit. This is easier to explain to house guests and friends if it is a group decision. (One group member dubbed this the "No Aunt Bessie Clause.")

Dream content and work is confidential.

One of the surest ways of undermining your purpose is to let intimate sharing become interesting conversation outside the group. Respect for the highly personal nature of dreams not only gives the dream a necessary freedom but helps build a spirit of belonging and warmth within the group.

After presenting the contract allow ample time for questions and revisions.

Problem Areas

As in other human affairs things often don't work out as planned. Here are some questions and issues that arise:

Are there limits to the length of a dream that the group can work with?

As we have seen, shorter dreams work better for beginning groups. But as the group gains experience and learns how to gauge the time necessary for dream work, it will feel comfortable with longer dreams and may even work with several sequences from the same night.

There is no limit to how short a dream can be. Dreamers will often apologize for having just a fragment or only an image from a longer dream, only to find that the group will spend a rewarding hour or more with it.

Occasionally someone will present a dream that takes as long as twenty or thirty minutes to tell. It is usually better to seek a shorter dream.

How about dreams that are several years old?

These are best tackled after the group has had some experience with recent dreams. When older dreams are important to the dreamer there is usually some recollection of the associated context. The problem is that one cannot probe the context for additional memories as easily as with a recent dream. When an old dream is also a repetitive one, it is important to look for any similarities in the contexts that trigger the dream.

Are there any dreams which the group should not work with?

The general rule is that, within the limitations noted above, the group should consider working with any dream that is offered. There is one proviso, having to do with the stability of the person offering the dream. While it is unlikely that anyone actively psychotic would come undetected into a group, if it should happen there may be accompanying distortions and misperceptions of the process that may set too difficult a task for the group and create the risk of deepening the psychosis. It then becomes a matter for professional help and management. This qualifying statement does not

mean that people with emotional difficulties, even severe
ones, should not be in dream groups. I have had successful
groups with seriously ill patients. The important criterion is
their ability to relate realistically to the process.

What if no one has a dream?

It sometimes happens that no one has a recent dream. If
this happens and the group waives the time factor, then
someone usually will come up with an older dream to work
on. If there is still no dream forthcoming, the group can
always generate a general discussion about dreams and what
they have learned about them so far.

Can two people have the same dream?

People may have similar dreams, but I've never known
identical dreams to occur. What happens sometimes is that,
on listening to another person's dream, you get the gut feeling that you could have had the very same dream yourself.

What are the points to be monitored at each stage of the process?

STAGE I (in which the dreamer presents the dream while the
group listens):

No one must be put on the spot and made to feel that he
must share a dream. The dreamer must be limited in presentation at this stage to the remembered dream only. The group
should check any tendency to get into context or associative
data.

STAGE II (in which the group moves into the dream, first
expressing personal feelings and then exploring the metaphors):

The group must not deviate from the rule that they are handling the dream as if it were their own. They should address each other rather than the dreamer. In the beginning there is a tendency to look at the dreamer and offer some kind of interpretive comment.

The dreamer must not be allowed to engage actively with the group at this time and should try to avoid cueing the group as to the accuracy of their responses. Sometimes it is difficult for the dreamer to control his nonverbal behavior as he experiences the excitement of discovery, so some allowance must be made for this.

There are times when two or more members have strong but opposing feelings about an aspect of the dream and get into a disagreement about who is right. This kind of argument must be checked. Remember that everyone has the right to say what he or she thinks without being challenged. From the point of view of the process both opposing feelings are right and there is no basis for argument.

STAGE III (in which the dreamer makes connections between the emotions and the images of the dream and the immediate life situation that gave rise to the dream, and the group then enters into dialogue with the dreamer):

It is important that the dreamer be given all the time he needs for an initial response without fear of interruption.

The group members must be aware that although they can ask any question they wish concerning the dream or the dreamer's response, they are obliged to accept any limitations imposed by the dreamer on level and degree of self-disclosure. But the dreamer, on the other hand, should not have told the dream *if he knew ahead of time* that he did not feel free to share the pertinent personal events that gave rise to the dream.

No one must be allowed to assume an authoritative interpretive stance toward the dreamer. No one should be allowed to become the dreamer's therapist.

The group must pursue the context in as thorough a manner as may be possible.

The group should question what they consider to be compliant responses by the dreamer.

They must learn to be in tune emotionally with the dreamer as the process unfolds so as to pick up any distress signals should they occur.

What kind of group tensions are apt to arise and how should they be handled?

If the process is followed carefully, few tensions will arise. But, since we are working in an area of subtle emotional crosscurrents, there are occasional tensions. They may result from the behavior of a single person who tries to dominate the group. Or they may occur between two or more members.

Each group will have to work out for itself the best approach to the problem. In the weekly groups I have conducted I have encountered few situations in which internal tensions were an interfering factor. On no occasion has it been necessary to ask anyone to leave the group. Obviously any process can be abused. People are open to hurt from others and dream groups are no exception. The only person who should not be in a dream group is someone the group feels is disruptive to the process.

Do feelings generated by dream work carry over into the days that follow?

The whole purpose of dream work is to have an impact on your life. Good and bad feelings will spill over. Hopefully the good ones will outweigh the bad. There are times when some degree of aftercare may be necessary; the person involved often seeks the support of another person in the group. There have been some occasions in my groups when members have sought private sessions. On one occasion the work in the group did lead to the decision to go into therapy.

How long should people continue in dream groups?

There is no set rule. Groups can be time limited or ongoing. Several of my groups are now in their third year. My arrangements are for people to contract for four weekly sessions at a time and then to keep renewing if they so wish. Nan's workshops last six weeks and her groups, too, renew if they wish.

What happens as people get to know each other better?

As the group gets to know more about one another, perceptions will sharpen. This will be most helpful in the third phase of the process when the group works directly with the dreamer. To some extent this awareness will shape the group's projections in the second stage as well.

What kinds of problems arise when people are in individual therapy while working in a dream group?

Theoretically problems can arise if a person is inclined to be manipulative or to set people against each other. It has been my experience that such manipulativeness is minimal. Most often the two processes complement each other very well. The essence of dream work is the search for an honest relationship with oneself. This tends to expose or diminish any manipulative tendencies.

In the usual course of events the dreamer will feel more in touch with the dream after group work and can then pursue it at a more intimate level with the therapist. Conversely, it may be possible to give only cursory attention to a dream in therapy in which case the dreamer can explore it further with the group. On occasion the group may, through a dream presented to it, help the dreamer form a deeper understanding of what is going on in therapy.

Is this form of dream work therapy?

Broadly speaking, any beneficial experience can be defined as therapeutic. In this sense then, the answer is yes. But if the question refers to the issue of psychotherapy in its more limited technical meaning, then the answer is no.

How does dream work differ from group psychotherapy?

Psychotherapy implies the notion of an expert or specialist trained along theoretical and technical lines in the use of skills to help people with emotional difficulties. The therapist has certain expectations of the patient or client (that he will not keep back any disclosures, for example) and in many ways controls and directs the process.

Very different circumstances prevail in the operation of a dream-appreciation group. The assumption is that dreaming is a normal healing mechanism that can be understood and used by everyone without special theoretical or technical skills. The dreamer is the only expert in the picture. If is he alone who controls the process. The dreamer's expectations alone prevail.

Although the leader, if there is one, guides the process, he does not stand in a special relation to the group. He participates in all aspects of the work, including the sharing of dreams. In fact, it is this egalitarian atmosphere that helps generate trust and freedom in self-disclosure.

There are more specific ways in which the processes differ. In a dream-appreciation group the focus is on the dream exclusively. Sufficient time is made available for the dream work to proceed at its own pace. In the therapeutic hour there are many other pressures contending for time.

The group affords a great range of possibilities and productive interplay in the pursuit of the metaphorical meanings in a dream. That goes beyond what a single person can do with the imagery, even if the person knows the dreamer very well, as in the case of a therapist. This is not to minimize the help that the knowledge of the therapist can bring to the dream but, rather, to emphasize that, for much of the imagery, the collective imagination of the group may prove a richer and more versatile resource.

Perhaps the essential point of difference between psychotherapy and group dream work lies in the focus of the two processes. In group psychotherapy the focus is primarily on the interpersonal field—the relationship within the group— set up by the interaction of the various participants and only secondarily on personal motivational patterns. In dream work the focus is on the relation of the dreamer to the dream. The dynamics of the interpersonal field are minimized as the group members seek to become an extension of the dreamer's ego in the effort to connect with the imagery created.

These same differences apply between dream-appreciation and encounter groups. Although the latter tend to be flatter hierarchically than therapy groups, again the focus is on the interpersonal field. The individual is held accountable for his behavior, verbal and otherwise, in the group, and that behavior determines the nature of the interpersonal field. In the dream group the dreamer sets the level of accountability to the group.

What aspects of the group approach can be carried over to individual work with the dream?

What if you don't want to belong to a group, but prefer to appreciate your dreams on your own? Can it be done? Yes. It isn't easy, but it isn't impossible, and it can be enormously rewarding. After all, most of us, most of the time, are on our own when it comes to working on our dreams. The preceding chapters can serve as a structure and a simple technology for getting on with the task. The main features of our dream life —its honesty, its relevance, and its uniqueness—demand a structure that takes into account each of these qualities and the difficulties involved in relating to them while awake.

Those who have had the experience of working with dreams in a group have found it helpful to apply aspects of that experience to their own individual work with dreams, and there is no reason why you cannot adopt their technique. What the group approach does, as we have seen, is to objectify the dream, make it an "object out there" which others can work on. A distance is created between the dreamer and the dream which is then filled in by the feelings and metaphors supplied by the members of the group. The creation of this temporary distance gives the dreamer the opportunity to test the input he has received from others. Working on your own, you can pursue a similar course, but it will take some imaginative role playing. The first step is to try to objectify the dream, to hold it at a distance and, if necessary, to try to see it as someone else's dream. Then think about the feelings and the metaphorical responses you might come up with if it were, in fact, someone else's dream. Finally, search out the waking event that precipitated your dream.

People relate to different aspects of the process in different ways:

"I can get into the feelings but seem to push the images

away. I have trouble even toying with the images. I have found it helpful to write down the meanings that occur to me, even wrong ones."

"It is helpful to me to treat the dream as if it were the dream of another and then to feel my way into it. I find it hard to identify feelings. I've drawn up a list of all the possible feelings I could think of and find that helpful when I have difficulties."

Useful questions to put to yourself are:

What am I not seeing that is there to see?

What would I be apt to see if it were someone else's dream?

What have I learned about my own biases and personal myths from past work with dreams that may be helpful in tackling a new dream?

Anyone doing dream work for any length of time becomes aware of certain built-in biases. These are tendencies that, rather than issuing from the dream, are superimposed on it. A helpful hint in objectifying the dream is noted in the following comment from one group member: "I find I can work better with a dream if I let a little time elapse after waking up. It's better if I don't try to engage with it in the heat of the emotions it leaves me with."

This approach can work but the dream should be written down before letting go of it.

What can I expect to learn through dream work?

The most significant change you will experience is the awareness of a larger dimension of yourself that seems to be nudging you in the direction of greater emotional health— so that you neither flinch from the problems involved nor underestimate the resources available. You will have a greater appreciation of yourself as the source of such an informative display of imagery. You will begin to be able to

rely on your dreams to disclose much-needed truths about
your life, truths that are hard to come by in waking life. Here
is how one person put it:

> Prior to learning this technique, dreams had been a
> fairly abstruse, if not opaque, language for me. Now
> I find that even without the help of a dream group
> I am far more able to communicate with the greater
> pattern of myself and to absorb the wisdom con-
> tained therein.

Certain skills evolve, particularly those having to do with
the identification of subtle and elusive feelings, as well as the
art of exploring the metaphorical potential of dream imagery.

> I find this work has provided an interesting side effect
> for me. It has increased my verbal skill as a result of
> my attempts to put my feelings into words.

You will become adept at recognizing familiar themes and
the kind of dream vocabulary you have developed to reflect
them. Perhaps you use the same image over and over to
express the same or a similar meaning. For one dreamer an
automobile figured prominently during times of impending
change. When he felt in control of a situation he would be
in the driver's seat. Another dreamer in a situation involving
some kind of forward movement would dream of a house
with new rooms when the move was associated with a sense
of freedom and expansion. But remember to be cautious
about your dream vocabulary and aware always that there
may be subtle variations in the way a particular image is
used.

14

A One-Year Journey
Nan's Tower House Experience

If you still question the efficacy of a group working on dreams without the benefit of a resident psychoanalyst, I offer you Nan's Tower House experience. Let her tell it in her own words:

My prime credential for the dream work Monte Ullman and I have been describing is that I am *not* a professional psychologist. Nor is my involvement in dream work a pretense at professional status. I am a writer, teacher, mother, et aliae, but not a member of a "helping" profession. Precisely because I am a nonprofessional, however, I could do what Monte could not: test our belief that a dream group will work well without professional leadership. I qualified for the position of "nonprofessional dream appreciator."

Following the procedures which Monte and I had worked on together, my husband and I began an eight-week workshop. It was offered as a class in an existing adult-education

school located in a white frame Victorian mansion: the
Tower House. Eight people enrolled in the dream workshop.
After the school term ended, we continued on a monthly
basis in the homes of the members. Our byname, Tower
House Group, outlived the original location.

Given our varied schedules it was not possible for all of us
to meet more frequently on a consistent basis. We wanted to
stay together. Generally we worked on a dream dreamt
within the week of our meeting. Procuring fresh dreams was
never a problem.

The dreams I have chosen, and the work presented on
these dreams, reflect, but by no means exhaust, our discoveries about ourselves and the techniques which made them
accessible.

Some of us were strangers before our first meeting. We
were cautious, yet genuinely eager to explore our dreams—
or eager at least about the *idea* of exploring. In the group
were three married couples (Tish and Weston, Lenore and
Ben, Howard and myself), a recent widow (Dotty), and three
married people who came without their spouses (Mike,
Mary, and Jenny). Among us were a naval captain, three
government workers, a teacher of disturbed children, a camp
director, and two artists. On our fourteenth night Tish
summed up the change that had occurred. "When we began,
we cared about our own dreams. Now we care about each
other."

Several days before the first class Carolyn, who had
planned to join our group, canceled her registration. Acute
bronchitis kept her homebound, but as it turned out, she was
our first dream reporter. The morning after our initial meeting she called to find out how things had progressed. At the
close of the conversation she said, rather shyly, "I had a
really peculiar dream last night . . . about Lisa [her young

daughter who had died of leukemia several years before]. I can't imagine why I'd start dreaming about her now."

Carolyn's Dream:

Lisa and I were at school to try out for a musical. All of a sudden Lisa said she didn't feel well. Her blue eyes reflected her fear that she wouldn't make it in the production because of her illness. I put her in bed and checked to see if she felt feverish. She didn't. I went out a side door of the school and cried.

Workmen across the alley noticed my crying but didn't approach. In my frustration I picked up a log and began to pound on the side of the building. A male nurse asked what was wrong. When I told him that Lisa was not feeling well he said he would tell another nurse, Miss Z. Part of my frustration was— how could I explain Lisa's presence? Everybody knew she had died, but here she was, still sick.

I knew that Carolyn had been eager to join the dream class, but I was, nevertheless, astonished by the dream's reflection of the extent to which she was depending on the group to help her grapple with her inner life. As she reflected on her feelings of the day before, she realized that she was very upset over not being well enough to participate in the dream class, just as in the dream Lisa's illness keeps Lisa from participation in the *production*. She wanted to *try out* new possibilities for self-expression. Canceling her registration was lost opportunity (one of the most poignant aspects of a young child's death). Around her it was life as usual. No one responded to the urgency of her feelings (the indifferent workmen in the alleyway). She resolved her isolation by deciding to call me, the dream nurse, *Miss Z*. This would expose the fact that some suffering part of herself had not been laid to rest, but was hurting and in need of attention.

Carolyn's candid appeal for help through her dream reinforced my own belief that we have within ourselves sources of renewal as well as the pain of our defeats—and that it is not always essential to have a doctor on hand to tap into these sources. We simply have to work with the techniques honestly and consistently, and be willing to listen and respond.

And Carolyn made it clear that it was the *class* from which she anticipated help. She called on *Miss Z.* only because her health would not free her to participate in the group. We all needed one another. I certainly needed Carolyn's dream.

At the second meeting Dotty (a widow with grown children and a highly responsible job with the Federal Government) recounted an experience of that week.

Dotty's Dream

Nan said I must dream a short dream. No way, I thought. All of mine are long and complicated. I went to bed and my dream was this:

"I am alone."

I woke up and walked around to be sure I could distinguish between dreaming and being awake. I went back to sleep and dreamed again:

"I am alone."

I woke up and thought, "Aha! I've dreamed two short dreams." I didn't give them any consideration, just wrote them down. Then I had a third dream:

I was introducing my group to someone else. I cut two round circles of white paper as representing them. They were like small, luncheon-size place mats.

> There were two square napkins. I started to trim
> them round, then realized they were O.K. as they
> were.
> I dreamed three short dreams!

The group agreed there was obvious loneliness, and beyond that the desire for acceptance and belonging. Dotty
cared very much that she produce a dream which fit the
necessary criteria for the group's attention. It was as if the
first two fragments carried out the injunction to present a
short dream. Having accomplished her task of producing a
dream of suitable length for the class she was free to express
her feelings in a somewhat longer dream.

Lenore asked if circles had a universal meaning. In response Dotty told us what she had been reading before going
to sleep:

> I had been studying John Sanford's book *God's For-
> gotten Language.* He's a priest in the Episcopal
> Church who attended the C. G. Jung Institute in
> Switzerland. Sanford said that persons developing
> both inwardly and outwardly will have balance. In
> circles all points are equidistant from the center.
> Squares have four sides of equal length.
>   When I think of small circles I think of a small
> group of people. White means pure and clean . . .
> whiter than snow . . . forgiveness. These are the only
> thoughts that seem to go with the dream at all. But
> I never came up with anything that hangs right.

Ben suggested that Dotty was trying to fit something (the
squares) into a small group and it wasn't working. What did
the squares represent? After a good deal of speculation about
this Dotty shared some additional day residue.

The night before the dreams I was with my church group and was in a devastating discussion of our life together. I felt that most of us didn't feel any "real" sharing had taken place. Recently I've been much alone, far removed from family and without closeness anywhere.

Dotty traveled farther than any other member to attend our sessions, driving some forty-five minutes alone. We knew that the dream group was an important experience for her. And we knew that her church group also gave her a vital sense of belonging. She was concerned over her place in both groups. She needed a place. This connected with the image in her dream, place mat. We also noticed the importance of the number two: two circles; two squares; saying two times, "I am alone."

The two short dreams create the setting for evaluating her relationship to the two groups to which she belongs. She felt herself alone and lonely. She made a point of saying this twice, once for each group. After affirming that she was a part of two groups (the white circles) she asked what her place was in the groups (circular place mats) and saw herself as a square napkin. This was not enough to certify her belonging. Her sharp edges didn't fit into the circles. The temptation was to force herself to look exactly like her conception of the group image. Then she realized that was not necessary. By combining both square and circle she made a new setting, a new place; a setting for eating, where needs may be satisfied, and quite often with pleasure.

We talked about how dreams confront situations that are not fully dealt with in waking life. Dotty raised the question, "When I dream, 'I am alone,' I'm not dreaming something I don't fully know. I *am* alone. Why do I dream about it? There is nothing further to be learned."

We decided there were two facets to knowing: that which we recognize in the seclusion of our own thoughts and feelings, and the expansion of our understanding through the sharing of it with others.

We asked Dotty how she responded to the work we had done with her dream. "Incredible—it fits like a size-ten dress!"

Many of our dreams were riddles, nagging at us until we figured them out. Jenny reported what she called a "one-framer":

> A friend was sitting in a chair scowling at me. She was very, very fat.

The week of the dream Jenny (a married woman with two teenagers) had tried, unsuccessfully, to lose weight; but why should this particular friend, who was well-proportioned and exceedingly unjudgmental, be fat and scowling? We asked Jenny all the reasonable questions we could think of. Was she certain this friend was not critical of her, perhaps in some area other than weight? Did she remind Jenny of some authority figure? Was Jenny envious of the friend's build?

We were beginning to think Jenny was withholding some feelings that were blocking the dream work. Then someone asked who the friend was. "Anita Cook." We were convulsed.

Mike explained, "As long as you *need to cook,* you're not going to lose weight!"

We soon learned that although the dominant emotion of a dream might come easily into focus, sometimes that very transparency of emotion encouraged us to jump to general conclusions that splashed away the precise value of the particular dream. A case in point was what came to be known as Jenny's "Coffin on the Hill."

Jenny's Dream:

I dreamed of pushing my mother up a hill in a coffin. It was terrible. I was pushing her up this dirt road in front of the house where I was raised. I got the coffin to the top but I couldn't take it over the crest of the hill. I had the feeling of struggle, struggle.

Jenny's word *struggle* epitomized the group's reaction to the dream's effect. Heavy. Laboring.

We asked her: "Could it be that you carry around something representative of your mother that you want to get rid of, bury? It's hard for you to function with this dead weight." This sounded logical.

But from Jenny there was unenthusiastic silence.

We returned to the images of the dream and tried "green-lighting": freewheeling with our own suggestions as to what the images might mean. "Mother" reminded some of us of home, warmth, security, love, and being cared for; others thought of possessiveness. "Coffin" conjured up images of death, container, final rest, and womb. The mother *in* the coffin left us with two interpretations: the stifling sensation of never escaping the mother's womb, and an attempt to bury the past.

When Jenny added that the coffin was plain pine, Dotty said, "There's something primitive about the entire scene. Pushing a pine coffin up a hill gives me the image of extreme poverty."

We felt we could go no further without the day residue:

The day before my dream I had gone to Capitol Hill
to see a congressman concerned with the rights and
plight of migrant workers. This is a problem close to
my heart, and although it was quite difficult to do,
I drummed up the courage to go talk with him. I'd
heard him give a speech in the House which seemed
to speak directly to the migrant problems. I thought
he was genuinely concerned about the realities of
their situation. I dreaded going, but felt it would be
better once we started talking. I had carefully considered the things I wanted to ask about and had written
down some of my ideas.

I had to wait outside his office before seeing him.
And then, well, I couldn't believe it. He shook my
hand, mumbled something you'd say on the cam-
paign trail, and walked away! At first I felt like a
country bumpkin. A little nothing. Now I'm getting
mad!

Jenny responded to Dotty's impression of extreme poverty
in the image of the pine coffin being pushed up a hill: "The
image of extreme poverty does creep into my dreams. My
growing-up years on a farm in Mississippi were years of great
poverty. The congressman represented a section in his state
that is one of the poorest regions in the country, very akin
to my background."

Suddenly Lenore jumped up and shouted, "The Hill!" At
last we had gotten past general comments and were linking
the metaphors to Jenny's present and personal dilemma.

Jenny had struggled to go to Capitol Hill because she felt
the lives of hardworking people trapped in an environment
of death were worth the extreme effort. She knew firsthand
the effects of deprivation and of the assumption of inferiority.
Such evils recalled her own roots. In wanting to help others,

was she also attempting to bury some pain from her own past? (The mother in the coffin.) She made it up to the Hill, but nothing was accomplished. In the end she was left standing beside the pine coffin. She was denied the support she had assumed would be hers. (The mother was dead.) No hope for the future of the migrants had been left with her, and her past feelings of inferiority were not disposed of. (Unburied coffin.) The images of poverty were mirroring the plight of the migrants, her own lack of power to mitigate their plight, and the poverty of her childhood. Trying to attract the genuine attention of this congressman was as difficult as attempting to raise the dead.

It was evident from the beginning of our group that we had come with varying degrees of skepticism. Cultural conditioning had done its job well on some of us—those who demonstrated a reluctance to trust any group not professionally manned. They turned to me for hunches and suggestions because of my work with Monte Ullman. But as the group matured, the feeling grew that a variety of backgrounds could bring invaluable freshness to each dream. Our shared dream-work techniques, imagination, and honesty were quite often successful catalysts for releasing a dream's meaning.

We had been meeting for several months when I received a call from Mary, an English artist who is married to an American psychologist. She had had a dream with a lot of "queer happenings" and wanted to talk with me about it. Five weeks before the call our own adopted daughter had arrived from Korea and between our toddler's adjustment to a new time frame, a new language, and her night fears, I had averaged about two hours sleep a night. So I listened to Mary's dream, but I couldn't really muster enough alertness to respond. I told her I'd think about it and call her back, and our next meeting arrived before I returned the call. I suspect that was lucky, for if Mary and I had worked on this particular dream alone, the dream's richness might never have been tapped—and certainly, the group would have missed one of our most invigorating times together. From then on, when camaraderie was high, we referred to ourselves as the Hanseatic League.

Mary's Dream:

I was in a very old medieval house, in a bedroom with a bathroom attached to it. Quite often the toilet flushed all by itself and a shelf in the bathroom moved around. Some children came to the door and asked for Jeffrey [her son]. They were nine or ten years old, not the age Jeffrey is now. I said to them that it was too early in the morning for Jeffrey to play and could they come back later. They went away, but I noticed some of them went through a door in the bathroom, going down into a room in the cellar.

My mother came to the house and I told her that strange things were happening. While I was talking to her a large, brown paper sack came flying out of the bathroom.

Then we heard a parade going down the street. We looked out of the window and I could see in a very old house opposite ours—the streets were quite narrow—the same children who had come to the house earlier. They were watching the parade from the window and laughing. My mother said, "Perhaps you had better move from this house."

In volunteering her day residue, Mary said:

A friend of my husband's dropped dead at the bus stop. The day before this dream we had been to the funeral home. I have a thing about funeral homes. I had never seen one before I moved here from England. When I first came over I asked Jason [her husband] what they do at funeral homes. After he explained it I said, "Never let me get into one of those places." In England the dead are taken to the undertaker and then to the church but none of these arrangements are carried out in a strange parlor and place labeled Funeral Home. I haven't gone in all the years we have been married, but I was so upset for Jason . . . it was a colleague whom he saw every day . . . that I went.

The wife of this man is a difficult person. Her younger daughter locked herself in the bathroom and refused to go to the funeral home, but the wife said to me, "Tomorrow she *will* be here!" I told her perhaps the girl didn't want to see her father lying in a coffin—because I didn't want to see him either. I felt the mother was vindictive. She then told Jason she wanted us to talk to her daughter. I thought that was going to be pretty much. We're not so hot with our own children. The whole thing upset me a great deal.

I returned from all this feeling absolutely like a rag. I had sunk into a chair in a sort of stupor when Jeffrey said, "This is your man, Mother." And there was Dr. Ullman on the TV conducting this dream class in New York! I was rooted to the chair. Here he was doing everything Nan does. Not only that . . . the people's dreams were about their anxiety over telling them to the dream class, just as ours had been. It was very exciting. Now I know what Dr. Ullman looks like and I know Nan is doing everything she should be.

My presleep thoughts really were about Nan and Dr. Ullman and the dreams.

I know I've said a lot, but I must tell you one association from the past. A few years ago in Bergen we were in the old Hanseatic houses that German merchants lived in. The German apprentices were not allowed out of that area. They were apprenticed to a merchant and stayed right in the houses. The houses were all joined: Each led into the next. The tiny bedrooms held four to six bunks where the apprentices slept. They were not allowed to mix with the Norwegians, not allowed to fraternize with the people of the country where they were training. I had a crushed feeling when I came out of the houses. This was the sort of house I saw in my dream.

Mary's dream stimulated considerable discussion. We talked about *The American Way of Death.* We talked about isolation and being cut off from the traditions and familiarities of one's native country. We talked about poltergeists and "things that go bump in the night." We talked about our dream class, and Monte Ullman's. It took us two meetings to sort through all our responses and bring them together in a satisfying way for Mary.

We concluded that the dream under the guise of a single "scenario," had joined two issues that were part of her day residue: her funeral-home experience and her viewing the dream class. A key to the dream was her association of the dream house with the houses of the Hanseatic League apprentices.

The most forceful images were drawn from the following metaphors: *The old house:* Mary's emotional domain where a great deal of hard work is done. There is a sense of estrangement and at the same time invasion of privacy. *Bathroom:* A place for private activity is invaded by some alien energy. Things are out of control. *A shelf moves about:* an unsuccessful attempt to shelve the day's unpleasantness and fatigue. *The toilet flushes on its own:* another attempt at eliminating the experience in a way which will not appear to implicate her. How could she be responsible for the contents of a self-flushing toilet! *Group of children* who invade her privacy: They are we, her dream-class playmates. We ask for Jeffrey, whom she reduces to ten or eleven years old, the typical age of the Hanseatic League apprentices. To play our game she must adopt some of the spontaneity of childhood, at the same time accepting the hard work involved. Mary thinks it is too early to play the game of more visibility. Some of us slip by anyway. (She is ambivalent about our being put off.) The children penetrate her territory in an alarming fashion. We get underneath the bathroom. That's where the stuff is which she's been attempting to eliminate surreptitiously.

Mary's conflict—that between her need for privacy and the urge to reveal her emotions—is now out of the bag . . . in fact the *bag* flies out of the bathroom. One member added, "When you're *sack*ed out (in bed and dreaming), your feelings don't stay in their accustomed niche." *Parade:* If Mary parades her feelings before others, all those children (dream mates) will be watching. What if they *laugh* and see it as something amusing, when for her it is quite serious?

Move from the house: What should she do? Habitual reserve suggests she leave all this behind and recreate an inner psychic distance where the dream-class poltergeists can't threaten to set her house awry.

Mary's day had been emotionally draining. She had had to face a dreaded funeral home, lend support to her husband, be attentive to a widow who was vengeful toward her daughter. We felt some of the dream's metaphors expressed her impressions of *The American Way of Death.* The toilet flushes on its own—her feeling that we try to hide the unpleasant aspects of death by the fakery and fuss of funeral homes. Impersonal forces *flush* dead matter away. All that we see is the container, the coffin or *brown sack.*

This might have been the primary thrust of her dream had she not seen Monte Ullman's dream-class film just before retiring. She was intrigued and excited about seeing his techniques in action. She was also amazed at the similarity between our class and his. In particular she mentioned that the content of the dream had to do with anxiety over participation in the dream class. Our dream class began to take on larger stature because our approach paralleled his. Perhaps she could trust the class with more of her deepest feelings, like those experienced that day. This resurrected the old bugaboo—if I go more public I experience more dis-ease. Should I or shouldn't I?

At the close of this meeting Weston said, "Any one of us could have dreamed our own version of that dream. We all wonder whether to tell it like it is or not. We have these doors connecting each of us to the other person's house. And we certainly are all seriously trying to learn from our dream work. I dub us Apprentices of the Hanseatic League!"

We had worked together on our dreams for eight months when Lenore (a teacher of underachievers and disturbed children) gave us her version of the shared-identity dilemma.

Lenore's Dream:

There is a little child, a toddler. I think it might be
Kerry [Howard and Nan's daughter], about her age,
two. Many people are sitting around in a circle and
there is a huge fireplace with a blazing fire. Dotty
says, "We can climb inside the screen and get closer
if we're cold." So I do. I have the feeling my church
friends are there, a warm fellowship. There is a toilet
convertible to a child's potty chair. Someone says,
"You can pray on it, too." When I go to look at it
I see there is a bowel movement on top of it. Nobody
notices it or says anything. The child wanders from
one to another. The feeling is of warmth and furni-
ture and wood. A good feeling.

Lenore added that the place was like the farmhouse owned
by her church as it had been several years ago. When the fire
was lit and people were sitting around, it was warm and cozy.
She had been there for a service a few days before and
thought how disappointing the atmosphere was now. It had
lost its warm, cozy feel.

Our last Tower House meeting had been held at Lenore's
house. She had this dream the night before we came.

Ben (Lenore's husband) thought the dream was describing
the precompany housecleaning process. Maybe Lenore felt
they couldn't quite get everything put away in time (bowel
movement on the toilet), and yet nobody would notice. This
sort of acceptance would be indicative of a warm fellowship.

Lenore used part of that idea to clarify her feelings about
the bowel movement. "I think this means, Don't worry about
who you are with this group. That kind of evacuation and
mess is acceptable."

HOWARD: To share something that is private and traditionally unacceptable is a childlike thing to do. A child sees a bowel movement as part of himself, not something to be concealed.

NAN: Did you have a dream that you wanted to share with us that night? Could the bowel movement have been a specific dream?

LENORE: I have a dream that I have debated sharing. I told Ben I wasn't going to tell it, and he said go ahead if I wanted to. But I didn't (short laugh). You never know about these dreams.

JENNY: Did you think you'd better *pray* about it first? (The convertible potty chair.)

NAN: What would going on the other side of the screen signify?

LENORE: Going all the way. I very much identify with going all the way, commitment.

TISH: Weren't you seeking warmth?

LENORE: The warmth is worth the burning.

JENNY: What about the convertible potty chair?

LENORE: That goes back to when Ben and I had our babies. We were always talking about whether to buy something that could do a multitude of jobs or buy something for what it was. We would end up with this complicated contraption and ask, "Why did we do this?"

NAN: Could it be you are feeling some sort of loss in your church group—the farmhouse isn't like it was several years ago—and you would like for this group to function as both a dream-appreciation group and an overtly spiritual group? The other day Dotty said she had left one of the core groups of your church. In the dream she suggests that if you feel out in the cold, get closer to this fire. You're wandering around trying to find where to settle in, like the toddler.

WESTON: Maybe you see us as a confessional group. Putting our inner movements out where everyone can see it is like confession.

LENORE: I think that's getting to it. I do feel a belonging and freedom in this group. I have to decide what this means to me, without making it mean too much. I want to be totally involved in what it does mean.

The Tower House group had fostered a setting wherein Lenore experienced acceptance and warmth. This gave her a base of support from which to reevaluate other significant relationships. Her dream expressed her commitment to the dream-appreciation group; however, we had a distinct identity and purpose which might not be a satisfactory substitute for her other involvements.

One evening Lenore's husband, Ben (a civilian working for the armed forces), gave us a lesson in the importance of including all details in our dream reporting.

Ben's Dream:

I was in a classroom or office. The hall outside was like one of the halls in the Pentagon where I work. People were breaking for lunch. Two boys that I had gone to school with came up to me and said, "Let's go to lunch together." I was flattered that they should ask me and I said I would meet them in the hallway.

I went out into the hall. There was a lot of confusion. I didn't see the boys so I thought I'd get lunch by myself. As I walked down the hall they both came running up to me and said, "We were worried about you." I felt good about that and walked off with them.

We worked with Ben's dream in the light of his reported day residue, but came up with nothing that was helpful. Then Howard asked about the boys in the dream. Ben said, "I lived at a boy's school and grew up with them. They always sat together in school because their names put them next to each other alphabetically. They weren't particularly close themselves but both of them, at one time or other, had been close friends of mine. It's been ten years since I've seen either of them."

LENORE: This is like another dream you had where you were asked to lunch and it made you feel good.

NAN: In that dream you were invited to join a group but there was no place left at the table so you had to hold the plate of food in your lap. You were glad to be close even though you weren't admitted up to the table. This dream takes acceptance a step further. You're much more a part of something here—not just looking for a place, but sought out.

BEN: Eating is a form of social intercourse. It represents a form of acceptance. When the guys disappeared I thought I would go ahead and eat alone, but I'd rather eat with them.

LENORE: Growing up in an orphanage you got anxious about where you were going to have Christmas, weekends, and things. You had to be invited or else you ate alone in a restaurant.

BEN: Yes, I had many of those times. . . . But that was years ago. I can't make much of this. It's not really a full-fledged dream. I guess the main thing I got from it was acceptance. This time I didn't have to look on my own. I had someone seeking me out.

One other thing did occur to me. About a month ago I received an OPR—Outstanding Performance Rating. Actu-

ally I won it a year ago but it took this long to go through.
JENNY: *Confusion in the halls* of the Pentagon.
BEN: I was also notified about two weeks ago that I was in
for a promotion. We've reached the place where the little
raise in salary doesn't mean that much, but I guess we all
need some form of recognition.
DOTTY: Could these two forms of recognition be your two
friends?
BEN: It's possible because in neither case did I seek these out.
LENORE: What were the boys' names?
BEN: I don't think you know them. One was named Salter
and the other Saltonstall. Similar names.
DOTTY: Similar forms of recognition.
LENORE: Hey, the organization you work for is SALT!
BEN: I never mentioned the names because I didn't think
they'd mean anything. Amazing. . . . I really wasn't going to
run this dream by. It didn't seem significant enough. I guess
you better not take anything about your dreams for granted.

We agreed at the outset of our meetings that we would
confine ourselves to working only with the waking-life problems depicted in our dream metaphors. Sometimes in our
search for the specific message, we touched on areas which
proved of little value in understanding a particular dream.
We dropped these areas as the focus of the dream problem
became clearer. We began with the dream and let its metaphors guide us to the waking dilemma. It was not until our
tenth month that this format was altered.

Howard had mentioned some experimentation done in a
dream workshop led by Robert Van de Castle, in which there
was an attempt at dreaming about the problems of other
members. Weston, a naval captain, listened intently and
asked if we would do this for him. He was struggling over

whether or not to take his comprehensives for a master's degree. The pros and cons were rather complex and we spent some time trying to comprehend the situation. Although most of us were baffled over how to "dream another person's problem" or recognize it if we did, we agreed to try. Perhaps because we were vague about both the process and our expectations the results were disappointing. However, the night of our meeting Weston had a dream that revealed his reaction to what had transpired that evening and gave us all a clearer picture of some dynamics operating within the group.

Weston's Dream:

Tish and I arrive at a social event. It seems to be an officers' club and to get in is like going through a turnstile at a stadium. Someone known to me greets us as we are going in and points out where the parking is. I brush him off and state I have already parked closer (really not an authorized spot). My impression is that the route to the party was similar to going over the Wilson Bridge and leading North on 295.

"The night of the dream we had attended this class. On the way home Tish said I was really 'coming down' to join the group. I told her I was glad I had joined. I liked the people —thought them a compatible group."

From our first meeting Weston had been struggling against feelings of aloofness; he really wanted to be a participating equal in the dream group. As a naval officer he was accustomed to having aides respond to the authority of his commands and decisions without reservation. It was not surprising that this sort of detachment and authority often appeared in his dreams.

Weston had a problem in relation to the group. The manner of his attempt to resolve the problem was symbolically described that night in his turnstile dream. Weston wanted to get inside the officers' club where the dream-work party was going on. To do that he imagined himself, as an officer of the dream club, with the familiar privileges and prerogatives of his waking life; so that the group—our group— became in effect his aides. He asked us to do the work ordinarily done by the dreamer: Here is my problem, dream me an answer. This was a turnabout from our usual procedure (turnstile entrance into the officers' club). Asking the dream group to do his hard inner work was like parking himself in an *unauthorized spot.* In the dream he brushes off the attendant who points out that the parking is in another place. It is more difficult to park in the lot and walk to the officers' club (i.e., record your own dream, bring in your day's events, presleep thoughts, and metaphors).

Weston wanted to bridge the gap (Wilson Bridge) between himself, his problem, and the members of the group. Without having the credentials of the dream material he pulled rank and gave us directions to get inside his head (North on 295) and determine the dream resolution.

The condition that he implicitly laid down for agreeing to be a member of the group—that he should in effect be regarded as an officer among enlisted men—created a familiar frame of reference. In his own way he was trying to join us and we accepted his "condition" as a step toward deeper belonging. But we had to recognize that it was limited in its effectiveness for both himself and the group. We were all apprentices in the Hanseatic League: each with our own bed, our own dreams, our own work. We could help each other to the extent that we revealed ourselves honestly and accepted one another without condescension.

In a second dream that night Weston turned the tables on himself and dreamed specifically about the "comprehensive" problem. In that dream he did for himself what he had asked us to do for him.

Though we might wish it otherwise, we all have our spot in the societal wasp's nest, and there is a great deal of buzzing when someone disturbs the order of things. Howard and I were caught in one local commotion. In our area the real estate taxes had soared. Our property was assessed at twice the figure of the previous year, and Howard called the county authorities to have it reassessed. Several days later a building inspector appeared at our door to inspect our two-year-old shed dormer. His report listed a number of minor offenses including the astonishing fact that our windows were a fraction of an inch under regulation. Unless they were torn out and enlarged, these spaces could not be used as bedrooms. What was maddening was that prior to Howard's challenge of our property assessment, we had seen no inspectors and suspected no problems. Obviously Howard had stuck a stick in the nest. The wasps were swarming. Out flew our files. Howard, quite exercised, wrote a letter to our county supervisor describing the sequence of events. He decided to "sleep on it" before mailing the letter. That night he dreamed.

Howard's Dream:

Nan and I were driving up the Parkway in our Opel. We passed the Fourteenth Street Bridge and went under the Memorial Bridge heading toward the juncture leading to Key Bridge. The Potomac was overflowing its banks and was coming up over the Parkway. Cars continued to go through it without making any splashes. Where the roads merged there was a muddy torrent of water from a heavy rainstorm. The other cars went through it as if the road were there and it didn't seem to hurt them. I wasn't apprehensive, but I slowed down and stopped at the edge. There was this powerful flow of water. All sorts of vehicles were in it, cars, trains, and flatbed trucks with building materials loaded on them. I decided I wasn't going to try that. I backed the car up and went the other way.

We had no difficulty identifying the torrent of water as the powerful, impersonal forces of the bureaucracy. People who didn't make a *splash* proceeded meekly and safely on their way. Howard was considering whether it was worth the risk to challenge the system by bringing our situation to the attention of the county supervisor (that is, drive into the torrent toward the Key Bridge). He didn't feel apprehensive about the possible outcome but rather demoralized by the powers of the government. He was angry and wanted to move away from the entire business: sell the house, forget about the higher taxes.

What gave this dream report an added punch was Howard's recalling a second dream of that same night.

I was talking to a man. It was an agitated conversation. I remember thinking, I have two choices how to relate to him: either continue talking, or hit this guy. I thought, so what, and hauled off and hit him. The thing was, I actually banged my hand on the back of the bed. I woke up and my knuckle ached and was skinned.

Next day Howard made minor diplomatic revisions in his "hard-hitting" letter and sent it to the county supervisor. Our assessment was lowered (albeit a fraction), and the inspection report ended up in the *closed* file. After this dream sequence we all had greater respect for the adage, "Sleep on it."

We all have our artful maneuvers which we slide into from time to time to evade admitting what we already know. Tish, Weston's wife and a preschool teacher, was no exception. She was a master of the multimetaphoric misadventure. She would unravel a tale of Homeric proportions dating from a dream far enough removed from our meeting that only the obvious day residue could be remembered. At first the group felt guilty about our flat responses to these odysseys. Then one painful evening it came to us that the dreams were being presented in a manner which insured our fitting them together without conviction. Tish was hurt and felt attacked by this disclosure. Fortunately we had been together long enough for trust to supersede the feeling of invasion. She was willing to accept our assignment: Next meeting she was to report on her most recent dream, no matter what length. The dream she presented was, as Lenore said, "a challenge to all of us as women." We called it the "Wifely Dream."

Tish's Dream:

I kept trying to get to a train. I was walking down through the woods. There was a lot of snow. I kept meeting up with the train, but every time I met up with it the conductor informed me I could go only one way. I said that was all right. I only wanted to go one way. I was going to pick up my car at the other end and drive back. The message kept being, "One way. I can only go one way." I would go up into the woods and back down, meeting the track at different spots.

Without knowing the day's events, we might have prematurely concluded that the dream was clarifying Tish's relationship with the group: wanting to get on the right *track* by presenting dreams in a workable fashion and at the same time confusing us with a *snow* job (her excursions into the dark woods). An account of the events of the previous day, however, took us much further into the frustrations pictured in her dream.

Tish had had a busy morning: preschool open house and orientation for new parents, picking up her mother-in-law at the hairdresser, and rushing home in time to fix Weston's lunch before he flew to Florida. She had wanted to buy a birthday present for Weston to take to her mother in Florida, but Weston was angry at her last-minute idea and refused to take it, even if she should manage to return before he left. Later in the afternoon Tish and her mother-in-law (who had looked at her wardrobe and said it was awful) went shopping to buy Tish clothes. They found several possibilities, none of which they bought because Tish always waited for Weston's approval of anything she wore. Her mother-in-law stayed with friends overnight and Tish had "a typical rest-of-the-evening, without Weston." To which Weston added, "Totally disorganized."

Dotty observed that Tish and Weston talked a great deal about how terribly disorganized Tish was, but that she seemed to get a lot done.

Tish answered, "Yes, but I'm an eggbeater in motion. I get a lot done, but there's utter chaos where I'm doing it."

That certainly put her relationship with the group in perspective. If she whirled through a long complicated dream, spinning images off in all directions, she accomplished what she wanted without our getting too close. No one is going to stick a hand in the bowl with an eggbeater! But how did this relate to Tish's dream?

Tish's dilemma in the dream is how to get done what she wants while doing what Weston wants. She not only has to go around fast, but go up and down, back and forth—from the woods, where she can function privately, to the track. And what is the track? Being Weston's wife. Weston's military *train*ing influences him to feel there is *one way* to *conduct* his household. Tish is the antithesis of the military order. As Weston's wife she has to keep track of the way he wants her to go. She must scurry back and forth between her style and his. In the dream she attempts to convince the conductor that she wants to go his way. Actually she hopes to use his way to get to her own car (that is to say, to the end of the day when she will be alone to handle her household as she pleases).

In her dream Tish spends a great deal of energy trying to maintain a hold on both the woods and the track. She never gets on the track, nor does she settle down and enjoy her walk in the woods. It seemed to the group that both the egg-beater technique and the one-way track needed evaluation. What did Tish want as a woman, a wife, a mother? Why did her car have to be at the end of the line? These are questions that are not answered in an evening.

During our year's journey together we had moments, deliberate and spontaneous, when we reviewed the significance of our dream discoveries. Jenny's leaving the group after nine months generated one period of reevaluation. She felt she had a handle on effective dream work. She was comfortable with our techniques and the language of metaphors was no longer strange. The group could always be summoned if she were stumped by a dream. For her the Tower House had served its purpose.

Jenny's perception helped us realize how wrong it would

be to keep the Tower House group alive as an artificial support system. There were already too many groups around that had begun with vitality and now had outlived their usefulness. At one point we held a disbanding session. It ended with a renewed appreciation of the group's value for each of us.

What Dotty said was expressive of the continual value of our meetings. "More than ever before, I look forward to dreams as help with my problems. Understanding my dreams has made me more conscious of my thoughts. Before we got together I was too bound by what I thought dream interpretation should be. We've opened the scope of my thinking about dreams to be as big as life. The other thing is the group: It's crucial for me to have our regular meetings. It makes me be active in my own dream work . . . apart from the ones I bring to you. I'm very bad about letting important dreams drop through the cracks, but because I know you're working on your dreams, I'm not as sloppy."

Our delight in the process could not be credited solely to insights or clever metaphorical associations. We developed an understanding of and appreciation for each other that could have come about in no other way.

Scientists sometimes speak of theories as possessing an "elegance." Rollo May refers to an "inner consistency . . . the character of beauty that touches your sensibilities—these are significant factors in determining why a given idea emerges."[1] So it was with our dream work. An elegance was evident when the dreamer was struck with the unique meaning of a dream. Even the painful disclosures were shot through with a leap of recognition. Of course! That's it! How could I have labored so long for the truth? We experienced release, and I do not think it is superlative to add, joy.

Whatever doubts we entertained about the future of our group (as of this writing we meet bimonthly), we knew our dreams were always with us: an internal reckoning agent. We were at liberty to ignore them. No matter; they relentlessly addressed themselves to the state of our psyches. We were talking about this one night when Ben said, "Let me quote a dream I had a month ago. It didn't make any sense to me at all. I told Lenore and she saw it right away.

> We had a lot of company in our house. In the living room was my bed. Under the pillow was a bunch of mail. I hadn't bothered to look at it. Some of it had fallen on the floor. There were dollar bills mixed in with it.

"I thought—what does this mean? But Lenore lit up. 'You're not reading your dream mail and you're not cashing in on it.'

"She was right, I haven't been disciplined in trying to capture my dreams and write them down. They keep coming and I keep ignoring them. For me they're an untapped gold mine. I guess my dream was saying—don't forget it!"

R. D. Laing says, "What we think is less than what we know; what we know is less than what we love; what we love is so much less than what there is. And to that precise extent we are so much less than what we are. . . ."[2]

We couldn't leave it at that—not with our dreams to help us.

15

Dreaming Across Space and Time

We have noted a great many remarkable features of our dream life. Among these are our sensitivity to triggering events in our lives and their potential importance (the day residue), the powerful backward scanning mechanism at our disposal that lights up hidden recesses in our memory, and the magnificently appropriate way in which we manage to locate and use images to express the drama we are experiencing. But while all these data are truly remarkable, there is still another rather puzzling fact about our dreams, namely, our ability under certain circumstances to include in them information about events going on in the outside world, now or in the future, about which we could have no knowledge through ordinary channels of communication. I am referring to paranormal dreams and the dreamer's ability to pick up information telepathically (from someone else's mind), clairvoyantly (events not in anyone's mind), and precognitively (events that have not yet happened). (These abilities are collectively and popularly referred to as ESP. Researchers in the field often prefer a more neutral designation, the Greek letter "psi," to include the various forms of ESP and other paranormal effects such as psychokinesis or the influence of mind over matter.)

The evidence that dream telepathy and precognitive dreaming actually occur comes from several sources. These include published accounts that have been carefully investigated and documented by reliable observers, accounts by psychiatrists and psychotherapists of patients' telepathic dreams, and from successful attempts to produce telepathic and precognitive dreams in the laboratory.[1]

The following dream experiences are not offered as proof of the reality of telepathy, clairvoyance, or precognition in dreams. There has been no attempt to validate the examples given here. Many of them came to my attention in response to an article I had written on dream telepathy for *Family Circle.* In some cases a more mundane explanation might replace the paranormal assumption if the incident were investigated more thoroughly. Nevertheless, based on my knowledge of the evidence from well-documented cases in the literature, the accounts that follow do illustrate in a fairly typical way how paranormal dream phenomena enter our lives.

I will begin with one of my own dreams. These are my notes on it written February 11, 1972, the day following the dream:

> I awoke during the night with a very vivid dream. It seemed unusually real. I had received first one check for a million and a half dollars, and then another for the same amount from an unknown donor. I was overjoyed. I realized the laboratory was saved. I couldn't believe it, yet I held the check in my hand.

1 P.M.: I told the dream to Lester.

2 P.M.: I told the dream to George, Gene, and Phil.

3 P.M.: The mail arrived with a check for five hundred dollars from an unknown donor who had responded to an appeal that had appeared in the magazine *Psychic*. A note wishing us well accompanied the check. The note was made out in duplicate. Strangely enough, both the original and carbon copies were sent.

Our laboratory was the only one exploring the problem of extrasensory communication and dreaming. It had been in dire financial straits since September 1971. We were concerned that after years of pioneering and productive experimental work we would be faced with the prospect of closing unless additional funds came through by the summer. The appeal in *Psychic* had resulted in donations of five or ten dollars coming sporadically during the two-month period before the dream. The plight of the laboratory was on my mind as well as the hope that someone would come to our rescue. The fact that the dream came the night before the large check may have been more than coincidental. Are there any other features to suggest that it was more than that? In the dream the duplication involved the receipt of two checks. In reality the duplication involved the receipt of two letters.

Not all vivid dreams have a paranormal content. But often paranormal dreams do stand out in a special way. The names in my diary were colleagues at the hospital where I worked. It was most unusual for me to share my dreams with them. I cannot recall having done it before or since.

I had been living and teaching in Sweden for seven months when my wife, Janet, had the following dream:

> Monte and I were visiting Ely and Norma (a medical-school classmate and his wife). The house was busy and crowded with many people, including children. During the visit Norma's old and feeble mother arrived—then Ely's old and feeble mother. Norma fussed over them in her own unique way. Ely called down from the floor above, where an old man, either his or her father, lay very ill. Monte went upstairs to see him.

On the morning following the dream we got the first and only letter we have ever received from Ely and Norma. We had written to them about four months before. Among the items in the letter were the news that Norma's father had died the past summer and an account of their involvement in resettling her mother in a town close to them. We have never met her parents. Janet's attachment to her own mother was and remains a very powerful one. Was this instrumental in creating a channel linking her dream thoughts to our friends and their preoccupation with Norma's deceased father and elderly mother?

Several years ago I gave a workshop on dreams at Esalen during which I met the writer of the following letter. I had helped her with a dream and we had subsequently corresponded, usually about dreams. This was the first time she had mentioned a paranormal dream.

> A week ago Sunday I dreamed of something that looked as if it had a long white cloud across the

center of it. The next day, during my hour with my therapist, I associated the cloud with an umbilicus, and kept speaking of Marian. Then my sister, Mary, came to mind. She is thirty-nine, pregnant, with three children, aged eleven, fourteen, and sixteen. I felt such anxiety about her that I phoned. She had recently moved to Glen Falls, New York, and had a general practitioner taking care of her. She told me her water had broken but she was not in labor. Her doctor said everything was perfectly all right, and that she should stay active. I asked if she would consider seeing a specialist for consultation and she said she would think about it.

The next day when I saw my therapist, he said, "She is not taking appropriate action. You must prepare for bad news." I had a knot in my stomach, especially when phone calls on Tuesday and Wednesday evenings found her still at home; she had talked with her doctor by phone and he said he believed everything was normal. Thursday night I was leaving for Philadelphia. The plane was late and I used the time to phone her again. I told her that ever since my dream on Sunday I had had a feeling of urgency about her condition and I hoped, just to put my mind at rest, that she would see a specialist. She said she had seen her doctor that afternoon and that he didn't feel a specialist was necessary since "he would probably want to confine you in some other hospital."

Somehow this time my words got through to her. Mary arranged to see an obstetrician who, half an hour after she arrived, performed a Caesarian on her. The baby was transverse, not in very good shape, and

Mary herself had problems. The baby is now out of the incubator and they are both improving every day. At midnight, the day of Mary's Caesarian, the nurse discovered that Mary had mumps: It's really a grotesque footnote! The doctor said if he had known that at the time of surgery, it would really have put him under a great deal of stress—although he would have had to go ahead anyway.

This is one of a category of cases in which the emotional residue of the dream impels the dreamer to take action and the disquiet is not dispelled until effective steps have been taken.

Issues of life, death, and survival often hover in the background even when the content of the dream itself seems quite removed from them. One day I received the following memorandum from a member of my staff, a psychiatrist who had had no prior experiences in ESP, but who knew of my interest.

TO: Montague Ullman, M.D.
FROM: Hans J. Nieporent, M.D.
SUBJECT: ESP (?) and Dreaming

Situation:

On June 27, 1972, my alarm clock went off at 6:30 A.M. I got up to shut it off and decided I could still spend some time in bed. I next awoke at 7:20 A.M. and during that time had the following dream:

Dream:

I am in the haberdashery section of a department
store (Alexander's ?). I see a group of people milling
around a counter and feel that a special sale must be
going on there. I see a rack of suits (yellow with black
stripes) that attract me. I force my way to the
counter and a woman remarks that I am very rude.
When I get to another side of the counter I see that
the suits are gone. I start looking at some polo shirts.
A salesgirl tells me that the shirts are slightly soiled
and therefore are reduced from $8.90 to $4.90. I look
at four of them but cannot make up my mind. I feel
that they may be too warm for the summer. At this
point I wake up.

ESP?

Five minutes after I awaken, my wife awakens.
She says, "I want to sound you out on how you
feel about this. Last night when I visited L., she
told me that she had been going through her husband's clothing and he had many beautiful things,
many only slightly worn, that she has been thinking about giving to men of her acquaintance who
were about her late husband's size, and she has
been thinking of you. Are you interested?" I replied that I was not.

Background:

L.'s husband, F., died on June 23, 1972. He was a
forty-year-old psychiatrist who had had a heart at-

tack the November before. I attended his funeral service two days before the dream.

The next series of dreams are those that came in response to my article in *Family Circle*. While I cannot vouch for their authenticity, I think the sincerity of the writer comes through in each case.

Most paranormal dreams are precognitive and do seem to be linked to tragic events. The following dream is typical:

I have often wanted to tell someone directly connected with research on precognition about a dream I had some years ago. Now that I have your address, I will tell you of my own experience. I am forty-three years old, a housewife, with four teenage children. I am normal, perhaps a little oversensitive. Born in England, I came to the United States in 1956 with my husband and three children. The following January we were about to move to another house, and I was too busy to take much notice of this disturbing dream which occurred at about 5:00 A.M. one Friday morning.

I suddenly felt that I was standing in the living room of my parents' home in England where they were still living. It was very dank and warm because they had not gone to bed too long before (I thought) and the fire was banked in the covered fireplace. It was very quiet.

I suddenly felt afraid for my family—for all of them. Then it seemed that the cold light of dawn was coming and I was standing at the window and looking out into the back garden. Then I knew that it was only my father that I had to worry about. I looked and dimly saw his body lying out there on the grass and I knew that he was dead. The ground all around seemed sprinkled with white and I thought it was frost.

That day and the next I forgot the dream in my preparations to move. On the Sunday following the Friday dream I received a telegram from England. It said that my father had been taken ill suddenly on Saturday and was in the hospital. I spent the rest of that week in a daze but still, for some reason, did not expect it when the following Sunday I received another telegram to say that he had passed away—just one week later.

Sometime after this, when my mother came out to live with us, I discussed the dream with her, and she told me that my father had been spreading lime all over our garden just prior to becoming ill (hence the appearance of frost in the dream?).

We cannot with any degree of assurance say that this is precognitive unless we knew for certain that the father was in good health at the time the dream was occurring. He may have been experiencing some distress that only he was aware of, in which case the dream may have been telepathic.

The next correspondent reports three unusual dreams, the first of which appears to be precognitive, the other two telepathic.

I have recently read an article written by you on dreams. I would like to relate to you three instances that have happened to me recently that might be of interest to you in your research:

First Dream:

This occurred on September 14, 1970. I had a terribly bad and frightening dream in which I saw my husband in an auto wreck. I saw the corner where the wreck occurred, the car that struck him, and could even see some of the people standing around at the time. The following morning I related the dream to my husband and warned him to refrain from driving the car for a few days.

On the morning of September 16, my seventeen-year-old son asked for permission to attend a statewide church meeting that was being held in our city, at which he planned to sing in the youth choir. The moment he mentioned being absent from his morning classes, I saw very vividly the wreck scene in my dream, only it was he driving the car and not my husband. Since we had a guest at breakfast that morning, I did not mention it to him, but pleaded with my husband to withhold his permission for my son to attend. He assured me that our son would be all right since he was a very cautious driver. I was terribly upset but I *did not* let my son know. Scarcely two hours passed before we received a phone call telling me that my son had, indeed, been in a terrible wreck. The identical wreck of my dream. The only difference was in the color of the car that had hit him. In

the dream it was blue and actually the car that hit
him was green. My son's car was totally demol-
ished but, luckily, everyone escaped severe inju-
ries.

Second Dream:

This happened on August 20, 1971. I awakened at
5:20 A.M., screaming and waking everyone in the
house. I did not at the time know just what was the
matter. Something terrible had happened and I was
aware of it. At 5:30 A.M. my brother-in-law phoned
me from Memphis, Tennessee. When the phone rang
I remarked to my husband that my mother was dead;
she had suffered a terrible accident. Indeed, the call
affirmed that my mother had just fallen down an
entire flight of stairs and had broken a bone and was
cut. She had fallen at exactly 5:20 A.M. I could actually see her injured. She had a laceration on the left
side of her forehead and a broken left arm.

Third Dream:

On August 26, 1971, I awoke at 12:05 A.M., again
screaming and crying aloud. This time I saw my
mother holding her head and pleading for relief. My
own head was throbbing painfully, with the pain
more severe on the left side. It was a period of hours
before I could return to sleep, since I felt that my
mother might be dying from a cerebral hemorrhage.
The next morning, upon awaking, I was still unable
to completely shake the effects of the "nightmare" I
had had the night before. I *telephoned* my mother
and found that she had awakened the night before at

exactly 12:05 suffering with a terrible headache
. . . on the left side of her head.

I had had numerous dreams previously that
seemed to be a warning and came true. Most of the
dreams were connected directly to my own immediate family, but I have also had warnings about people
that I have never met.

I don't know if any of this can be of help to you
in your research but I am convinced that we have
some sort of warning system built into our brains
that sometimes alerts us to impending disaster.

In the first dream the dreamer is impelled to take action,
but, because of the circumstances, stops short of taking it.
The first two dreams deal with near tragedies, the third with
illness. The kind of sympathetic pain experienced by the
dreamer at the time of the mother's headache is not uncommon.

In the following situation a mother is impelled to action
because of the strong feelings generated by the dream:

In 1964 my only child, a mongoloid son, was admitted to Gracewood State School and Hospital, 280
miles from Valdosta, Georgia, where I lived at the
time. One night I dreamed he was deathly ill and
burning up with fever. The dream was so intense that
I could actually feel the heat of his body next to my
chest. I aroused my husband and told him of the
incident. He said I was crazy and told me to go back
to sleep; that it was my overactive imagination. The
next morning I *knew* my child was sick and needed
me. I was afraid to mention this to my co-workers at

the Lee Street Baptist Church for fear they'd think
me crazy. At noon I could no longer stand the stress,
so I told them my dream and called the school where
my child was. Dr. William Sanders answered the
phone and said, "How are you?" I replied, "I am
worried sick that Douglas is deathly ill and burning
up with fever." He said, "You're right. We admitted
him to the hospital last night with a fever of 104."

In the next example the dreamer's estranged husband appears in a dream on the night that he died.

I want to tell you about a dream I had. It was not
a warning of danger, but a dream that told me something, although I didn't realize that at the time.
   In my bedroom, my bed faces my dresser. The
dresser has twin mirrors. I dreamed that the telephone rang (the phone was by my bed). I answered
it and it was my ex-husband, whom I had not seen
in five years. While I was talking to him on the phone
I was facing the mirror. He started walking out of
one of the mirrors, putting on the coat to his suit and
fixing his tie. I put the phone down, got out of bed
(still dreaming), and I said, "Roger, what are you
doing here?" He answered, "I just wanted to see
you." I woke myself up and walked around the
apartment for a while. It was still dark outside, but
when I went back to bed and then to sleep, it seemed
only a short time had elapsed and it was time to get
up—so I feel that I dreamed this early in the morning. When I awakened this time, I had a depressed
feeling—something I couldn't describe.

At 9:00 A.M. my brother-in-law called to tell me that my husband had died of a stroke at 3:30 A.M. in Mississippi. I believe he told me good-bye. We had lived together for twenty-three years, but were divorced because he was an alcoholic and could not keep a job. I can't say that I knew I would get that message, but I was not surprised. This may not be unusual but I will never forget it.

As we have seen, a premonition strong enough to impel one to action can be life saving. This was so in the following instance where the premonition occurred during the day and a dream suggestively related to the actual disaster followed the same night.

We were living in Erlanger, Kentucky. My husband traveled as service manager for a large company. On this particular occasion he had traveled all day to reach home—get clean clothes, etc., and take the 8:00 A.M. flight out of Cincinnati for Cleveland where he had an appointment. When I reached home at 5:00 P.M., I did not know about any of these arrangements. I prepared supper for us and my daughter-in-law. While we were doing the dishes my husband mentioned his intention of flying to Cleveland the next morning. My reaction was strange, even to me. I lashed out in anger, said he wasn't flying anywhere in the morning . . . if he had to be in Cleveland it would be by some means other than plane. A real argument followed. My embarrassed daughter-in-law went to her room. My husband, seeing I was quite upset, made arrangements with a neighbor to drive him to the railroad station and he took the 11:39 P.M. train to Cleveland. I felt guilty about all this, so when I went to bed I could not sleep. Toward morning I fell asleep and dreamed that I was floating in air with strange objects, and then I started to fall. I woke with a start and as I did, I felt the house shake. I got up, made coffee, and felt I did not want to be alone in the house. It was a Tuesday and my day off from work, so I took the car and just drove around awhile. I shopped and returned home by lunch time. My daughter-in-law had been trying to reach me by phone. She asked me if I had the radio on. I told her no and told her of my dream and how I felt. It was then she said there had been a collision between the 8:00 A.M. plane and a private plane—everyone had been killed!

The following is a clear-cut example of a precognitive dream of a disaster:

I am nineteen years of age and I firmly believe that last summer I had a precognitive dream.

One night in early June of 1970 I dreamed a boy I was dating was driving in the mountains when suddenly his car went over a cliff and he was killed. The dream was so vivid that I awoke, terrified, and had trouble returning to sleep. The next morning I mentioned the dream to my mother and sister and then put it out of my mind. In mid-June of the same year the very boy I had dreamed about was killed in circumstances almost identical to those of my dream. He was driving in my home town of Winter Park, Florida, when suddenly the car he was driving went over a steep embankment into a drainage ditch and he was killed.

It is of interest in dreams of this kind that the dreamer feels impelled to share it with one or more people.

The following illustrates three common features of dreams of this type—the emotional closeness of the people involved, the occurrence of a sudden potentially or actually serious event happening to one of them, and the compulsion to act or contact the other.

On April 28, 1971, I experienced a vague feeling of uneasiness all day—enough so that I called a friend to come over, since my husband was out of the state at the time. That night I had a horrifying dream that I was going to my sister's funeral; she was in Germany and I saw her in a casket, but as I approached, she moved and we were all so joyful that she was alive. Immediately after this I awoke, remembered the dream precisely, and was unable to sleep anymore that night.

The next morning I called my parents even though I knew they would probably laugh it off because I *felt certain* something terrible had happened to my sister and that they had been notified. They hadn't heard anything. However, my next letter from my sister indicated that she had been rushed to a hospital on April 28 for an emergency appendectomy. An astute surgeon had refused to operate, though, and it was later discovered that she had a tumor in one of her tubes. My sister and I have always had a close relationship which made me think twice about it. I have had numerous bad dreams in the past, but none of them ever affected me as this one did, and none occurred in actuality at a later date.

Let us turn from the tragic and near tragic to a lighter vein of precognitive and telepathic dreams which are illustrated in the next three examples:

This is a precognitive dream and although it happened years ago, I still remember it vividly. Early on a Sunday morning on Father's Day I woke both myself and my husband by laughing out loud. The dream consisted of one scene and no dialogue. My sister, ten years my junior, stood before me in a bulky coat, put her hands in the coat pockets, and, when she pulled them out and extended her arms toward me, I could see each hand was filled with bottle caps. That was the complete dream. I told my husband about the silly dream and later we told my father about it at the breakfast table.

Around noon my sister, her husband, and two sons arrived for Father's Day dinner. My sister, who was pregnant, was wearing a very full, lightweight summer coat. As I was hanging up her coat she called to me to bring her cigarettes from the coat pocket. I returned to her with the coat, and while I still held it, she reached into the pockets and came out with—not cigarettes—but two handfuls of bottle caps. As you can see, the only difference was that in the dream she was wearing the coat, while in reality I was holding the coat. When she saw the bottle caps she exclaimed, "Look at what the boys put in my pockets." The sensation that my husband, my father, and I felt at that point is indescribable!

Christmas Eve of this year I had a dream. My brother Clayton, who is principal of Westmore High in Westlake, was wearing a caftan in his office. I thought to myself, boy, is my brother getting wild! Imagine him wearing a caftan. He is ultra-conservative and this dream really amused me, so I told my sister and nephew about it. The next day I went to Clayton's house and he and his wife gave me a caftan for Christmas. I cannot believe that this was just a coincidence!

Soon after this I had another short dream and at the end of the dream, upon awakening, I heard these words ringing in my ears: "Read to me anything as long as it's by Dickens, it's got to be by Dickens—I just love Dickens!" Now, when I woke up I kind of laughed to myself for, while I am a "voracious" reader, Dickens is scarcely one of my favorites. About the only thing I have ever read by him is "A Christmas Carol," and that most definitely is not noteworthy in my memory.

That night I was watching television and Rod Serling's *Night Gallery* came on—I don't remember the name of this particular episode but could find the date of this show if you desire such information. It

was a show with Agnes Moorehead in which she was
a bedridden invalid. In it she said to her brother,
"Will you please read to me?" I think at first he
declined, but she begged and he said, "All right,
what will it be this time?" She said, "Read something
by Dickens—anything as long as it is by Dickens—
I just love Dickens!"

Precognitive and telepathic dreams are more commonly
reported by women than by men. Perhaps women tend to be
more open to, and accepting of, their reality. While some
people report paranormal occurrences just once in their lives,
others seem to have accumulated a number of such experiences.

Even for those who seem to have premonitory dreams
from time to time, there is no certain way of identifying a
dream as precognitive until the prefigured events actually
occur. There are in the literature many instances in which
the accompanying feelings were so compelling that there was
no doubt in the dreamer's mind that some kind of preventive
action had to take place. These are, however, the exception
and quite often feelings of certainty do not prove a reliable
guide to the precognitive nature of the dream.

We know that a number of different states of consciousness other than dreaming—for example hypnosis, trance,
and states of sensory deprivation—facilitate these effects.
These states are collectively known as "altered states" of
consciousness. In such states changes occur in the way we
experience time and space. Those of us who experience such
states seem to have a degree of openness to extrasensory
contact with other people, particularly to those who play a
significant role in our lives. It may be that the evolution of
more reliable or practical forms of communication have led

to a kind of disuse atrophy of this ability so that it tends to come out of hiding only under rather unusual circumstances. The less skeptical one is about the possibility of ESP, the more apt it is to occur.

Even under the most receptive circumstances, paranormal effects in dreams remain elusive and ephemeral. And there are many occasions when strong premonitions turn out to be wrong.

These abilities do not lend themselves to any controlled, practical application—at least not yet. There are occasional reports in the literature of the names of horse-race winners appearing in dreams, but this is a rather rare occurrence and unlikely to provide the dreamer with a secure source of income. We did have one such report of a dreamer picking out horse-race winners in her dream.

I would like to tell you I have dreamed who would win at the harness races and they did win. In June of this year I dreamed three nights in a row who would win the perfectas (this is the first and second horse in one race). The first night I dreamed the numbers 7-2 would win the first perfecta, the second night 5-2. It did, and the third night, 6-2. It did. The first night I ever dreamed of horses was about four or five years ago. The horse's name was circled *Jimmy Cannon,* as such. I had never heard of this horse. The next day it was listed and ran and won! I have wanted to tell someone about this. This was a race horse. I also recently went to Latonia in Florence. I dreamed 4-7 would win the perfecta; 7-4 won and paid $225. I bet this both ways and therefore won. The next night I dreamed 2-1. It won the double and I won. I told the teller at Latonia and he was fascinated. I later found out he was a reporter for a newspaper and he wrote an article about me. He called me "The Dream Girl."

I hope this will be of some help to you. As you can see, sometimes I dream numbers and sometimes names, but usually numbers. It sort of frightens me to think I can do this.

The existence of these phenomena suggests that while asleep, we are not only able to scan backward in time and tap into our remote memory, but are also able to scan forward in time and across space to tap into information outside our own experience. Regardless of how seldom they occur, these manifestations cast a new light on the range of our psychic abilities. They persuade us to look at dreams as events occurring in a much larger and more complex reference frame than we are accustomed to viewing them. A good deal more investigative work will have to be done before we can begin to understand the role telepathy and precognition play in our lives.

16

Toward a Greater Appreciation of Dreams

Colleagues of mine have raised two kinds of questions about the effort to extend serious dream work beyond the clinical setting. The first concerns the effectiveness of the effort: Isn't it apt to remain superficial? The second touches on risk: Isn't it dangerous to pursue dream work without professional guidance?

The charge of superficiality is unwarranted. If dream work does anything, it moves the dreamer beyond appearances into the deeper aspects of the psyche. How "deep" a level depends on the persistence and honesty with which the dreamer pursues dream work.

The distinction between professional and nonprofessional work with dreams does not involve the issue of superficiality. The only valid distinction is that, in the hands of a therapist, the dream becomes an instrument for probing, confronting, etc. It becomes a matter of treatment, not dream appreciation. The skills of the professional may facilitate dream work for those who are resistive to it, but they don't alter the nature of dream work itself. Whenever such work is carried out properly, whether under professional auspices or not, it always provides us with a more penetrating glimpse of what lies beneath the surface.

All we ever deal with is what is in our awareness at the moment. We are never aware of all the intricacies of our own connections to the world at any given moment—just of a fraction of them. Working with personality is like working at an archaeological dig. We start on the surface and go deeper. The dream images are indicators of what we may come upon. They hint at the existence of underlying complexity. And every time the dreamer—with or without the help of a group—can breathe meaning into the image, he reaches deeper into himself. This is the nature of dream work. Superficiality implies the attempt to conceal or ignore these complexities. Through dream work we can learn about and come to terms with what lies beneath the surface.

Those who feel that a professional must be present for work with dreams are, as I have noted, concerned that a dreamer with a fragile self-concept might produce a dream which could reveal the dreamer as abnormal in some way. Yet the very thing that sets off anxiety in such a dreamer is often the weight given to the interpretation by the authority and prestige of the professional. Nonprofessionals who work together invite less anxiety because they are free of that image of authority as well as of the necessity to abide by any particular theoretical position. In a group setting, if something is said which is unduly threatening, the dreamer can say, "Who do you think you are? You don't know any more about dreams than I do." But if a psychotherapist presents that same interpretation, the dreamer may tell himself, "This professional who knows about dreams is telling me I am this way. It must be the way I am." And that can have a very unsettling impact.

The issue of danger is not inherent in the nature of dream work unless that work is pursued without respect for the authority of the dreamer. When we have a dream we are ready to deal with it. The danger, as far as I'm concerned, is not of any threat unleashed by the dream but of failing to see what the dream sets before us.

There is, though, another kind of danger to dream work: the danger of seeing through sham and pretense. Dreams generate knowledge: self-knowledge and social knowledge. As we have said, working on dreams is as dangerous as thinking. Don't take that lightly. When we ponder an issue we frequently come up against ideas and feelings that are novel and alien to our present understanding. We may be thrown off balance and plunged into disturbing emotions which force us to reevaluate the meaning and effectiveness of many of our routine performances. Dread of this fosters in us the attitude that we dare not think without the guiding hand of an authority to ensure that we remain within safe bounds. Yet most of us do not need this sort of protection. We can tolerate large doses of change, with discomfort perhaps, but without damage. The support and encouragement needed for self-discovery through dreams can come from anyone, professional or nonprofessional.

Dreaming is as normal, physiological, universal, and human as childbirth. More so; it has no sexual limitations. And the help of specialists is as little needed with most dreams as with most normal births. But some help is needed, and I hope that this book will serve as a midwife to the truths inherent in our dreams.

To sum up how dreams can help us enlarge and enrich our lives:

Our dreams don't lie. They use the simple expedient of

truth to monitor our struggle to be human. Whatever our defensive structure, the truth of a situation is displayed honestly in a dream. We can count on it.

Waking life confronts us with many surprises and challenges and our dreams try to absorb some of the impact by bringing to bear a greater number of personal resources than we are generally aware of possessing. As we pursue dream work we become more and more appreciative of how the dreamer in us keeps urging us on to greater wholeness.

Dreams are sensitive to the state of our relationship with others. When we are awake we view ourselves as separate creatures, concerned with our own individuality and our own identity. Our dreaming self, however, focuses on our connections to others, the intactness of those connections, and how what has happened during the day has disturbed those connections—hurt or enhanced them.

In dream work, especially when it takes place in groups, the binding forces between people become more palpable, the sense of connections more real. Our attitudes toward self-disclosure begin to change. It no longer seems threatening to us, no longer makes us feel vulnerable. In dream work self-disclosure becomes the pathway to honest and helpful exchanges with others. As a consequence we become more open to others as well as to ourselves.

Sharing of our self begins to happen with greater frequency and in greater depth. We find that we are able to identify with others in the struggles that characterize their everyday lives. We see people as becoming, in process, unfinished. They evoke more interest, support, and tolerance. Relationships with others seem to move into a more balanced perspective.

How these characteristics of dreaming are put to use will depend on our own propensities and circumstances. In my experience the dream comes to light most easily through group work. In a group we feel the goodwill, trust, support, interest, and concern of others. They provide us with the help we often need to explore the possibilities of the images we have created, without putting us on the defensive or pushing us to explain or reveal anything beyond any self-determined point. Under these conditions we feel safe in exposing ourselves to a greater range of personal truth. And because we feel safe we make the truth our own. Although the content may be negative and painful at times, the act of ownership is a positive step.

Dreams never give up on us. They are with us every night, urging us to face the issues that restrict and discourage us, or that limit our inventiveness. They remind us of the responsibility we all have to free up our emotional life. They are, in their own way, our personal spokesmen for saner living.

Nan and I have tried to pass on the message that more can be done with our dreams than most of us are now doing. Our hope is that the process developed in this book will make its way into the systems that shape so many of our choices—into industry and institutions, into school programs at all educational levels. For parents and teachers who agonize over the distance between themselves and their children, dreams offer a warm and honest connection. Dream work could find its place in halfway houses or prisons. It could open up something new for senior citizens at a time when society tends to disregard or discard them. Dream appreciation can become accessible to everyone in any setting where understanding and compassion are valued.

We hope that our book provides the inspiration and the guidance for those who wish to learn to appreciate their dreams by themselves as well as for those who want the rewards of a group approach to dreams. It will not transform any reader into an expert as a dream-group leader—only a great deal of experience can do that—but no expert leadership is needed when people come together as peers in the art of working with dreams.

Notes

Chapter 2

1. MacKenzie, Norman. *Dreams and Dreaming.* New York: Vanguard Press, Inc., 1965.
2. MacKenzie, *Dreams and Dreaming,* p. 30.
3. Freud, Sigmund. *Interpretation of Dreams.* New York: Modern Library, 1950.
4. *The New English Bible.* New York: Cambridge University Press, 1971. Genesis 37: 7-8.
5. Woods, Ralph L., and Herbert B. Greenhouse, eds. *The New World of Dreams.* New York: Macmillan Publishing Co., Inc., 1974, p. 153.
6. Woods and Greenhouse, *New World of Dreams,* pp. 157–158.
7. *New English Bible.* Daniel 4: 10–16.
8. Sanford, John A. *God's Forgotten Language.* Philadelphia and New York: J.B. Lippincott Company, 1968.
9. *New English Bible.* Daniel 4: 27–34.
10. Woods and Greenhouse, *New World of Dreams.*
11. Meier, Carl Alfred. "The Dream in Ancient Greece and Its Use in Temple Cures," in G.E. Von Grunebaum and Roger Caillois, eds., *The Dream and Human Societies.* Berkeley and Los Angeles: University of California Press, 1966.

12. MacKenzie, *Dreams and Dreaming.*
13. Freud, *Interpretation of Dreams,* p. 5.
14. MacKenzie, *Dreams and Dreaming.*
15. Creel, H.G. *Chinese Thought from Confucius to Mao Tse-tung.* Chicago: University of Chicago Press, 1953, p. 104.
16. MacKenzie, *Dreams and Dreaming,* p. 58
17. *Encyclopaedia Britannica.* Macropaedia. Vol. 5, p. 1011.
18. Artemidorus Daldianus. *The Interpretation of Dreams.* White, Robert J., translation and commentary. Park Ridge, New Jersey: Noyes Press, 1975, p. 25.
19. Kelsey, Morton T. *Dreams: The Dark Speech of the Spirit.* New York: Doubleday & Company, Inc. 1968.
20. Kelsey, *Dreams.*
21. De Becker, Raymond. *The Understanding of Dreams.* New York: Hawthorn Books, Inc., 1968.
22. Kelsey, *Dreams.*
23. Kelsey, *Dreams.*
24. MacKenzie, *Dreams and Dreaming.*
25. Eliot, Charles W., ed. The Harvard Classics, Vol. 15, John Bunyan, *Pilgrim's Progress.* New York: P.F. Collier & Son Corporation, 1965, p. 13.
26. *Poe's Poems and Essays.* Lang, Andrew, introduction. New York: E.P. Dutton, Everyman's Library, 1964, p. 73.

Chapter 3

1. Jung, Carl G. *Modern Man in Search of a Soul.* New York: Harcourt, Brace and World, 1933, p. 11.
2. Jung, *Modern Man,* pp. 10–11.
3. Stekel, Wilhelm. *The Interpretation of Dreams.* New York: Liveright, 1943.
4. Gutheil, Emil A. *The Language of the Dream.* New York: Macmillan, 1939.
5. French, Thomas M., and Erika Fromm. *Dream Interpretation.* New York: Basic Books, 1964.
6. Fromm, Erich. *The Forgotten Language.* New York: Rinehart, 1951, p. 33.
7. Boss, Medard. *The Analysis of Dreams.* New York: Philosophical Library, 1958.

8. Lowy, Samuel. *Foundations of Dream Interpretation.* London: Kegan Paul, Trench, Trubner, 1942.
9. Jones, Richard M. *The New Psychology of Dreaming.* New York: Grune & Stratton, Inc., 1970.
10. Perls, Frederick S. *Gestalt Therapy Verbatim.* Lafayette, California: Real People Press, 1969.

Chapter 4

1. Stevens, Wallace. "Thirteen Ways of Looking at a Blackbird." From *The Collected Poems of Wallace Stevens.* New York: Alfred A. Knopf, Inc., 1977.

Chapter 6

1. Green, Celia. *Lucid Dreams.* Oxford: Institute of Psychophysical Research, 1968.

Chapter 10

1. Bergom-Larssom, Maria. Tre kvinnors drömmar, *Ord & Bild.* April, 1975.

Chapter 14

1. May, Rollo. *The Courage to Create.* New York: W.W. Norton & Company, Inc., 1975, p. 132.
2. Laing, Ronald D. *The Politics of Experience.* New York: Ballantine Books, Inc., 1967, p. 30.

Chapter 15

1. Ullman, Montague, Stanley Krippner, with Alan Vaughan. *Dream Telepathy.* New York: Macmillan, 1973.

Index

A

T